T5-CVO-830

Contemporary Ethical Issues
in the
Jewish and Christian Traditions

Stanley M. Wagner, General Editor

EDITORIAL COMMITTEE

Ralph R. Covell
Cecil L. Franklin
Nicholas E. Persich, C.M.
John D. Spangler

Publication of this volume has been made possible
by the Rabbi C.E.H. Kauvar Publication Fund.

Contemporary Ethical Issues in the Jewish and Christian Traditions

Edited by
Frederick E. Greenspahn

Ktav Publishing House, Inc
Hoboken, NJ

COPYRIGHT © 1986
Center for Judaic Studies at the University of Denver

Library of Congress Cataloging-in-Publication Data

Contemporary ethical issues in the Jewish and
    Christian traditions.

    Includes bibliographies and index.
    1. Ethics, Jewish.   2. Christian ethics.
3. Social ethics.   I. Greenspahn, Frederic E.,
1946–
BJ1280.C63   1986   241   86-7315
ISBN 0-88125-085-6

Manufactured in the United States of America

Table of Contents

Foreword

The secular world is impressed with efforts to introduce ethical dimensions to confronting human problems. For religious communities this is no new quest; yet never before have God-ordained standards of morality been so seriously put to the test in so many and diverse terrains.

Western civilizaton refers often to the Judeo-Christian heritage which shapes and informs our society. The hyphen implies a commonality which is not always present. In fact, the ethical orientations of Judaism and Christianity are often contradictory. It is well, therefore, that we bring to a wider reading audience a study of *Contemporary Ethical Issues in the Jewish and Christian Traditions,* which emerged out of the Phillips Symposia sponsored by the University of Denver's Center for Judaic Studies.

This volume completes a trilogy. Already published are *Scripture: Authority, Interpretation, Relevance* and *The Human Condition,* in which Jewish, Protestant and Catholic positions were presented, analyzed and compared. In these works we have brought together the views and scholarship of outstanding intellectuals of these faiths. This volume is no exception.

Again, we recognize our indebtedness to Dr. Paula Bernstein for her efforts in acquiring the Phillips Foundation grant which enabled us to pursue our goal of understanding the mainstream religious traditions on problems of contemporary relevance. We are also grateful to Dr. Frederick E. Greenspahn for his editorial competence and for his dedication and commitment to seeing our project to its completion.

Finally, we acknowledge the encouragement, support and cooperation of the University of Denver which in no small way has enabled the Center for Judaic Studies to expand its program, especially in the field of interfaith activities. The Talmud records that "a part of the dream may be fulfilled, but never the whole" (*b. Ber.* 55a). To all those who assisted us in fulfilling this part of our dream, we express our profound thanks.

Dr. Stanley M. Wagner, Director
Center for Judaic Studies
University of Denver

Contributors

Sid Z. Leiman—Professor of Jewish History and Literature and Chairman of the Department of Judaic Studies, Brooklyn College of the City University of New York

Richard A. McCormick, S.J.—Rose F. Kennedy Professor of Christian Ethics, Kennedy Institute of Ethics, Georgetown University

Roger L. Shinn—Reinhold Niebuhr Professor of Social Ethics, Union Theological Seminary

Timothy E. O'Connell—Director of the Institute of Pastoral Studies and Associate Professor of Theology, Loyola University of Chicago

James B. Nelson—Professor of Christian Ethics, United Theological Seminary of the Twin Cities

David Novak—Adjunct Associate Professor of Philosophy, Baruch College of the City University of New York

George G. Higgins—Professional Lecturer, Catholic University of America

Eugene B. Borowitz—Professor of Education and Jewish Religious Thought, Hebrew Union College—Jewish Institute of Religion (New York)

Orlando E. Costas—Dean of the School and Judson Professor of Missiology, Andover Newton Theological School

General Introduction

Frederick E. Greenspahn

In his play *Nathan the Wise*, the eighteenth-century German dramatist Gotthold Ephraim Lessing wrote of a ring with the magical power to make its bearer universally loved. According to Lessing, the ring had been handed down for several generations until it reached a man who could not decide which of his three sons should have it next; as a result, over the years he promised the ring to each of them. As death drew near, the man confronted the implications of his indecision and, to solve his dilemma, had two copies made so that each son could receive a ring. When his sons discovered what had happened, they sought a court determination, but the judge refused to intervene. Noting the ring's power, he suggested observing the brothers' behavior; the authentic ring would be that which belonged to the one most loved and respected.[1]

This story serves a didactic as well as a literary purpose. For Lessing, the rings represent Judaism, Christianity, and Islam. The true faith, he asserts, should be determined by its adherents' behavior, since they will be those who live most meritoriously. The story thus reflects the belief that the primary purpose of religion is to affect human behavior. This attitude is also prevalent in our time, as in the view that religion is, in one writer's words, "morals helped out by mythology."[2] We could note also the popular belief that the Ten Commandments (especially the last six) lie at the center of both Judaism and Christianity, as well as the common claim that being a good person is more important than one's religion.[3] Underlying all of these is the

1

widespread conviction that ethics are the essence of religion and that there is some universal ethical standard by which all people should live.

As Lessing's parable demonstrates, such ideas are not particularly new. The Jewish reformers of the eighteenth and nineteenth centuries provide an illuminating example. Born during the Enlightenment and pluralistic almost by definition, Reform Judaism rejected the concept of a personal messiah, arrogating to its collective self the messianic mission of spreading the gospel of ethical monotheism.[4] Whether monotheism is always ethical or ethical people are always monotheistic was never seriously questioned. For our purposes, however, the theological presuppositions of this view are less important than its social consequences. For it was from this milieu that the Ethical Culture Society developed. Founded by the son of a leading nineteenth-century Reform rabbi, this movement teaches that one can be ethical without being religious in the conventional sense and, as often occurred, without being particularly Jewish.[5] Whether a viable ethical system can survive on its own remains a separate but troubling question for those who hold this view. In any event, the emergence of Ethical Culture out of Reform Judaism demonstrates how the belief that a universal ethical system lies at the heart of all valid religions can easily lead to the denial of religious theological systems and rejection of the distinguishing characteristics of individual traditions in favor of universal ethical norms. Unitarianism exemplifies a similar process within the Christian community.[6]

Although the position of Lessing and the early Jewish reformers finds a contemporary voice, a rather different evaluation of this issue prevails in our time, one which stresses religious differences and thus the distinctive characteristics of each religion's ethics. This approach is exemplified by the view, shared by many Christians and Jews, that Christianity emphasizes love whereas Jewish ethics is based on justice.[7] Similarly, Christianity is frequently regarded as stressing the spiritual dimension of reality more than does Judaism. If true, such radically different orientations should affect the way these traditions handle ethical problems.

In fact, neither of the traditions can be characterized simply, nor can their ethical conclusions be so readily predicted. Judaism is not always harsh and vindictive, nor is Christianity's attitude toward bodily pleasure invariably negative. Moreover, within each there is no single view, as is readily apparent from the internal disputes that can be found in every denomination— ranging from questions of foreign policy to those relating to private behavior, all justified by appeals to their various traditions.

Ethics is more a process than a product, and the conclusions drawn within a particular tradition are often governed by a wide variety of factors, extending even to the way in which an issue is framed. Here abortion can provide a useful case in point. Some traditions prefer to phrase the question in physical terms—"At what point can a fetus exist outside of its mother?"— others are more "spiritual"—"When does the fetus become a person?" Moreover, although the fundamental problem of whether to terminate a pregnancy is the same for all groups, their answers will also be conditioned by their decision whether to focus on the mother or the fetus. A tradition which emphasizes the mother as a person in her own right will tend to respond quite differently than one which views her primarily as a means for creating new life. Finally, one must recognize the role of such concepts as God (transcendent or personal), humanity (sinful or obedient), and even life itself (inherently valuable or only a prelude to something more important).

All this is not to imply that the various traditions do not consult their sources of authority. Quite clearly they do. But such sources are not unequivocal.[8] Moreover, the role and meaning of such authority is frequently less clear than one might suppose. For example, the Bible seems quite explicit in its condemnation of homosexuality. "Do not lie with a male as one lies with a female; it is an abomination."[9] Yet one could deflect the *apparent* force of this statement by focusing on the Bible's intention instead of its words. If the underlying concern is not the same as our own, then the prohibition may be directed against a different kind of homosexuality than that which exists in our society. One could, therefore, argue that the biblical prohibition does not apply to us.

A comparison of the ethical stances taken by various religious traditions cannot settle for a mere catalog of positions. We must focus on methods as well as results. An inductive approach can accomplish this by posing similar questions to each tradition and observing *how* they respond. The results may not be pleasing either to those who believe that all religions have a common ethical stance or to their rivals who think that each religion has its own characteristic ethic. Despite their ostensible differences, both groups share a mistaken assumption regarding the proper role of ethics within a religious tradition. What we shall find is different communities applying their own perceptions of the world to common problems. Ironically, the conclusions may differ despite common presuppositions, even as different approaches may occasionally yield the same result.

Notes

1. *Nathan the Wise*, Act III, scene 7, trans. Bayard Quincy Morgan (New York: Frederick Ungar, 1955), pp. 75–80
2. R.M. Hare, "The Simple Believer," in *Religion and Morality: A Collection of Essays*, ed. Gene Outka and John P. Reeder, Jr. (New York: Doubleday, 1973), p. 408.
3. This probably accounts for remarks such as that ascribed to President Eisenhower, "Our government makes no sense unless it is founded in a deeply religious faith—and I don't care what it is." (Cf. Patrick Henry, "'And I Don't Care What It Is': The Tradition-History of a Civil Religion Proof-Text," *Journal of the American Academy of Religion* 49 [1981]: 35–49.) The underlying premise would seem to be that some sort of belief in God is necessary for people to live moral lives, even though the specifics of that belief make little difference.
4. Cf. Samuel Holdheim, "It is the Messianic task of Israel to make the pure knowledge of God and the pure law of morality of Judaism the common possession and blessing of all the peoples of the earth," in W. Gunther Plaut, *The Rise of Reform Judaism: A Sourcebook of Its European Origins* (New York: World Union for Progressive Judaism, 1963), p. 138.
5. Cf. Benny Kraut, *From Reform Judaism to Ethical Culture: The Religious Evolution of Felix Adler* (Cincinnati: Hebrew Union College Press, 1979).
6. Interestingly, Felix Adler himself drew the analogy between Reform Judaism and Unitarianism (ibid., p. 219).
7. Common as an anti-Jewish slur, this same position was espoused as Judaism's greatest virtue by the turn-of-the-century

thinker Ahad Ha-am (pseudonym of Asher Ginzberg) in "Jewish and Christian Ethics," in *Ahad Ha-am: Essays, Letters, Memoirs*, ed. Leon Simon (Oxford: East and West Library, 1946), pp. 127–37.

8.   Cf. F. Greenspahn, *Scripture in the Jewish and Christian Traditions: Authority, Interpretation, Relevance* (Nashville: Abingdon, 1982), for diverse ways in which this can be done; note esp. p. 16 regarding the possibility of deriving contradictory conclusions from Scripture or using Scripture to justify contradictory positions.

9.   Lev. 18:22; see also Lev. 20:13 and Rom. 1:26–27.

Part I
Science and Technology

In our own time, scientific progress seems constantly to create new and difficult problems. Nowhere is this more vividly demonstrated nor the results more confusing than in the realm of medicine, with its potential to create and destroy life. One might wish that a clear consensus on the use of these skills could be achieved prior to the scientific breakthroughs on which they rely. In fact, our ability to do often seems greater than our ability to anticipate or comprehend. Therefore, ethicists often find themselves debating questions which are already being dealt with in laboratories and hospitals. Sid Leiman's enumeration of all the issues relating to so seemingly simple a problem as *in vitro* fertilization demonstrates how complex this can become.

What is the role of religion in this process? Richard McCormick reminds us that religions are not computers, for which one need only enter the relevant "facts" in order to receive an ethical conclusion. Rather, he suggests, religions help to identify the values one should consider before making an ethical decision. So conceived, religion provides the language into which ethical questions should be encoded rather than an official response to a particular dilemma.

Finally, Roger Shinn cautions us to remember that such discussions are neither so abstract nor so theoretical as they may sometimes seem. Ethical deliberations cannot take place in a vacuum, but must reckon with the real world and the ways in which they will be imposed. What is at stake are lives and people—and power.

Jewish Ethical Teaching and Technological Advance

Sid Z. Leiman

The aim of this presentation is to bring Jewish ethical teaching to bear on problems raised by recent technological advance. After some preliminary remarks about the nature of the Jewish ethical enterprise, I shall focus on the two extremities of modern bioethical discussion: the beginning of life, or more precisely, *in vitro* fertilization and embryo transfer; and the end of life, or more precisely, the comatose patient and euthanasia. A brief concluding comment will attempt to analyze how Jewish ethics works in the light of the two issues we will explore.

Perhaps the first matter to be noted with regard to Jewish ethics is that the term "Jewish ethics" was foreign to Judaism and unknown to Jewish literature prior to the latter half of the nineteenth century. Indeed, biblical and classical Hebrew have no term for "ethics." The creators of modern Hebrew perforce had to borrow *ethica* from the Latin or invest new meanings into the older Hebrew terms *musar* ("chastisement") and *middot* ("virtues").

The study of Jewish ethics, then, is in a sense anachronistic. When we speak of Jewish ethics, however defined, we are imposing a modern category of thought upon an ancient, yet still vibrant tradition. Classical Judaism did not imagine that one could isolate the ethical from all other strands comprising the complex matrix of Judaism. But this is precisely the basic assumption of modern scholarship: not only is it possible to isolate that strand which treats of Jewish ethics but, having isolated that strand, scholars can proceed to examine it, categorize it, and make judgments about it. This enterprise is not without its dangers. By isolating one strand of values, namely Jewish ethics, and contrasting it with an alien configuration of values, namely contemporary ethical discussion, one risks losing still another configuration of values, namely Judaism. In the case of Jewish ethics, scholars risk falling into the trap of searching Judaism for its parallels to modern ethics, when in fact Judaism may be offering an alternative worldview, one which does not separate out ethics from law and theology.

Having said that, we affirm that the risk is well worth taking—for the scholarly benefits to Jew and non-Jew alike are salutary. First and foremost the pursuit of Jewish ethics is significant because its teaching is historically significant. R.G. Collingwood said it well: "The value of history, then, is that it teaches us what man has done and thus what man is."[1] Judaism is a major repository of the ethical teaching of the past. We have much to learn from the Hebrew Bible and from the teachings of the rabbis in the Talmud and Midrash about ethical issues and about how they were resolved by the ancients. The point here is not that the Hebrew Bible and rabbinic teaching are necessarily authoritative for modern man. Rather, it is incumbent upon mankind to learn from its collective experience. If the Jews have preserved the protocols of four thousand years of ethical discussion and decision-making, it would be ludicrous for modern man to overlook such a treasure trove of ethical insight and experience. One can agree or disagree with the material; one cannot afford to ignore it. Secondly, as the precursor of the ethical teaching of Christianity and Islam, the Hebrew Bible introduced a basis for moral obligation that moves beyond prudence, reason, and nature. Why be ethical? Because ultimately one is held accountable for his deeds in this world. Other biblical teachings include the brotherhood of all mankind (all humans are created in the divine image) and moral duty (one must love one's neighbor and come to his aid; it is not enough that he does not hate him and that he causes him no harm). These and many other teachings relating to ultimate values have been elaborated upon by the rabbis in every generation to this very day. A voluminous Jewish literature exists on almost every ethical issue. The best of this material should be made available to, and utilized by, all scholars interested in contemporary ethical discussion. It is not enough to pluck fruits from the branches; one needs to examine the roots as well.

In Vitro Fertilization

The first successful laboratory fertilization of human egg by human sperm—what is generally known as *in vitro* fertilization- was reported in 1969.[2] Since then progress has continued unabated and has led to the successful reimplantation of an *in vitro* fertilized human egg into the uterus of a previously infertile woman, resulting in childbirth. Such technological achievement was unthinkable before this century, and one would naturally be inclined to think that classical religious teaching would be ill-equipped to grope intelligently with the enormous ethical implications of such technological advance. I trust that the discussion that follows will persuade some, at least, that religious teaching is not quite as sterile as it is sometimes made out to be.

For heuristic purposes, I have found it convenient to structure this presentation in scholastic form, attempting to provide Jewish responses, however brief, to a series of questions. The answers to the last questions will, in effect, summarize several Jewish perspectives on *in vitro* fertilization and incorporate some personal opinion as well. At best, whatever I say is provisional, even with regard to Jewish teaching, for Jewish teaching is an ongoing process. And one can say with certainty regarding *in vitro* fertilization that more remains to be said than has been said.

The first question is whether *in vitro* fertilization and embryo implantation are not an interference with nature and thus, *ipso facto,* to be viewed with suspicion? Is not sexual intercourse the only natural setting for procreation? Will not *in vitro* fertilization and embryo implantation lead to various kinds of abuse, ranging from host-mothering for profit to the public auction of celebrity ova and sperm?

From a Jewish perspective, much of medical practice, and certainly surgery, is a kind of interference with nature. But such interference is welcome when it is therapeutic. In the Midrash

(Jewish homiletic literature from the second through the twelfth centuries) we are told about Ishmael and Akiba, two distinguished second-century Palestinian rabbis, who were walking through the streets of Jerusalem when they chanced upon a sick man. The sick man asked: "Masters, how can I be cured?" The rabbis responded: "Take such and such medicine and you will be cured." The sick man then asked: "And who afflicted me with disease?" "The Holy One, blessed be He," replied the rabbis. The sick man asked once again: "Do you then interfere in matters that are not your concern? God afflicted, and you heal?" The rabbis responded with a question: "What is your occupation?" The sick man responded: "I am a tiller of the soil, and I prune trees." "But who created the soil and the trees?" asked the rabbis. "The Holy One, blessed be He," answered the sick man. The rabbis continued: "Did you then interfere in a matter that is not your concern? He created the trees as they are, and you have the audacity to prune them?" The sick man responded: "Were I not to weed the field and prune the trees, it would bear no fruit." "So too," answered the rabbis, "with regard to the human body. Without proper medical care it cannot function properly."[3]

Another rabbinic passage tells the following story: When Hillel (a first-century rabbi and contemporary of Jesus) completed the lesson with his disciples, he accompanied them on their way. They asked him, "Master, where are you going?" He replied, "To perform a religious duty." "Which religious duty?" they asked. Hillel answered, "I am going to take a bath." "Is taking a bath a religious duty?" they asked. Hillel explained, "If the statues of the emperor in the public domain are regularly scraped and cleaned, how much more so should I, who am created in the divine image, take care of my body."[4] Thus, classical Judaism looked kindly upon the internal and external care of the body. Interference was welcome when it was beneficial to the patient.

While sexual intercourse was viewed as the natural setting for procreation, it was not the only one. Thus, Jewish sources from as early as the fourth century discuss efforts upon the part of some rabbis to create humans without engaging in sexual intercourse.[5] Indeed, the Talmud claims that the rabbis succeeded in their efforts! Regarding artificial insemination, the rabbis discussed its legal implications as early as the fifth century of the common era.[6] The rabbis did not proscribe efforts to create humans without engaging in sexual intercourse, nor did they view artificial insemination as being unnatural in a pejorative sense. In general, it is worth noting that classical Judaism viewed sex and procreation as independent values.[7] Sexual intercourse during pregnancy, for example, was a wife's privilege and a husband's duty. It mattered not that she was pregnant. Similarly, procreation was viewed as a value independent of the sexual act.[8] Thus, it is not surprising that many contemporary rabbis find human in vitro fertilization palatable, when warranted. This is not to say that rabbis have no preferences. To be sure, they viewed natural sexual intercourse as the primary means of procreation; but they acknowledged other possibilities.

Regarding possible abuse, it would be the responsibility of the federal, state, and local governments to prevent or control serious abuse. But this should in no way lead us to throw out the baby with the bathwater. Drug abuse abounds in this country, but no one is seriously considering abolishing drugs. In vitro fertilization may be likened to a box of matches, a kitchen knife, or an automobile. When used properly, they are a boon to mankind; when used improperly, they are destructive. It is the manipulator, and not the object, that must bear the blame for any wanton destruction.

Human in vitro fertilization experimentation, as presently practiced, involves the fertilization of ova that will deliberately not be brought to term, thus raising the second question: Should such life be created and aborted in order to advance science? Should such life be created and aborted to enable the infertile to become fertile? Here, much depends on how one views the moral worth of the conceptus in its earliest stages. Some Jewish authorities rule that during the first forty days of gestation, the conceptus has little or no moral status, and therefore could be aborted for any constructive purpose, such as medical experimentation.[9] Other, more stringent Jewish authorities accord moral status to the conceptus from the moment of conception on. They advocate confining human in vitro fertilization to one ovum at a time (instead of the practice of extrapolating and fertilizing numerous ova), thus obviating the wanton destruction of unused fertilized ova.[10]

The next six questions are really all of a kind, serving to underscore the legal ambiguity that abounds in *in vitro* fertilization and in embryo implantation:

— If an ovum is provided by X, and is then fertilized *in vitro*, and then implanted in Y, who brings the fetus to term, who is its legal mother?

— In cases of surrogate mothers, who would have the right to decide for abortion or amniocentesis? Would either the provider of the ovum or the surrogate mother have a right of refusal?

— X and Y are sisters happily married to their respective spouses. X is infertile and, in order to procreate, agrees to the implantation into her uterus of a fertilized ovum of Y. X's husband has provided the sperm for the *in vitro* fertilization. Is the husband guilty of either an incestuous or an adulterous relationship?

— Assuming an *in vitro* fertilized ovum could be brought to term *in vitro*, would the donor of the ovum or the scientist who conducted the experiment be the legal mother?

— If a conceptus is brought to term *in vitro*, what would be his or her legal birthday? Consequences here can sometimes be a matter of life or death, e.g., determining whether or not it was a minor or an adult who committed a murder, or whether or not someone was eligible for the draft.

— If a scientist engages in *in vitro* fertilization without the prior consent of the male and female donors, who is legally and morally responsible for the conceptus when brought to term? Is rape possible *in vitro*?

In Judaism, no decision regarding such a weighty matter as *in vitro* fertilization would be rendered until all the legal consequences were explored and resolved. It seems to me that the Department of Health and Human Services should not approve a research application in these areas unless the desired or expected results are free and clear of legal encumbrance and ambiguity. Thus, if the desired result of an experiment is an embryo transplant which will be brought to term by a surrogate mother, the legal status of the infant-to-be needs to be determined before the experiment is funded, not after. Similarly, if the desired result of an experiment is a conceptus brought to term *in vitro*, a new legal definition of birth needs to be promulgated before the experiment is funded, not after. Another sample of legal ambiguity comes from a less pressing area, but one that nonetheless merits mention here. I have seen numerous discussions of human cloning. Inevitably it is argued that one of the important benefits of human cloning will be the availability of spare parts for organ transplantation. If what is intended is the creation of human clones whose organs would be designated for transplantation purposes, I fail to see by what ethic or law any clone could be designated a donor rather than a recipient. And if experiments are being undertaken whose intended result is the cloning of a human being, we had better legislate now regarding the rights and privileges of such clones.

Instead of responding directly to each of the questions, which at this stage of Jewish discussion would in any event be premature, I should like to focus on the question of surrogate mothers, and hopefully a Jewish response to some of the questions will begin to emerge.

The earliest Jewish discussion relating to embryo implantation dates back to 1928 and was authored by an East European rabbi[11] who reports that the status of a child born from an ovarian transplant was discussed at a medical conference held in Chicago in 1911.[12] Was its mother the donor of the organ, or the recipient mother who brought the child to term? After drawing several dubious analogies to talmudic passages, the rabbi ruled (in theory, of course, since he was not involved in the case) that the recipient of the ovary was the child's legal mother. He reasoned that since in the case in question fertilization occurred after the transplant, clearly it was the recipient's ovum that had been fertilized. And in humans, "the seed of the father and the mother who is impregnated and gives birth is decisive." The learned rabbi was perhaps a poor biologist (for while it is clear that a transplanted ovary becomes the property of the recipient, it is by no means clear that an ovum fertilized after the transplant is to be genetically related to the recipient); but the principle he enunciated seems to be clear: parentage is determined by genes. The providers of the sperm and ovum that form the zygote are the legal parents of the conceptus. Kamelhar did not envision the possibility that one mother could provide the genes and another could provide the locus for impregnation; nor is it altogether clear how he would have ruled in such a case. It may well be that he would have drawn a distinction between the implantation of a fertilized and an unfertilized ovum, motherhood being determined genetically in the former case and by locus in the latter case. Recent rabbinic discussion is divided on the issue,[13] but there is every indication that at least in the case of implantation of a fertilized ovum, the emerging consensus will be that motherhood is determined genetically.[14] This does not rule out surrogate motherhood. It simply indicates that from a Jewish perspective surrogate motherhood does not necessarily carry with it the maternal obligations and privileges (e.g., filial responsibility) that genetic motherhood does. Judaism clearly would not look kindly upon surrogate motherhood when it is resorted to "as a convenience in order to avoid the encumbrances of pregnancy."[15] But such moral judgments, it seems to me, are not the concern of public policy makers. It is the business of the United States government to protect the rights of, and to prevent tangible harm to, its citizens. It is not the business of the United States government to comment upon the morality or immorality of surrogate mothers-for-profit, so long as no one's rights are compromised and all agreements entered into are by mutual consent, and actionable in a court of law. From an American perspective, I see little difference between a wet nurse and a surrogate mother, assuming procedures are perfected so that there are no extraordinary dangers to the surrogate mother's health.

In recent rabbinic discussion, parallels are drawn between artificial insemination and embryo implantation.[16] Recipients of donated ova or sperm assume legal responsibility for their progeny only by contract.[17]

From a Jewish perspective rape and incest are crimes against persons; they are integrally bound up with sexual intercourse. Where there is no physical contact between male and female, there is neither rape nor incest.[18] Thus, the mad scientist who expropriates an ovum and fertilizes it *in vitro* has committed an actionable offense and can be sued by the mother and child for child support, and perhaps for other damages as well, but he has not committed rape.

The final questions pertain to the role of the government:

> Should the federal government support human *in vitro* fertilization research? Should the federal government subsidize human *in vitro* fertilization and embryo implantation as a health care delivery service? Is infertility a disease requiring medical attention? Is making the infertile fertile therapeutic?

These bring me to my conclusions: Research in human *in vitro* fertilization for purposes of enabling the infertile to become fertile should be supported by the federal government if—

— appropriate preliminary research has been done on non-human primates;

— risk-benefit analysis is favorable—ideally, the state of the art should be that no greater risk be involved for the conceptus and the mother than in normal pregnancy and childbirth;

— informed consent of all participants is obtained;

— appropriate liability and compensation for research related injuries is assured;

— the legal consequences of the desired or expected results are free and clear of encumbrance or ambiguity;

— human zygotes and embryos are not destroyed wantonly.

The federal government should subsidize health care delivery services for the needy as, for example, through medicaid. These services should include *in vitro* fertilization and embryo transplant, if such procedures are necessary in order to render an infertile patient fertile, and if such procedures prove to be safe.[19] It would be a sad commentary on the American ethos if federal funds could subsidize the taking of human life (i.e., therapeutic abortion), but not the creation of human life (i.e., therapeutic conception). I am aware that some strict-constructionists will not view infertility as a medical need and its cure as therapeutic. They overlook the fact that it is to the physician that the infertile have turned for centuries seeking a cure. Now that physicians can, at least in some instances, administer the cure, it is hardly the time to label that cure nontherapeutic.

Surely, *in vitro* fertilization and embryo transplant are a cure for dis-ease, if not disease. The rabbis put it this way: Four are considered as if they were dead: the poor, the blind, the diseased, and the childless.[20]

Euthanasia

If I had to select that area of scientific advance that has wreaked most havoc with traditional ethical teaching, it would be the new techniques available for prolonging life. Despite a landmark decision by New Jersey's Supreme Court—which ruled in 1976 that Karen Ann Quinlan's respirator could be disconnected with impunity if her attending physicians and a panel of hospital officials, an "ethics committee," agreed that there was no reasonable possibility that she would recover—the issues are hardly settled. For the purposes of our discussion, I should like to focus on four specific problems which will enable us to formulate a Jewish perspective on euthanasia in general and, more specifically, a Jewish response to the Karen Ann Quinlan case.

    1.   May a patient hasten or induce his own death in order to relieve physical suffering or in order to reduce the financial burden on the family savings?

This raises the issue of suicide in Jewish law. Do people have a "right to die" when and if they so choose, so long as they harm no one else while in the process of dying? The rabbinic response would be an unequivocal no. Jewish teaching proscribes suicide in no uncertain terms. Not only is suicide proscribed, but even the right to injure oneself. The rabbis derived these teachings from Genesis 9:5 ("for your lifeblood I will surely require a reckoning"), from Deuteronomy 30:19 ("therefore choose life"), and from elsewhere in Scripture. The underlying theory seems to be that man is created in God's image; to injure man, even oneself, is to diminish God's image. Moreover, since God provides man with body and soul, they are not man's possession to do with as he pleases. According to Jewish teaching, then, one is obligated to safeguard his personal well-being, to live, and to live well. While suicide in general was banned, the rabbis were sensitive to the complexities of life and made it virtually impossible for anyone to be considered a legal suicide. The rabbinic attitude is reflected in the following:

> Rabbi Akiba ruled: Neither praise nor blame a suicide.
>
> (Semahoth 2:1)

> If one climbs the highest tree and falls to his death, or falls from the highest roof and dies, he is not considered a suicide. One is considered a suicide only if he declares, "I shall climb a tree or go up on a roof and leap to my death," and then witnesses see him carry out his threat immediately after the declaration.
>
> (Semahoth 2:2)

Occasionally, the rabbis condoned suicide. An aggadic passage in the Talmud describes how four hundred Jewish children drowned themselves at sea rather than submit to rape at the hands of the Romans (B. Git. 57b). Despite their mass suicide, all were assured a share in the world-to-come. For our purposes, it is crucial to determine whether or not the rabbis considered physical pain a sufficient justification for suicide. In the Babylonian Talmud we read as follows:

> The Romans found R. Hanina b. Tradyon sitting and occupying himself with the Torah, publicly gathering assemblies, and keeping a scroll of the Law in his bosom. Straightaway they took hold of him, wrapped him in the scroll of the Law, placed bundles of branches around him, and set them on fire. They then brought tufts of wool, which they had soaked in water, and placed them over his heart so that he would not expire quickly. His daughter exclaimed, "Father, woe to me that I see you in this state!" He replied, "If it were I alone being burned, it would be a hard thing to bear; now that I am burning together with the scroll of the Law, He who regards the plight of the Torah will also regard my plight." His disciples called out, "Rabbi, what do you see?" He answered them, "The parchments burn but the letters soar on high." "Open your mouth," they said, "so that the fire may enter into you." He replied, "Let Him who gave me my soul take it away, but one should not injure oneself." The executioner

then said to him, "Rabbi, if I raise the flame and remove the
tufts of wool from your heart, will you guarantee me a share
in the world-to-come? "Yes," he replied. "Swear to me," he
urged. He swore to him. He thereupon raised the flame and
removed the tufts of wool from his heart, and his soul
departed speedily. The executioner then leaped into the fire.
An oracle exclaimed: R. Hanina b. Tradyon and the executioner have been assigned a share in the world-to-come.

(B. Abod. Zar. 18a)

Clearly, R. Hanina b. Tradyon did not consider physical suffering
a sufficient justification for suicide. Hanina's view was codified
in the thirteenth-century code of the Jewish pietists in Germany,
called Sefer Hasidim (the Book of the Pious), where we read:

If a man suffers unbearable physical pain, and he knows that
he is terminally ill, he may not commit suicide. We derive
this ruling from the account of Rabbi Hanina b. Tradyon,
who refused to open his mouth, lest he contribute toward his
own death.

(ed. Wistinetzki, p. 100)

In sum, Jewish teaching proscribes suicide. Under extenuating
circumstances it is sometimes condoned. Neither physical pain
nor serious financial loss is considered sufficient justification
for suicide in rabbinic sources. It follows, then, that a patient
may not hasten or induce his own death in order to relieve
physical suffering or in order to reduce the financial burden on
his family.

2. May a physician hasten or induce the death of a patient
   for any of the above reasons? May he do so only with
   the patient's consent or even without the patient's permission?

This problem is easily resolved. From a biblical and rabbinic
perspective, the prohibition against homicide applies despite
the victim's consent. In general, human life is inviolate. In the
rare instances where a life may be taken, such as capital punishment in biblical-rabbinical times, or self-defense to this very
day, there must be sufficient warrant to take a life. Where there

is sufficient warrant, the victim's consent or lack of it is irrelevant. Conversely, if there is not sufficient warrant, life may not be taken *even at the victim's request*. And so the following ruling, also from the *Book of the Pious:*

> If a man suffers unbearable physical pain and informs another party that he is terminally ill, and requests the other party to perform an act of euthanasia in order to relieve him of his pain, the second party may not do so.
>
> (p. 100)

Similarly, Maimonides (in the twelfth century) and Joseph Karo (in the sixteenth century), in their respective codes, rule that "one who is near death is regarded as a living person in all respects. Whoever lays a hand on someone near death and hastens his death is guilty of shedding blood. To what may one who is near death be likened? To a flickering flame, which becomes extinguished as soon as one touches it."[21] Thus, a physician may not hasten or induce the death of a patient, even at the patient's request.

3.   Should a patient suffering from severe brain damage, and having entered an irreversible comatose state, be maintained alive indefinitely by artificial means?

This problem addresses itself to the Karen Ann Quinlan case and is not easily resolved. A rabbinic consensus has yet to emerge, nor is one likely to emerge, as indeed no Protestant consensus has emerged. The stakes are much too high and the issues much too complex for a clear and simple resolution. Two approaches to the Quinlan case have been suggested in recent rabbinic discussion, and they merit mention here. The first approach, espoused by Rabbi J. David Bleich of Yeshiva University, views all humans as being either alive or dead. If not dead, runs the argument, every effort—however artificial—must be maintained in order to prolong life. Since Karen Ann Quinlan was alive physiologically by almost any definition of the term, her life must be sustained at all costs. The respirator should not have been turned off until such time that she was declared legally, which is to say halachically, dead.

A careful examination of the classical Jewish sources suggests a second approach, which I shall espouse here. Classical
Judaism recognizes at least three stages in the life-cycle: life,
dying, and death. While every effort must be made to prolong
life, the rabbis saw no need to prolong the act of dying needlessly.
The rabbis valued biological life, but it was not always sacro-
sanct in their eyes. There was still another more important
value, namely, the quality of life. And so they ruled that a Jew
must lay down his life rather than take an innocent life, engage
in a sexually immoral act, or engage in idolatrous worship.
Their devalued regard for the biological life of those in whom
death was imminent, or for those who could no longer function
in any meaningful way, expressed itself in their reluctance to
engage in any activity which would prolong the act of dying.
Thus, under certain circumstances, the rabbis tolerated passive
euthanasia, that is, they were willing to allow nature to take its
course. Let us examine the rabbinic evidence:

> It once happened that a woman who had aged considerably
> appeared before Rabbi José b. Halafta [a second century C.E.
> tanna] She said, "Rabbi, I am much too old, life has become a
> burden for me. I can no longer taste either food or drink, and I
> wish to die." Rabbi José asked her, "To what do you ascribe
> your longevity?" She answered that it was her habit to pray
> in the synagogue every morning, and despite occasional more
> pressing needs, she had never missed a service. Rabbi José
> advised her to refrain from attending services for three con-
> secutive days. She heeded his advice, and on the third day
> she took ill and died.
>
> (*Yalqut to Proverbs*, §943)

I am not sure what the moral of this story is. Some will claim, no
doubt, it teaches that if life becomes a burden one should stay
away from the synagogue. Others, especially rabbis, will see
here a clear indication that those lax in synagogue attendance
are, in fact, courting death. In any event, Rabbi José's willingness
to hasten biological death by means of inaction is clear. He did
not deem it obligatory to prolong life needlessly.

> One may not prolong the act of dying. If, for example, someone
> is dying, and nearby a woodcutter insists on chopping wood,

thereby disturbing the dying person so that he cannot die, we remove the woodcutter from the vicinity of the dying person. Also, one may not place salt in the mouth of a dying person in order to prevent death from overtaking him.

(Book of the Pious, ed. Wistinetzki, p. 100)

These rulings from the Book of the Pious have been incorporated into the standard Jewish codes of law.

The rabbis did not hesitate to pray for death when they felt it was warranted:

On the day that Rabbi Judah was to die the rabbis decreed a public fast and offered prayers for heavenly mercy.... Rabbi Judah's handmaid ascended the roof and prayed, "The immortals desire Rabbi Judah to join them, and the mortals desire Rabbi Judah to remain with them; may it be the will of God that the mortals may overpower the immortals." When, however, she saw how often he resorted to the privy, painfully taking off his tefillin and putting them on again, she prayed, "May it be the will of the Almighty that the immortals may overpower the mortals." As the rabbis incessantly prayed for heavenly mercy, she took up a jar and threw it down from the roof to the ground. The rabbis were distracted from their prayers, and the soul of Rabbi Judah departed to its eternal rest.

(B. Ket. 104a)

Rabbi Simeon b. Laqish died, and Rabbi Johanan was plunged into deep grief. Said the rabbis, "Who shall go to ease his mind? Let Rabbi Eleazar b. Pedath, whose disquisitions are very subtle, go." So he went and sat before him; and on every dictum uttered by Rabbi Johanan he observed, "There is a baraitha which supports you." "Are you the son of Laqisha?" retorted Rabbi Johanan, "When I stated a law, the son of Laqisha used to raise twenty-four objections, to which I gave twenty-four answers, which consequently led to a fuller comprehension of the law; while you say, 'A baraitha has been taught which supports you.' Do you think I do not know that my dicta are right?" Thus he went on rending his garments and weeping, "Where are you, O son of Laqisha, where are you, O son of Laqisha?" He cried until his mind was turned, whereupon the rabbis prayed for him and he died.

(B. B. Meṣ 84a)

One day Honi was journeying on the road and he saw a man planting a carob tree; he asked him, "How long does it take for this tree to bear fruit?" The man replied, "Seventy years." He then further asked him, "Are you certain that you will live another seventy years?" The man replied, "I found ready grown carob trees in the world; as my forefathers planted them for me, so too I plant these for my children."
Honi sat down to have a meal and sleep overcame him. As he slept, a rocky formation enclosed upon him which hid him from sight, and he continued to sleep for seventy years. When he awoke, he saw a man gathering the fruit of the carob tree and he asked him, "Are you the man who planted the tree?" The man replied, "I am his grandson." Thereupon he exclaimed, "It is clear that I have slept for seventy years." He then caught sight of his ass who had given birth to several generations of mules, and he returned home. He inquired there, "Is the son of Honi still alive?" The people answered him, "His son is no more, but his grandson is still living." Thereupon he said to them, "I am Honi," but no one would believe him. He then repaired to the academy and he heard the scholars say, "The law is as clear to us as in the days of Honi," for whenever Honi came to the academy he would settle for the scholars any difficulty they had. Whereupon Honi called out, "I am he." But the scholars would not believe him, nor did they render him the honor due to him. This hurt him greatly, and he prayed for death and he died. Raba said, "Hence the saying: Either companionship or death."

(B. Ta'an. 23a)

From a rabbinic perspective, then, one could pray for divine intervention, one could in certain situations passively allow death to come, but one could not actively induce death. Under no circumstances would the rabbis allow the deliberate taking of innocent life.[22]

The crucial issue in the Karen Ann Quinlan case, from a halachic point of view, is her precise physiological as well as halachic status. Clearly, she was not dead by even the most liberal definition of the term. Was she among the living and to be accorded all the rights and privileges of any other ill patient, or was she moribund, i.e., one in whom death is imminent (and halachically termed a goses)? According to some halachic authorities, Karen Ann Quinlan was clearly to be numbered among the latter. She was qualitatively in a transition state between life and death, i.e., she was dying, and as such, those rabbinic authorities would rule that there is no moral or legal obligation to keep her alive artificially, since there is no possibility of restoring her to a nonmoribund state. The physician's obligation is to heal, to restore to cognitive life, and not to prolong the act of dying. With regard to the moribund, many rabbinic authorities would allow the withdrawal of any and all devices prolonging death needlessly. While the physician and hospital staff would no longer be obligated to engage in therapeutic activity, they would be obligated to care for the patient, to make her end as comfortable as humanly possible.

4. Is there ever justification for turning off a respirator once such treatment has begun?

Regarding this last problem, the initial justification for the use of a respirator was therapeutic. If this justification falls away, i.e., if the physicians determine that she cannot be restored to cognitive life, the respirator is, in fact, prolonging the act of dying. As just indicated, many rabbinic authorities would allow the withdrawal of any and all devices prolonging the act of dying needlessly. Three options present themselves at this point, with regard to the Quinlan case.

a. withdrawal of antibiotic treatment
b. pulling the plug
c. withdrawal of nourishment

Assuming Karen Ann Quinlan was a *goses*, many rabbis would sanction all these options, if necessary, with a clear preference for the withdrawal of antibiotic treatment, since it involves no direct action (such as pulling the plug) and allows for nourishment to continue until the end, an obligation some rabbis would extend to all the terminally ill, however advanced their moribund state. Since it is often difficult, well-nigh impossible to determine with certainty that a patient is moribund (i.e., halachically termed a *goses*), several rabbinic authorities have ruled that in all cases of doubt the patient's respirator be placed on a timer. If the patient shows signs of being moribund and, when the timer turns the respirator off, he cannot breathe independently of it, the physician is no longer obligated to turn the respirator on. This procedure obviates the possibility of the physician engaging in active euthanasia.

Lest anyone have qualms about the absolute biblical-rabbinic prohibition against active euthanasia, let me remind you, as indeed Paul Ramsey reminded me, of the judgment of Dr. Leo Alexander, a leading historian of Nazi medical crimes: "Whatever proportion these crimes finally assumed, it became evident to all who investigated them that they had started from small beginnings....It started with the acceptance of the attitude...that there is such a thing as life not worthy to be lived... its empetus was the attitude toward the non-rehabilitable sick."[23] It is sometimes exceedingly difficult to distinguish between active euthanasia as an act of mercy and a violation of basic human rights. So long as confusion reigns in the minds of some, Jews will be in no hurry to come down on the side of the act of mercy.[24]

What can we say then about Jewish ethical teaching and how it is brought to bear on problems raised by recent scientific advance? It is, perhaps, safe to say—even judging from the two issues we have explored—that several elements inform Jewish ethical discussion.

1. *Reason.* The *sine qua non* for all Jewish ethical reflection is reason. Passages are analyzed to see whether or not they are analogous. All options are carefully considered; those most consistent with Jewish values are selected as optimal. In our discussion, relevant distinctions were made between sexual intercourse and procreation, and between prolonging life and prolonging dying. Reason is the vehicle that makes all the above possible.

2. *Principle.* Principles are invoked, especially those grounded in what the classical Jewish tradition considers to be authoritative texts: Scripture and Talmud. Thus, the scriptural principle "man is created in God's image" and the talmudic principle "we neither praise nor blame a suicide" were adduced in the discussion of suicide as it relates to euthanasia.

3. *Context.* Context is carefully considered. Motivations of participants are examined. Are *in vitro* fertilization and embryo transfer being engaged in for therapeutic purposes or for convenience? Is there a morally relevant difference between active and passive euthanasia? The situation itself will often color the Jewish response.

No one element reigns supreme. Unbridled reason alone does not account for all of a Jewish ethical stance. A gut reaction does not by itself determine the direction of a Jewish ethical response. Neither rigid legalism nor context, by themselves, accounts for a Jewish ethical decision. All these elements inform each other, and serve as a built-in system of checks and balances against rigidity, stagnancy, and capriciousness in Jewish ethical thought. Doubtless, these very elements are largely responsible for the resiliency and sobriety of a four-thousand-year-old ethical tradition as it brings its values to bear on modern technological advance.

Notes

1. R. G. Collingwood, *The Idea of History* (New York: Oxford University Press, 1956), p. 10.
2. See Leon R. Kass, "The New Biology: What Price Relieving Man's Estate," *Science* 174 (1971): 780.
3. *Midrash Temurah* in A. Jellinek, ed., *Bet ha-Midrasch* (Jerusalem: Wahrmann Books, 1967), 1:107.
4. *Midrash Rabbah: Leviticus* 34:3, in H. Freedman and M. Simon, eds., *The Midrash* (London: Soncino Press, 1939), 4:428.
5. E.g., *B. Sanh.* 65b. In general, see A. Rosenfeld, "Religion and the Robot," *Tradition* 8, no. 3 (1966): 15–26.
6. E.g., *B. Hag.* 14b–15a. In general, see "Artificial Insemination in Jewish Law," in F. Rosner, *Modern Medicine and Jewish Law* (New York: Yeshiva University Press, 1972), pp. 89–106.
7. See D. M. Feldman, *Birth Control in Jewish Law* (New York: New York University Press, 1968), pp. 21–105.
8. See, e.g., Samuel b. Uri Shraga Phoebus (17th cent.). *Beth Shemuel* 1:10, in the standard editions of J. Karo, *Shulhan Arukh, Even ha-Ezer,* chap. 1.
9. Feldman, *Birth Control in Jewish Law*, p. 266, nn. 79 and 83.

10. J. D. Bleich, "The Problems of Creating a Test-Tube Baby from a Jewish Perspective" (Hebrew), *Or Hamizrach* 27 (1978): 14.

11. J. Kamelhar, *Ha-Talmud u-Madda'ey ha-Tevel* (Lvov: Czcionkami Drukarni, 1928), pp. 44–45.

12. The rabbi gives no details regarding the identity of the medical society that convened the conference, nor does he provide the names of the participants. That ovarian transplantation was a topic of discussion in Chicago in 1911 is clear from F. H. Martin, "Ovarian Transplantation in Lower Animals and Women," *Surgery, Gynecology and Obstetrics* 13 (1911): 53–63. Martin practiced in Chicago, though the paper on ovarian transplantation was read before the American Gynecological Society on May 24, 1911, in Atlantic City. It may be that the rabbi (or his informants) mistook Martin's place of residence for the location of the American Gynecological Society conference.

13. See, e.g., B.Z. Safran, *Sheelot u-Teshuvot Harabaz* (Jerusalem: Mosad Harav Kook, 1962), pp. 204–225; M. Klein, *Sheelot u-Teshuvot Mishneh Halakhot* (Tel Aviv: Machon Mishne Halakhoth, 1970), vol. 4, responsum 249; E. J. Waldenberg, *Sheelot u-Teshuvot Tzitz Eliezer* (Jerusalem: Itah, 1970), vol. 10, responsum 25, chap. 26, par. 3, p. 167; I. Liebes "On Organ Transplantation" (Hebrew), *Noam* 14 (1971): 28–111; J. Gershuni, "The First Test-Tube Baby in the Light of the Halakhah" (Hebrew), *Or Hamizrach* 27 (1978): 15–21; M. Hershler, "Test Tube Babies According to Halakha" (Hebrew), in M. Hershler, ed., *Halakhah Urefuah* (Jerusalem: Machon Regensberg, 1980), 1:307–320; J. D. Bleich, "Maternal Identity," *Tradition* 19, no. 14 (1981): 359–360; M. Drory, "Human Cloning" (Hebrew), *Assia* 2 (1981): 105–116; A. Steinberg, "Test Tube Baby" (Hebrew), *Assia* 2 (1981): 99–104; and D.I. Frimer, "Maternal Identity," *Tradition* 20, no. 2 (1982): 174.

14. So personal communications from numerous rabbinic authorities, including Rabbi Dr. Moses D. Tendler of Yeshiva University. On the genetic determinant of motherhood, see especially A. J. Horovitz, *Sheelot u-Teshuvot Tzur Yaakov* (Bilgoray: Kronenberg, 1932), responsum 28, end, who writes: "Do the female generative organs create the baby? They are simply a means for housing the conceptus. The essential factor in the creation of a baby is the seed of the father and the mother, as spelled out in the Talmud."

15. J. D. Bleich, "Host-Mothers," in his *Contemporary Halakhic Problems* (New York: Yeshiva University Press, 1977), p. 106; see also his *Judaism and Healing* (New York: Ktav, 1981), pp. 85–95.

16. See the references cited above in nn. 10, 13, 14, and 15. In a recent responsum, E. J. Waldenberg argues strongly against the analogy between artificial insemination and embryo implantation. Indeed, he concludes that *in vitro* fertilization and embryo implantation are

sufficiently different from artificial insemination that, from a Jewish perspective, they must be proscribed. See E. J. Waldenberg and D. Maeir, "In Vitro Fertilization" (Hebrew), Assia 9, no. 1 (1982): 5–13.

17. See M. Feinstein, Iggerot Moshe, Even ha-Ezer (New York: Sinai Offset Company, 1961), responsum 10, end.

18. See M. Feinstein, Iggerot Moshe, Even ha-Ezer (New York: Gross Brothers, 1963), vol. 2, responsum 11. Some rabbinic authorities, however, allow for incest and adultery even when no act of sexual intercourse has taken place (e.g., in cases of artificial insemination). See the sources cited by E. J. Waldenberg, Sheelot u-Teshuvot Tzitz Eliezer (Jerusalem: Itah, 1978), vol. 13, responsum 97, pp. 192–195.

19. Cf. the opinion rendered by the Sephardic chief rabbi of Israel, Rabbi Ovadiah Yosef, as reported in the Jewish Telegraphic Agency Daily News Bulletin, August 16, 1978.

20. B. Ned. 64b.

21. Mishneh Torah, Hilkhot Evel 4:5.

22. In extremis, some rabbis condoned the deliberate taking of innocent life. See, e.g., I. Z. Cahana, ed., Maharam of Rottenburg: Responsa, Rulings and Customs (Hebrew) (Jerusalem: Mosad Harav Kook, 1960), vol. 2, responsum 59, p. 54; and J. J. Weinberg, Sridey Esh (Jerusalem: Mosad Harav Kook, 1977), vol. 2, responsum 78, pp. 196–201. Such exceptions prove the rule.

23. Quoted by Paul Ramsey in The Patient as Person (New Haven: Yale University Press, 1970), p. 164, from "Medical Science Under Dictatorship," New England Journal of Medicine 24, no. 2 (July 14, 1949): 44–45.

24. For further study, see G. A. Rabinowitz and M. Koenigsberg, "The Definition of Death and Establishing Its Occurrence According to the Halakhah" (Hebrew), Hadarom 32 (1971): 59–76; I. Jakobovits, Jewish Medical Ethics, 2d ed. (New York: Bloch, 1975), pp. 275–276 and notes; J. D. Bleich, "Karen Ann Quinlan: A Torah Perspective," Jewish Life, Winter 1976, pp. 13–20; A. Cohen, "An Analysis on Whether Pulling the Plug Is Ever Permissible Under Jewish Law," Young Israel Viewpoint, November 1976, pp. 5–15; I. L. Liebes, "Medical Issues According to the Halakhah" (Hebrew), Perspective 3 (1976): 50–60; E. J. Waldenberg, Sheelot u-Teshuvot Tzitz Eliezer, vol. 13, responsum 89, pp. 172–180; F. Rosner and J. D. Bleich, eds., Jewish Bioethics (New York: Sanhedrin Press, 1979), pp. 253–348; J. D. Bleich, Judaism and Healing, pp. 134–145; and E. J. Waldenberg, "On Shutting Off a Respirator" (Hebrew), Assia 3 (1982): 458–462.

Biomedical Advances
and the Catholic Perspective

Richard McCormick, S.J.

We live at a time when nearly every morning's newspaper brings us another biomedical breakthrough—and problem. Some of the recent ones would include the following: surgery on the fetus *in utero* to correct bladder pathology; laparoscopic introduction of relief valves into the fetal cranium to prevent hydrocephalus and the subsequent retardation associated with neural tube defects; the transitional use of the totally artificial heart; *in vitro* fertilization procedures to overcome tubal occlusion. In the next few years we will witness the production of hybridomas (man-made hybrid cells that can be introduced into the body to produce swarms of disease-fighting antibodies). We will see the production of interferon from DNA technology as well as the development of nuclear magnetic resonance body imaging—to do what X rays do now. And on and on it goes.

With scientific and technological breakthroughs come the usual set of questions and concerns. Will this procedure promote or undermine the *humanum*? Is it overstepping the line of human stewardship? On what criteria do we decide? And who decides? Is public regulation called for? These questions are, of course, ethical questions. Their answers are not only important in themselves. They are also a paradigm. How we go about them will tell us how we will be acting twenty years from now. For the type of moral reasoning employed, its premises, its sensitivity, its precision, its combination of finality of commitment with appropriate tentativeness of formulation will reappear wherever bioethical issues reappear.

How does the Catholic tradition view and judge such developments? I can begin with two statements by colleagues. In a sympathetic and insightful article, Lisa Sowle Cahill notes: "McCormick forcefully correlates religious and similar values, but does not so clearly demonstrate the functional significance for ethics of his theology, precisely *as* Christian."[1] Alisdair MacIntyre concludes one of his essays on medical ethics as follows: "Theologians still owe it to the rest of us to explain why we should not treat their discipline as we do astrology or phrenology. The distinctiveness and importance of what they have to say, if it is true, make this an urgent responsibility."[2]

Both of these statements are, I believe, accurate. Theologians ought indeed to make clear the distinctiveness of their contribution. I also confess that in dealing with the practical problems of medical ethics I have not always done this.

Every theologian comes from a tradition and is deeply influenced by it. The Catholic tradition from which I come has held, at least since the time of Saint Thomas, that the sources of faith do not originate concrete obligations (thought to apply to all persons, *essential* morality) that are impervious to human insight and reason. Thus the Roman theologians F. Hurth and P.M. Abellan state: "All moral commands of the 'New Law' are also commands of the natural moral law. Christ did not add any single moral prescription of a positive kind to the natural moral law...that holds also for the command of love...the ethical demand to love God and one's neighbour for God's sake is a demand of the natural moral law."[3] In such a tradition, it is perhaps understandable how the specifically Christian dimensions of theological analysis might remain less explicit than is desirable.

Yet I write and think as a Catholic moral theologian. What does that mean? Three things above all: (1) Religious faith stamps one at a profound and not totally recoverable level. (2) This stamping affects one's instincts, sensitivities, imagination, etc., and hence influences one's perspectives, analyses, judgments. (3) Analyses and judgments of such a kind are vitally important in our communal deliberations about bioethics.

If Alisdair MacIntyre means to imply in his statement cited above that theology and theologians are out of place in these discussions, then I think he has it all wrong, difficult as it may be to specify the exact contribution of theology, especially in a very concrete problem of bioethics.

If God is present and self-communicative to us in His glorified Son—the exemplary human being—through His spirit, and if this presence is mediated to us by a historical religious community, then surely the faith in that presence as formed by this community will have a powerful influence on one who tries to sort out the complexities of modern scientific problems.

But how? There are any number of ways. For instance, James Gustafson develops three theological themes taken from the Judeo-Christian tradition.[4] They are: (1) God intends the well-being of creation. (2) God is both the ordinary power sustaining the well-being of creation and the power that creates new possibilities for well-being. (3) Humans are finite and sinful. These beliefs in turn impact on medical ethics by providing a fundamental moral perspective on medical care and research. Furthermore, these beliefs ground certain attitudes toward life (attitude of respect for life, of openness, of self-criticism) and form the basis of more concrete action-guiding rules.

Elsewhere Gustafson has made similar points.[5] Christian experience and belief qualify the reasons for being moral, the character of the moral agent (e.g., readiness to seek the interests of others is nourished by sharing the Christian story), the points of reference to determine conduct. An example of this latter: the Christian community ought to be willing to give up its own immediate interests for the sake of others.

In the past, I myself have tried to relate Christian belief to medical ethics by attending to the analysis of moral obligation. In doing this, I have found illuminating the neo-Thomist (Grisez, deFinance, deBroglie) understanding of the Thomistic inclinationes naturales. Here only a brief sketch can be outlined.[6]

How does the general thrust of our persons toward good and away from evil become concrete? In other words, how do we arrive at definite moral obligations? We begin by asking what are the goods or values man can seek, the values that define our flourishing. We can answer by examining our basic tendencies (*inclinationes naturales*). For it is impossible to act without having an interest in something, without some inclination already present. What then are the basic inclinations?

With no pretense at being exhaustive, we could list some of the following as basic inclinations present prior to acculturation: the tendency to preserve life; the tendency to mate and raise children; the tendency to explore and question; the tendency to seek out other men and obtain their approval—friendship; the tendency to establish good relations with unknown higher powers; the tendency to use intelligence in guiding action; the tendency to develop skills and exercise them in play and the fine arts. In these inclinations our intelligence spontaneously and without reflection grasps the possibilities to which they point and prescribes them. Thus we form naturally and without reflection the basic principles of practical or moral reasoning. Or as philosopher John Finnis renders it:

> What is spontaneously understood when one turns from contemplation to action is not a set of Kantian or neoscholastic "moral principles" identifying this as right and that as wrong, but a set of values which can be expressed in the form of principles as "life is a good-to-be-pursued and realized and what threatens it is to be avoided."[7]

We have not yet arrived at a determination of what concrete actions are morally right or wrong; but we have laid the basis. Since these basic values are equally underived and irreducibly attractive, the morality of our conduct is determined by the adequacy of our openness to these values. For each of these values has its self-evident appeal as a participation in the unconditioned Good we call God. The realization of these values in intersubjective life is the only adequate way to love and attain God.

Further reflection by practical reason tells us what it means to remain open and to pursue these basic human values. First we must take them into account in our conduct. Simple disregard of one or another shows we have set our mind against this good. Second, when we can do so as easily as not, we should avoid acting in ways that inhibit these values, and prefer ways that realize them. Third, we must make an effort on their behalf when their realization in another is in extreme peril. If we fail to do so, we show that the value in question is not the object of our efficacious love and concern. Finally, we must never choose against a basic good in the sense of spurning it. What is to count as "turning against a basic good" is, of course, the crucial moral question. Certainly it does not mean that there are never situations of conflicted values where it is necessary to cause harm as we go about doing good. Thus there are times when it is necessary to take life in defense of life, in our very adhering to this basic value. That means that taking life need not always involve one in "turning against a basic good." Somewhat similarly, one does not necessarily turn against the basic good of procreation (what Pius XII called a "sin against the very meaning of conjugal life")[8] by avoiding childbearing. Such avoidance is only reproachable when *unjustified*. And the many conflicts (medical, economic, social, eugenic) that justify such avoidance were acknowledged by Pius XII. Suppressing a value or preferring one to another in one's choice cannot be simply identified with turning against a basic good. My only point here is that particular moral judgments are incarnations of these more basic normative positions, which have their roots in spontaneous, prereflective inclinations.

Even though these inclinations can be identified as prior to acculturation, still they exist as culturally conditioned. We tend toward values as perceived. And the culture in which we live shades our perception of values. Philip Rieff, in *The Triumph of the Therapeutic*, notes that a culture survives by the power of institutions to influence conduct with "reasons" that have sunk so deeply into the self that they are implicitly understood. In other words, decisions are made, policies set not chiefly by articulated norms, codes, regulations, and philosophies, but by "reasons" that lie below the surface. This is the dynamic aspect of a culture, and in this sense many of our major moral problems are cultural. Our way of perceiving the basic human values and relating to them is shaped by our whole way of looking at the world.

"Our way of looking at the world" can, then, easily distort our perception of the basic human values, and hence affect our moral judgments. A symptom of this might be our treatment of the aged.

The elderly are probably the most alienated members of our society. More and more of them spend their declining years in homes for senior citizens, in chronic-disease hospitals, in nursing homes. We have shunted them aside. Their protest is eloquent because it is helplessly muted and silent. But it is a protest against a basically functional assessment of their persons. "Maladaptation" is the term used to describe *them* rather than the environment. This represents a terribly distorted judgment of the human person.

Love of and loyalty to Jesus Christ, the perfect man, sensitizes us to the meaning of persons. The Christian tradition is anchored in faith in the meaning and decisive significance of God's covenant with men, especially as manifested in the saving incarnation of Jesus Christ, his eschatological kingdom which is here aborning but will only finally be given. Faith in these events, love of and loyalty to their central figure, yields a decisive way of viewing and intending the world, of interpreting its meaning, of hierarchizing its values. In this sense the Christian tradition only illumines human values, supports them, provides a context for their reading at given points in history. It aids us in staying human by underlining the truly human against all cultural attempts to distort the human. It is by steadying our gaze on the basic human values that are the parents of more concrete norms and rules that faith influences moral judgment and decision-making. That is one way of understanding "reason informed by faith."

In summary, then, Christian emphases do not immediately yield moral norms and rules for decision-making. But they affect them. The stories and symbols that relate the origin of Christianity and nourish the faith of the individual affect one's perspectives. They sharpen and intensify our focus on the human goods definitive of our flourishing. It is persons so informed, persons with such "reasons" sunk deep in their being, who face new situations, new dilemmas, and reason together as to what is the best policy, the best protocol for the service of all the values. They do not find concrete answers in their tradition, but they bring a worldview that informs their reasoning—especially by allowing the basic human goods to retain their attractiveness and not be tainted by cultural distortions. This worldview is a continuing check on and challenge to our tendency to make choices in light of cultural enthusiasms which sink into and take possession of our unwitting, pre-ethical selves. Such enthusiasms can reduce the good life to mere adjustment in a triumph of the therapeutic, collapse an individual into his functionability, exalt his uniqueness into a lonely individualism, or crush it into a suffocating collectivism. In this sense I believe it is true to say that the Christian tradition is much more a value-raiser than an answer-giver. And it affects our values at the spontaneous, prethematic level.

While this attempt of the past may be true as far as it goes, the question remains whether it is all of the truth and whether it goes far enough. Perhaps not.

In what follows I wish to pursue this question. As noted, Gustafson refers to "theological themes" that form the basis of more concrete action guides. He refers to "points of reference to determine conduct." Similarly Franz Böckle of the University of Bonn argues that faith and its sources have a *direct* influence on "morally relevant insights," not on concrete "moral judgments."[9] I have referred to a "decisive way of viewing and intending the world" and to the stories and symbols that affect our "perspectives." These phrases seem to me to be referring to substantially the same thing.

Theological work in the past decade or so has rejected the notion that the sources of faith are a "thesaurus of answers." Rather they should be viewed above all as narratives, as a story. From a story come perspectives, themes, insights, not always or chiefly concrete action guides. The story is the source from which the Christian "construes the world theologically" (to use Gustafson's phrase).

To see what these perspectives, themes, insights—as related to medical ethics—might be, let us attempt to disengage some key elements of the Christian story and form a Catholic reading and living of it. One might not be too far off with the following listing:

—   God is the author and perserver of life. We are "made in His image."

— Thus life is a gift, a trust. It has great worth because of the value He is placing in it (Thielicke's "alien dignity").

— God places great value in it because He is also (besides being author) the end, purpose of life.

— We are on a pilgrimage, having here no lasting home.

— God has dealt with us in many ways. But his supreme epiphany of Himself (and our potential selves) is His Son Jesus Christ.

— In Jesus' life, death, and resurrection we have been totally transformed into "new creatures," into a community of the transformed. Sin and death have met their victor.

— The ultimate significance of our lives consists in developing this new life.

— The spirit is given to us to guide and inspire us on this journey.

— The ultimate destiny of our combined journeys is the "coming of the Kingdom," the return of the glorified Christ to claim the redeemed world.

— Thus we are offered in and through Jesus Christ eternal life. Just as Jesus has overcome death (and now lives), so will we who cling to Him place our faith and hope in Him, and take Him as our law and model.

— This good news, this covenant with us, has been entrusted to a people, a people to be nourished and instructed by shepherds.

— This people should continuously remember and thereby make present Christ in His death and resurrection at the Eucharistic meal.

— The chief and central manifestation of this new life in Christ is love for each other (not a flaccid "niceness," but a love that shapes itself in the concrete forms of justice, gratitude, forbearance, chastity, etc.).

If we are thinking *theologically* (I refer to Christian theology) about the ethical problems of biomedicine, it is out of such a framework, context, or story that we will think. The very meaning, purpose, and value of a person is grounded and ultimately explained by this story. Since that is the case, the story itself is the overarching foundation and criterion of morality. It stands in judgment of all human meaning and actions. Actions which are incompatible with this story are thereby morally wrong. In its *Declaration on Euthanasia*, the Sacred Congregation for the Doctrine of the Faith made reference to "Christ, who through his life, death and resurrection, has given a *new meaning to existence*."[10] If that is true (and Christians believe it is), then to neglect that meaning is to neglect the most important thing about ourselves, to cut ourselves off from the fullness of our own reality.

The Christian story tells us the ultimate meaning of ourselves and the world. In doing so, it tells us the kind of people we ought to be, the goods we ought to pursue, the dangers we ought to avoid, the kind of world we ought to seek. It provides the backdrop or framework that ought to shape our individual decisions. When decision-making is separated from this framework, it loses its perspective. It can easily become a merely rationalistic and sterile ethic subject to the distortions of self-interested perspectives and cultural drifts, a kind of contracted etiquette with no relation to the ultimate meaning of persons. (Indeed, even when our deliberations are nourished by the biblical narrative, they do not escape the *reliquiae peccati* in us.)

A medical symbol of this separation is a statement of Terry Kennedy, a spokesman for Nassau Hospital, in the Brother Fox case.[11] Kennedy stated: "Our mission is to do all that we can to maintain life." The implication is that mere life (ventilation and circulation) has a human value as such and must be maintained. The Christian story will not, in my judgment, support this. Once a value-judgment is separated from the story that displays our meaning, it begins to be controlled by mere technology. This is the crux of my problem with Paul Ramsey's "medical indications policy" with regard to the dying—as if such judgments were exclusively scientific in character.[12]

Here we happen upon the inherent danger of medicine practiced in a Western secularized society. In such a society (by definition), the story that reveals the meaning of life is no longer widely functional. Meaning must be derived from elsewhere, and decisions shaped in other ways. Thus in our secularized society we have (1) the assertion of autonomy as the controlling value of the person; (2) the canonization of pluralism as instrumental to it. The modern liberal secularized society sees its task as protecting the individual's autonomy to do his/her own thing. The function of the state is to guarantee and protect the right of noninterference. I am not attacking autonomy. It is surely a precious value. But it is the condition of moral behavior, not its exhaustive definition. To view it as exhaustive is to ask the state to remain neutral on our most treasured and basic values (e.g., the family). In this context Daniel Callahan has noted that "general solutions and binding group norms need to be worked out that are of more than a consensual or procedural kind."[13] He continues: "If personal morality comes down to nothing more than the exercise of free choice, with no principles available for moral judgment of the quality of those choices, then we will have a 'moral vacuum.'"[14]

It is precisely the secularism of Western society that makes the humane use of our technology seem so problematic. We have distanced ourselves from the very matrix (story) that is the only complete indicator of the truly human. How can we be humane without full knowledge of the human? Considerations such as these lead to the assertion that theology is utterly essential to bioethical discussions. It does not give us concrete answers or ready-made rules. But it does tell us who we are, where we come from, where we are going, who we ought to be becoming. It is only against such understandings that our concrete deliberations can remain truly humane and promote our best interests.

Vatican II put it as follows: "Faith throws a new light on everything, manifests God's design for man's total vocation, and thus directs the mind to solutions which are *fully human*."[15] It further stated: "But only God, who created man to His own image and ransoms him from sin, provides a fully adequate answer to these questions. This He does through what He has revealed in Christ His Son, who became man. Whoever follows after Christ, the perfect man, *becomes himself more of a man*."[16]

The Catholic tradition, in dealing with concrete moral problems, has encapsulated the way faith "*directs the mind to solutions*" in the phrase "reason informed by faith." Thus Pius

XII, when speaking of the suppression of consciousness, stated that it was "permitted by natural morality and *in keeping with the spirit of the Gospel.*"[17] The Congregation for the Doctrine of the Faith, in the *Declaration on Euthanasia*, referred to "human and Christian prudence." "Reason informed by faith" is neither reason *replaced* by faith nor reason *without* faith. It is reason shaped by faith, and in my judgment this shaping takes the form of perspectives, themes, insights associated with the story that aid us to construe the world.

What are some of these perspectives and insights that ought to inform our reasoning in the area of biomedicine? Hazardous as it may be to attempt this distillation, I should like to do so at least as a basis for further discussion.

1. *Life as a basic but not absolute good.* The fact that we are pilgrims, that Christ has overcome death and lives, that we will also live with Him, yields a general value judgment on the meaning and value of life as we now live it. It can be formulated as follows: life is a basic good but not an absolute one. It is *basic* because, as the Congregation for the Doctrine of the Faith worded it, it is the "necessary source and condition of every human activity and of all society."[18] It is not *absolute* because there are higher goods for which life can be sacrificed (glory of God, salvation of souls, service of one's brethren, etc.). Thus in John (15:13): "There is no greater love than this: to lay down one's life for one's friends." Therefore laying down one's life for another cannot be contrary to the faith or story or meaning of humankind. It is, after Jesus' example, life's greatest fulfillment, even though it is the end of life as we now know it. Negatively, we could word this value judgment as follows: death is an evil but not an absolute or unconditioned one.

This value judgment has immediate relevance for care for the ill and dying. It issues in a basic attitude or policy: not all means must be used to preserve life. Why? Pius XII, in a 1952 address to the International Congress of Anesthesiologists, stated: "A more strict obligation would be too burdensome for most men and would render the attainment of the higher, more important good too difficult. Life, health, all temporal activities are in fact subordinated to spiritual ends."[19] In other words, there are higher values than life in the living of it. There are also higher values in the dying of it.

What Pius XII was saying, then, is that forcing (morally) one to take *all* means is tantamount to forcing attention and energies on a subordinate good in a way that prejudices a higher good, even eventually making it unrecognizable as a good. Excessive concern for the temporal is at some point neglect of the eternal. An obligation to use all means to preserve life would be a devaluation of human life, since it would remove life from the context or story that is the source of its ultimate value.

Thus the Catholic tradition has moved between two extremes: medico-moral optimism or vitalism (which preserves life with all means, at any cost, no matter what its condition) and medico-moral pessimism (which actively kills when life becomes onerous, dysfunctional, boring). Merely technological judgments could easily fall into either of these two traps.

Thus far theology. It yields a value judgment and a general policy or attitude. It provides the framework for subsequent moral reasoning. It tells us that life is a gift with a purpose and destiny. Dying is the last or waning moments of this "new creature." At this point moral reasoning (reason informed by faith) must assume its proper responsibilities to answer questions like: (1) What means ought to be used, what need not be? (2) What shall we call such means? (3) Who enjoys the prerogative and/or duty of decision-making? (4) What is to be done with now incompetent and always incompetent patients in critical illness? The sources of faith do not provide direct answers to these questions in my judgment.

2.   *Extension to nascent life.* Paul Ramsey refers to the "shape of biblical thought" on nascent life.[20] Just as God called the world out of chaos (nothing), just as He created a people (Israel) out of next to nothing and the new Israel out of insignificant beginnings, so He calls into being each one of us. Thus Psalm 139: "Truly you have formed my inmost being; you knit me in my mother's womb." This is the thought-form that governs the biblical account of human life.

Of those sincere Christians who believe the Bible says nothing definitive to the abortion problem, Ramsey states that they have responded to the biblical account with "Speak, Lord, and thy servant will think it over."[21] Ramsey concludes that "far more than any argument, it was surely the power of the nativity stories and their place in ritual and celebration and song that tempered the conscience of the West to its audacious effort to wipe out the practice of abortion and infanticide." In other words, the biblical story teaches us to think of unborn children is a very special way. Albert Outler puts it as follows:

> One of Christianity's oldest traditions is sacredness of human life as an implication of the Christian conviction about God and the good life. If all persons are equally the creatures of the one God, then none of these creatures is authorized to play God toward any other. And if all persons are cherished by God, regardless of merit, we ought also to cherish each other in the same spirit. This was the ground on which the early Christians rejected the prevalent Graeco-Roman codes of sexuality in which abortion and infanticide were commonplace. Christian moralists found them profoundly irreligious and proposed instead an ethic of compassion (adopted from the Jewish matrix) that proscribed abortion and encouraged "adoption."

It should be noted that this does not settle the moral rightfulness or wrongfulness of any particular abortion. That is the task of moral reason when faced with desperate conflicts—but moral reason *so informed.* Or as Ramsey says: "Perhaps that conclusively settles nothing yet, but this is how we should *look on* the question."[22] A simple prochoice *moral* position is in conflict with the biblical story.

3. *What is to be valued in human life.* James Gustafson has stated of medical ethics that "the most important ethical task is to develop as precisely and thoroughly as possible the qualities of well-being...those qualities that are valued about human physical life as the condition *sine qua non* for other values."[23]

The Christian story can provide help here. Pius XII referred to a "higher, more important good," to "spiritual ends." What is this good, what are these ends? One answer—not the only one—can be given in terms of love of God and neighbor. Such love sums up briefly the meaning, substance, and consummation of life. As Matthew puts it on the lips of Jesus: "On these two commandments the whole law is based, and the prophets as well" (Matt. 22:40). One scarcely needs to belabor the point in the biblical accounts. Charity is the epitome of the entire law (Gal. 5:14). It is more elevated than all charisms (1 Cor. 13:13). It is the bond of perfection (Col. 3:14). It ought to be so characteristic of Christians that they are recognized by their love.

What can easily be missed is that these two goods are not separable. Saint John notes: "If any man says I love God and hates his brother, he is a liar. For he who loves not his brother, whom he sees, how can he love God, whom he does not see?" (1 John 4:20–21). This means that our love of neighbor is in some very real sense our love of God. The good our love wants to do Him and to which He enables us can be done only for the neighbor, as Karl Rahner has so forcefully argued.[24] It is in others that God demands to be recognized and loved. If this is true, it means that in Christian perspective, the meaning, substance, and consummation of life are found in human *relationships*.

In the Christian tradition, therefore, life is not a value to be preserved in and for itself. To maintain this would commit me to a form of medical vitalism that makes no human and Christian sense. It is a value to be preserved precisely as a condition for other values, and therefore insofar as these values remain at least minimally attainable or, as Gustafson puts it, "as the condition *sine qua non* for other values." Since these other values cluster around and are rooted in human relationships, it seems to follow that life is a value to be preserved only insofar as it contains some potentiality for human relationships.

These general reflections constitute the shape of, the informing of, our reasoning as we deliberate about the more concrete problems of biomedicine, especially the duty to preserve life. They do not replace reasoning; but moral reasoning ought to be compatible with them.

Two examples may help, one of incompatibility, one of compatibility. In the instance of Brother Fox, Dr. Edward Kelly, surgeon in the case, stated that once a respirator is employed "it should not be removed."[25] Implied—doubtless unwittingly—in such a judgment is the absolutization of physical life—and that is incompatible with the Christian story.

As an example of compatibility with Christian perspectives, I would propose the living will composed by Sissela Bok. It reads as follows:

> I wish to live a full and long life, but not at all costs. If my death is near and cannot be avoided, and if I have lost the ability to interact with others and have no reasonable chance of regaining this ability, or if my suffering is intense and irreversible, I do not want to have my life prolonged. I would then ask not to be subjected to surgery or resuscitation. Nor would I then wish to have life support from mechanical ventilators, intensive care services, or other life prolonging procedures, including the administration of antibiotics and blood products. I would wish, rather, to have care which gives comfort and support, which facilitates my interaction with others to the extent that this is possible, and which brings peace.[26]

Bok has identified the two conditions beyond mere circulation and ventilation that ought to be present before life makes life-sustaining claims upon us: some minimal potential for interrelating, absence of profound and intractable pain. I believe most of us, were we to construct a living will, would come close to the formulations of Bok.

4. *Our essential sociality.* In the Judeo-Christian story, God relates to and covenants with a people. Both the Old and New Testament stories yield such abundant evidence of this that it need not be documented. As Christians, we live, move, and have our Christian being as a believing group, an *ecclesia*. Our being in Christ is a shared being. We are vines of the same branch, sheep of the same shepherd.

This fact—attested by so many biblical images—underscores two aspects of our personhood that are highly relevant to medical ethics: our essential equality (regardless of functional importance) and our radical sociality. Let me emphasize this latter aspect. It suggests that our well-being is interdependent. It cannot be conceived of or realistically pursued independently of the good of others. Social insertion is part of our being and becoming. As Joseph Sittler words it, "personhood is a social state."[27]

This perspective provides the backdrop for our deliberations on such procedures as transplantation of organs and nontherapeutic experimentation. For instance, given certain conditions, I believe minimal- or no-risk experimentation on the incompetent (fetuses, babies) can be justified. When there is little or no risk to the incompetent and great potential benefit to others that cannot be had in any other way, it is reasonable to conclude that the incompetent would not object were they capable of giving consent. Such a construction seems a "connatural" aspect of sociability. Indeed, I have argued that those who proscribe all such experimentation on the grounds that it is "offensive touching" in violation of the canons of consent often define the rights of the incompetent in an individualistic and atomistic way, without consideration of our radical sociality.[28] The Christian story does not yield conditions and protocols for human experimentation. But in describing our status in Christ as a shared status, it makes it especially intelligible to think that our well-being and the rights that protect this flourishing cannot be conceived in isolation from others.

Our radical equality before our Heavenly Father should exercise a steadying and restraining influence as we face what are and will continue to be the biggest and most complex problems in biomedicine: the problems of distributive justice (use of limited resources, equitable national policy of health care, adjudication of competing interests in the biomedical field).

5. *The sphere of life-giving and love-making.* Paul Ramsey has repeatedly referred to the moral bond that exists between the procreative and communicative goods of marriage. He sees this as the nature of parenthood "in the first of it." Ramsey combines the prologue of John with Ephesians 5 to discover the nature of marriage and parenting. As he words it:

> We procreate new beings like ourselves in the midst of our
> love for one another, and in this there is a trace of the original
> mystery by which God created the world because of His

love. God created nothing apart from His love; and without the divine love was not anything made that was made. Neither should there be among man and woman, whose man-womanhood is in the image of God, any love set out of the context of responsibility for procreation or any begetting apart from or from beyond the sphere of their love. There is a reflection of God's love binding Himself to the world and the world to Himself to be found in the claim He placed upon man and woman in their creation when He bound the nurturing of marital love and procreation together in the nature of human sexuality.[29]

Clearly Ramsey believes that we may not put radically (in principle) asunder what God has joined together. In a similar vein Bishop J. Francis Stafford, auxiliary bishop of Baltimore, refers to the "ancient and momentous biblical insight of the inseparability of the procreative and unitive aspects of human sexuality."[30] This perspective of inseparability is common in Catholic theologians like Rahner and Haring. Where Ramsey restricts this inseparability to marriage (not individual acts), Bishop Stafford would apply it to individual acts.

Whatever the case (and I agree with Ramsey in his rejection of act analysis), it is clear that this perspective has significance for one's understanding of contraception, sterilization, and reproduction technologies (AIH, AID, *in vitro* fertilization, surrogate motherhood, etc.).

Let us take artificial insemination as an example. Vatican II affirms (GS 48, 50) that by their very nature marriage and marital love are ordained toward the procreation and education of children, that the child is the ultimate crown of marriage. In other words, the child is the fruit of marriage and marital love.

Applying this to AIH, Louis Janssens writes:

This can also be true when the child is conceived through AIH. Indeed it is still brought into being in the context of *marriage* and owes its life to the contribution of two persons who are united in marriage. It is also the fruit of *marital love*: in marital love it is desired by the couple and during the pregnancy it is waited for in a shared, joyful anticipation.[31]

Notwithstanding the condemnation of AIH by Pius XII, it is safe to say that the procedure is now accepted by very many theologians. The *spheres* of procreation and marital love are not put radically asunder.

Louis Janssens is of the opinion that even AID cannot be absolutely excluded. He is the first—and only—Catholic author I know of who has arrived at this conclusion. He sees AID as containing both a value and a disvalue. "The moral question is whether there is a proportionate reason (*ratio proportionata*) to make this activity responsible or balance the positive and negative aspects according to the rules of priorities."[32] Under certain conditions, Janssens believes there can be such a *ratio proportionata*.

I have not arrived myself at such a judgment. The basic analysis of Karl Rahner seems to me to remain persuasive. He writes:

> Now this personal love which is consummated sexually has within it an essential inner relation to the child, for the child is an embodiment of the abiding unity of the marriage partners which is expressed in marital union. Genetic manipulation [Rahner means AID], however, does two things: it fundamentally separates the marital union from the procreation of a new person as this permanent embodiment of the unity of married love; and it transfers procreation, isolated and torn from its human matrix, to an area outside man's sphere of intimacy. It is this sphere of intimacy which is the proper context for sexual union, which itself implies the fundamental readiness of the marriage partners to let their unity take the form of a child.[33]

This, plus a series of subordinate but supportive practical arguments, leads me to believe that there is not the *ratio proportionata* argued by Janssens.

6. *Heterosexual permanent marriage as normative.* Very close to the point just made is the normative character of marriage in the Christian story. In the Christian story, it is taken for granted that permanent heterosexual marriage is normative. This does not mean that every such marriage is a guarantee of happiness or success. Nor does it imply that every homosexual union is destructive, unstable, or necessarily morally wrong. It means simply that monogamous marriage provides us with our best chance to humanize our sexuality and bridge the separate-

ness and isolation of our individual selves. *Therefore* we all *ought* (= normative) to try to make this the context for the expression of our full sexuality. In this sense Roger Shinn refers to "a clear emphasis on the normative place of heterosexual love" in Christian theology.[34] Similarly Ralph Weltge refers to the man and woman joined together as one flesh in faithful love as "the biblical norm."[35]

This Christian norm will give shape to our deliberations about biomedicine's proper ministry to problems of teenagers, of homosexuals, and of transsexual surgery.

Thus far I have been discussing Christian perspectives or themes or insights that give shape to our ethical deliberations in biomedicine. I have mentioned six. (1) Life as a basic but not absolute value. (2) The extension of this evaluation to nascent life. (3) The potential for human relationships as that aspect of physical life to be valued. (4) The radical sociality of the human person. (5) The inseparability of the unitive and procreative goods. (6) Permanent heterosexual union as normative. There are probably many more themes that are woven into the Christian story. But I am confident that these are dimensions of our being pilgrims created in the image and likeness of God.

Above, the influence of these themes on biomedical ethics was rendered in the phrase "reason informed by faith." The question naturally arises about those who do not share this story, or even have a different story. If the theological contribution to medical ethics must be derived from a particularistic story, is not that contribution inherently isolating? Those who do not agree with the themes I have disengaged from the story need only say, "Sorry, I do not share your story." There the conversation stops. Public policy discussion is paralyzed in the irreconcilable stand-off of conflicting stories and worldviews. And public policy is increasingly the area in which the problems of biomedicine will be discussed and decided, a point sharply made by Daniel Callahan in his Shattuck lecture.[36]

That would be a serious, perhaps insuperable, problem if the themes I have disengaged from the Christian story were thought to be mysterious—that is, utterly impervious to human insight without the story. In the Catholic reading of the Christian story that is not the case. The themes I have lifted out are thought to be inherently intelligible and recommendable—

difficult as it might be practically for a sinful people to maintain a sure grasp on these perspectives without the nourishing support of the story. Thus, for example, the Christian story is not the only cognitive source for the radical sociability of persons, for the immorality of infanticide and abortion, etc., even though historically these insights may be strongly attached to the story. In this epistemological sense, these insights are not specific to Christians. They can be and are shared by others.

Roger Shinn is very close to what I am attempting to formulate when he notes that the ethical awareness given to Christians in Christ "meets some similar intimations or signs of confirmation in wider human experience."[37] Christians believe, as Shinn notes, that the Logos made flesh in Christ is the identical Logos through which the world was created. He concludes: "They [Christians] do not expect the Christian faith and insight to be confirmed by unanimous agreement of all people, even all decent and idealistic people. But they do expect the fundamental Christian motifs to have some persuasiveness in general experience."[38]

Since these insights can be shared by others, I would judge that the Christian warrants are confirmatory rather than originating. I have suggested elsewhere (on abortion) that "these evaluations can be and have been shared by others than Christians of course. But Christians have particular warrants for resisting any cultural callousing of them."[39] Particular warrants might be the most accurate and acceptable way of specifying the meaning of "reason informed by faith." If it is, it makes it possible for the Christian to share fully in discussions in the public forum without annexing non-Christians into a story not their own.

For many years there has been discussion framed in terms of how Athens relates to Jerusalem. Jerusalem, it is argued, tells stories but has no theology properly so called. Athens analyzes and rationalizes, without need of a story or in lofty independence of all particular stories. Thus, and in stark contrast, if you belong to Jerusalem, you have no need of reason. If you are of Athens, you have no need of a story.

The Catholic Christian tradition, as I understand it, refuses to accept the desperate exclusivity of these alternatives. Briefly, it reasons about its story. In the process it hopes to and claims to disclose surprising and delightful insights about the human condition as such. These insights are not, therefore, eccentric refractions limited in application to a particular historical community. For instance, the sacredness of nascent life is not an insight that applies only to Catholic babies—as if it were wrong to abort Catholic babies, but perfectly all right to do so with Muslim, Protestant, or Jewish babies. Quite the contrary. Reasoning about the Christian story makes a bolder claim. It claims to reveal the deeper dimensions of the universally human. Since Christian ethics is the objectification in Jesus Christ of what every person experiences of him/herself in his/her subjectivity, "it does not and cannot add to human ethical self-understanding as such any material content that is, in principle, 'strange' or 'foreign' to man as he exists and experiences himself in this world."[40] However, a person within the Christian community has access to a privileged articulation, in objective form, of this experience of subjectivity. Precisely because the resources of Scripture, dogma, and Christian life (the "storied community") are the fullest available objectifications of the common human experience, "the articulation of man's image of his moral good that is possible within historical Christian communities remains privileged in its access to enlarged perspectives on man."[41]

That is a bold claim, and even an arrogant one unless it is clearly remembered that Christian communities have, more frequently than it is comforting to recall, botched the job. It is a claim entertained neither by Jerusalem nor by Athens—but one which offers some modest hope of overcoming the partialities of either alternative.

Notes

1. Lisa Sowle Cahill, "Within Shouting Distance: Paul Ramsey and Richard McCormick on Method," *Journal of Medicine and Philosophy* 4 (1979): 398–417.

2. Alasdair MacIntyre, "Theology, Ethics and the Ethics of Medicine and Health Care," *Journal of Medicine and Philosophy* 4 (1979): 435–443.

3. F. Hurth and P. M. Abellan, *De Principiis, de virtutibus et Praeceptis* (Rome: Gregorian University, 1948), p. 43.

4.   James M. Gustafson, The Contributions of Theology to Medical Ethics (Milwaukee: Marquette University, 1975).

5.   James M. Gustafson, "A Theocentric Interpretation of Life," Christian Century 97 (1980): 754–760. See also his "Theology Confronts Technology and the Life Sciences," Commonweal 105 (1978): 386–392.

6.   Richard A. McCormick, How Brave a New World? (New York: Doubleday, 1981), pp. 3–17.

7.   John M. Finnis, "Natural Law and Unnatural Acts," Heythrop Journal 11 (1970): 365–387.

8.   Pius XII, Acta Apostolicae Sedis 43 (1951) 835–854.

9.   Franz Bockle, "Glaube und Handeln," Concilium 120 (1976): 641-647.

10.   Declaration on Euthanasia (Vatican City: Vatican Polyglot Press, 1980); also in Origins 10 (1980): 154–157.

11.   For details of the Brother Fox case, see R. McCormick and R. Veach, "The Preservation of Life and Self-Determination," Theological Studies 4 (1980): 390–396.

12.   Among other references, cf. Paul Ramsey, "Two-Step Fantastic: The Continuing Case of Brother Fox," Theological Studies 42 (1981): 122–134.

13.   Daniel Callahan, "Shattuck Lecture: Contemporary Biomedical Ethics," New England Journal of Medicine 302, no. 22 (1980): 1232.

14.   Ibid., p. 1233.

15.   The Documents of Vatican II (New York: America Press, 1966), p. 209.

16.   Ibid., p. 240.

17.   Pius XII, The Pope Speaks 4 (1957): 45; Acta Apostolicae Sedis 48 (1957): 129–147. In a latter speech on prolongation of life, Pius XII refers to "natural reason and Christian morals" as if they were almost identical. The Pope Speaks 4 (1958) 395.

18.   Declaration on Euthanasia (see note 10 above).

19.   Pius XII, Acta Apostolicae Sedis 49 (1957): 1031–1032.

20.   Paul Ramsey, "Liturgy and Ethics," Journal of Religious Ethics 7 (1979): 139–171.

21.   Ibid.

22.   Ibid., p. 161.

23.   Cf. Gustafson, Contributions of Theology to Medical Ethics, pp. 85–86.

24.   Karl Rahner, Theological Investigations (Baltimore: Helicon, 1969), 6:231–249.

25.   Cf. Theological Studies 42 (1981): 109.

26.   Sissela Bok, "Personal Directions for Care at the End of Life,"

New England Journal of Medicine 295 (1976): 367–369.

27. Joseph Sittler, Grace Notes and Other Fragments (Philadelphia: Fortune Press, 1981), p. 98.

28. McCormick, How Brave a New World?, pp. 87–98.

29. Paul Ramsey, in The Vatican Council and the World of Today (Brown University, 1966), no pagination.

30. J. Francis Stafford, "The Year of the Family Revisited," America 144 (1981): 399–403.

31. Louis Janssens, "Artificial Insemination: Ethical Considerations," Louvain Studies 8 (1980): 3–29.

32. Ibid., p. 28.

33. Karl Rahner, "The Problem of Genetic Manipulation," Theological Investigations, 9: (New York: Herder & Herder, 1972), p. 246.

34. Roger L. Shinn, "Homosexuality: Christian Conviction and Inquiry," in The Same Sex, ed. Ralph W. Weltge (Philadelphia: Pilgrim Press, 1969), p. 52.

35. Ralph W. Weltge, "The Paradox of Man and Woman," in The Same Sex, p. 57.

36. See above, n. 13.

37. "Homosexuality," p. 51.

38. Ibid.

39. See How Brave a New World?, pp. 197–198.

40. James F. Bresnahan, "Rahner's Christian Ethics," America 123 (1970): 351–354.

41. Ibid.

Old Traditions, New Decisions: Protestant Perspectives

Roger L. Shinn

Protestant Christianity, which thrives on controversy over many issues, has no united mind on modern science and technology, but it has a great awareness of the urgent ethical issues connected with contemporary scientific-technological achievements. A vivid example of both the diversity of opinions and the shared concerns was the World Council of Churches' Conference on Faith, Science and the Future, convened at the Massachusetts Institute of Technology in the summer of 1979.[1] Although the conference was not exclusively Protestant—there was strong Eastern Orthodox participation, and the speakers included Roman Catholics, Jews, Muslims, Buddhists, and agnostics—it was predominantly Protestant in makeup. And it is hard to say which was the more evident: the excitement of the controversies or the intensity of shared concern about the opportunities and perils of modern technology.

Public attention centers on a variety of specific issues, including discoveries in genetics, new medical achievements, the world energy problem, the population explosion, hunger and the green revolution, the exhaustion of critical resources, new sources of energy, and the heightening threat of new weapons. The traditional ethical sources do not explicitly address these problems, and contemporary religious communities are sometimes reinterpreting their heritages, sometimes creating new ethical codes and guidelines.

Behind the specific issues is a deeper grappling with the religious meaning of the new powers of human beings achieved through the scientific-technological enterprise. The theological and ethical judgments on such basic issues permeate all the debates on details. I begin this investigation by looking at some persistent themes in their interactions.

THREE STRANDS IN PROTESTANT THOUGHT

The variety of Protestant opinions on the value and importance of science and its technologies may be reduced to three general positions which run like threads through the fabric of contemporary discussions. One position applauds technology and claims credit for Christianity in nurturing it. A second position criticizes technology as inherently dangerous, possibly even demonic. A third, more recent position sounds a warning about the ecological destructiveness of technologies and calls for a revision of them.

Acclaim and Self-Congratulation

One prominent strand in Protestant thought sees science and technology as human accomplishments to be celebrated and committed to the improvement of life. Any serious thinking in this vein acknowledges that these achievements often are misused in predatory and destructive ways. But human rationality and creativity are acknowledged as divine gifts. God has empowered human beings to act upon nature and modify it for human purposes.

Furthermore, in this way of thinking, the Hebrew and Christian faiths have contributed indispensably to the rise of science. Alfred North Whitehead pointed out that modern science arose out of the background of "the medieval insistence on the rationality of God, conceived as with the personal energy of Jehovah and with the rationality of a Greek philosopher."[2] The Hebrews alone were not highly interested in science, and their prophets sometimes criticized the technological arrogance of societies that built their towers of Babel and lost their reverence for God. The Greeks had more of a gift for mathematics (in some of its modes) and theoretical understanding of the world, but usually so elevated theory above practice that they did little with experimentation and technology. However, the intermingling of Hebrew and Greek traditions prepared the way for scientific investigation.

One prerequisite for scientific investigation was the desacralizing of nature. Hebrew-Christian monotheism removed the divinities that populated nature in animistic and polytheistic faiths; it made possible the exploration of nature uninhibited by traditional taboos. Yet it so related the Creator and creation that eventually Puritan faith would understand science as a form of reverence in which the scientist seeks to think God's thoughts after him.

Scientific technologies require not only an intellectual basis but also a social context. When Hero of Alexandria built a steam engine, he and his society did nothing with it except to enjoy it as a novelty.[3] But when Thomas Newcomen and James Watt developed the steam engine of the eighteenth century, society immediately put it to industrial use. If we wonder why the Alexandrians did not exploit Hero's invention, the reasons are complex. One probable reason is that metallurgy was not sufficiently developed to make a truly practical engine. But a cultural reason is that a society which separated intellectual inquiry from muscular work and economic production had no powerful incentive to drive a technology. People who believe that God is a creator and worker,[4] who also enjoys rest, are able (like the Benedictine monks) to see productive labor as part of their spiritual discipline.[5] Then, even though they put a value on physical work, they have motivations to make work easier through technology. Human ingenuity, emancipated from the Platonic-Aristotelian disdain for the humdrum practical, finds expression in technology.

Social causation is infinitely complex, and much of what I have described is rationalization after the fact. But in the twentieth century some Protestants, impressed by the liberating power of technology, raised a paean of praise for it and congratulated the religious traditions that contributed to it. They saw the "disenchantment" that Max Weber had described[6] and the secularization that many religious people deplored as opportunities for human freedom and achievement. Thus Arend van Leeuwen, the Dutch theologian with experience in Egypt and

Indonesia, acclaimed the gift of Christianity as "liberation ... from the fetters of 'sacred' tradition, together with the renewal of society in the direction of a truly secular and man-made order of life."[7] In the United States, Harvey Cox, in his influential book *The Secular City*, argued that biblical faith, particularly as interpreted by Barthian theology, overcame myth and ontology in such a way that "man's freedom to master and shape, to create and explore now reaches out to the ends of the earth and beyond."[8]

Those writers also had a passion for justice and, far from merely cheering on technology, recognized its misuses and urged its redirection. But their basic mood was affirmation. Christians, they held, should rejoice in technology and the contribution of their faith to its successes.

Criticism of the Demonic

The Christian enthusiasts for technology were consciously refuting a differing, in some ways an opposing tradition. Both the Hebrew Scriptures (as I have already noted) and Christian theology have often resisted technological innovation. Sometimes the resistance has been only an inertia. One task of faith is to jar people out of nostalgic affection for their past and into awareness of possibilities for their future. When a religion has developed its cult, doctrine, and metaphysics in a prescientific, pretechnological age, its progressive formulators will often have to break up encrusted traditions. Given the blundering resistance of the church to Copernicus, Galileo, and Darwin, twentieth-century Protestantism has been right in learning to welcome some scientific and technological changes.

But skepticism about the values of technological change has not been merely nostalgic. Reinhold Niebuhr made perceptive criticisms of various forms of the modern faith in progress, including scientific-technological messianism. He insisted that "progress" is usually an enhancement of human powers for evil or for good.[9]

Christians concerned about social justice and forms of social organization have shared some of the ambivalence of Karl Marx toward technology. Before Marx, Adam Smith argued that technology and the division of labor were key contributors to productivity and human betterment. Marx, by contrast, saw the division of labor as a contributor to the dehumanization of laborers and to class struggle. Yet in his materialism he fully endorsed the desacralization of nature. He shared with Smith the eagerness "to increase the total of productive forces as rapidly as possible,"[10] and he assumed that the future socialist society would be built upon the productive achievements already made by the bourgeoisie. In a somewhat similar way, many Christians tried both to appropriate technology and to criticize the dynamics that they saw lurking in it.

The most eloquent and prolific critic of technology among contemporary Protestant writers has been Jacques Ellul, the French sociologist, sometime politician, and theologian. Precisely speaking, his target is "technique," not technology. But Ellul defines *la technique* as "the *totality of methods rationally arrived at and having absolute efficiency* (for a given stage of development) in *every* field of human activity."[11] It is, in effect, technology applied not only to engineering problems but to the whole of society. And Ellul sees it as profoundly demonic.

In past history, says Ellul, technique was an element in civilization. But that is no longer the case. "Today *technique has taken over the whole of civilization.*"[12] The result is the loss of human freedom and subordination of persons to technology. "The human being is no longer in any sense the agent of choice.... He is a device for recording effects and results obtained by various techniques."[13]

The intense, even strident insistence on a demonic fatalism in technology is by no means a majority opinion in contemporary Protestantism. But it is a theme that emerges frequently in open or veiled ways.

Ecological Warnings

A third strand in Protestant Christianity, although it has old roots, leapt into prominence with the heightened ecological consciousness of the 1960s. Lynn White, Jr., who had been quietly teaching and writing medieval history for a long time, suddenly became almost a household name. Because of its timeliness and its scintillating style, his address to the American Association for the Advancement of Science in 1966, "The Historical Roots of our Ecologic Crisis," caught the ear of scientists, theologians, and journalists. At the time when van Leeuwen and Cox were arousing wide attention, White accepted their historical premises, yet turned a sharp criticism upon their conclusions. His differences with Ellul were equally sharp. Although White mentioned none of these writers, his own statement led to many reconsiderations of their positions.

"The victory of Christianity over paganism," said White, "was the greatest psychic revolution in the history of our culture." Even in our contemporary era, often called "post-Christian," he saw the consequences of that revolution in the consciousness and the practices of a world that subordinated nature to human desires. Christianity, he said, especially in its dominant Western formulations, "is the most anthropocentric religion the world has seen." The results are today terribly threatening. "By destroying pagan animism, Christianity made it possible to exploit nature in a mood of indifference to the feelings of natural objects."[14] Now we are suffering the consequences.

A few years later Arnold Toynbee took up the same theme. The monotheism of the Book of Genesis, he said, "has removed the age-old restraint that was once placed on man's greed by his awe." As a result, nature "is taking her revenge on us unmistakably in our time."[15]

Lynn White proposed as an answer to our ecological predicament a recovery of the Christian insights of Saint Francis of Assisi: "His unique view of nature and of man rested on a unique sort of pan-psychism of all things animate and inanimate, designed for the glorification of their transcendent Creator, who, in the ultimate gesture of cosmic humility, assumed flesh, lay helpless in a manger, and hung dying on a scaffold."[16] Then (surely with tongue in cheek, since he was addressing America's greatest scientific organization) he proposed that Saint Francis be made "a patron saint for ecologists." To complete the story, Pope John Paul II did exactly that on April 6, 1980.

In response to White, René Dubos made a counterproposal. He nominated Saint Benedict of Nursia as "a patron saint of those who believe that true conservation means not only protecting nature against human misbehavior but also developing human activities which favor a creative, harmonious relationship between man and nature."[17] Benedict, unlike Francis, developed an ethic and a system of economic production.

The Protestant interest in two medieval Catholic monks is a sign of the ecumenical climate of our time. And the serious ecological concerns of this era have led some Protestants to renewed interest in those of their own modern theologies that emphasize the intimate relation between the human and nonhuman creation. Before most of the church had become sensitive to ecological issues, Joseph Sittler, in his address at the 1961 Assembly of the World Council of Churches in New Delhi, pointed out the *theological* importance of "the care of the earth, the realm of nature as a theater of grace, the ordering of the thick material procedures that make available to or deprive men of bread and peace."[18] Process theologians (Daniel Day Williams and John Cobb, among others) had long been emphasizing the relation of human nature to the rest of nature. Paul Tillich had looked at the meaning of human being in the context of all being. H. Richard Niebuhr in his "radical monotheism" had gone through a dialectical movement of the secularization of nature (because it is not God) and then the resanctifying of it (because it is the creation of God).[19] More recently James Gustafson has urged a return from excessively anthropocentric to theocentric faith and ethics.[20] Most of these theologians were not preoccupied with issues of technology. For theological reasons they set a direction that called for reconsideration of the meaning and uses of technology.

FROM BASIC BELIEF TO CONCRETE SOCIAL DECISIONS

The three themes I have described do not of themselves directly prescribe answers to concrete questions about the uses of technology in the contemporary world. But they express the eagerness, the skepticism, or the caution with which people respond to new technical possibilities. Since the processes that produce new technologies are not the processes that judge the value of those technologies, the basic beliefs and attitudes of people and societies have much to do with their decisions on what to do with new technical opportunities.

As broad case studies I shall look at (1) the controversies over the exploitation of natural resources, especially of energy, and (2) the burgeoning field of bioethics. Both are examples of issues where fundamental religious attitudes interact with new information and new achievements. Both are cases where urgent practical decisions relate to religious sensitivities and commitments. I here neglect a third equally important case, the issue of nuclear weapons, because it is different in kind: there is virtual unanimity that nuclear war is inherently evil, even though there is great controversy about the ways of preventing it. In the two areas I am choosing for discussion, there are lively debates about the desirability of many new goals and practices as well as about the ways of achieving or stopping them.

Use of Limited Resources, Especially Energy

The contemporary worries about shortages of energy, both in intermittent emergencies and in the long-term future, are the most visible evidence of a far wider concern about the question of the natural resources that support technological societies. The emergence of the ethical issues in Protestant thinking belongs to a recent history that, for convenience, I can here trace from 1966. That was the year when the World Council of Churches (WCC) called a conference in Geneva, Switzerland, on "Christians in the Technical and Social Revolutions of Our Time."[21] The conference was noteworthy both for the large participation of laypeople from many walks of life and for the impressive representation from areas beyond the North Atlantic countries that then dominated technological power.

In relating to the two revolutions of the title of the conference, the delegates found themselves more verbally adept on social revolutions than on technical revolutions. Eloquent speakers—especially from Africa, Latin America, and Asia—denounced the injustices of colonialism and neocolonialism. Discussion of technology was less pointed, partly because there were far fewer physical scientists and technologists than social scientists in attendance. One recommendation of the conference was that the churches give more attention to the impact of technology on society.

In the following years the Department of Church and Society took up that task. It soon discovered that it had to face ethical issues that were then neglected by most of the world. At a meeting in Nemi, Italy, in 1971 it heard a report from Jørgen

Randers, one of the authors of *The Limits to Growth*, a book yet to be published and to leap into international controversy.[22] This book, the product of an international study project centered at the Massachusetts Institute of Technology and sponsored by the Club of Rome, was the most dramatic of many studies that called the world's attention to the conflict between inexhaustible human desires and exhaustible resources.

The thesis was that technological societies, which had made stupendous achievements in increasing human production and consumption, were consuming resources at an exponentially rising rate that *could not* continue. For a time the problem had been obscured by the seeming ability of technology to create new resources. Although technology did not actually create petroleum, it created systems in which petroleum, which had been largely unused through most of human history, became a resource for industry. But technology was consuming that finite quantity of petroleum at spectacular rates—more in the decade of the 1950s than in all past history, and more again in the 1960s than in all the past, including the 1950s. That tempo of increase could not possibly persist, and the time was sure to come, within a few decades, when consumption must decrease. The world was not preparing for so stark a change.

Energy is the most prominent of many problems that compose the whole picture of human life in a finite world. There are limits to other resources, notably water, forests, agricultural land, and some metals. Rising population, rising consumption, and rising pollution push against the limits. But from here on I shall concentrate on energy, especially nuclear energy, as the case study within the wider case study. And I shall look especially at the developments within the WCC, as these illustrate the process of relating a religious ethic to technological problems that were never envisioned by the religious tradition.

The process, extending over several years and still continuing, included several major stages: a Conference on Science and Technology for Human Development, in Romania, 1974;[23] an Ecumenical Hearing on Nuclear Energy in Sweden, 1975;[24] the work of an Energy Advisory Group that formulated recommendations in 1976 and presented them to a conference of the International Atomic Energy Agency in Salsburg in 1977;[25] a Consultation on Ecumenical Concerns in Relation to Nuclear Energy, in Switzerland, 1978.[26]

The participants in this process included some of the world's foremost nuclear scientists and engineers, both advocates and critics of nuclear energy. They included citizens of many nations, industrialized and agricultural, rich and poor, oil-exporting and oil-importing. They included physical scientists, social scientists, political leaders, theologians, representatives of people's protest movements. They included enthusiasts for industrialization and enthusiasts for simple lifestyles. At times it seemed as though the process were designed to make agreement impossible. But any less intricate procedure would have encouraged glib conclusions.

Each stage in the process had its distinctive character, but some common themes ran through all. One was recognition of the bearing of technology, human values, and social and international systems upon any attempt to answer the issues of energy. Another was agreement on the importance both of conservation and of the development of many sources of energy. Still another was the growing consensus that an appropriate social goal was the development of a "just, participatory and sustainable society"—with the realization that each of those adjectives represented a difficult goal and the relating of each to the others was still more difficult.

All these stages of international study fed into the Conference on Faith, Science and the Future in 1979. That conference reaffirmed the agreements of the past meetings. Then it took up the controversy on nuclear energy. The awareness of the events at Three Mile Island just three months earlier colored the discussions.

After heated debate the conference adopted the position that "for the long term no options should be excluded," but that "for the short and medium terms" there should be much greater emphasis on "soft" energy options (small-scale, decentralized sources, including solar energy).[27] And, in a divided vote, the majority advocated "a moratorium on the construction of all new nuclear plants for a period of five years," for the purpose of encouraging "wide participation in a public debate on the risks, costs and benefits of nuclear energy in all countries directly concerned."[28] Some supporters of the moratorium were clearly opponents of nuclear power but accepted the moratorium as a compromise. On the other side, advocates of nuclear power filed a dissenting report, arguing that nuclear-generated electricity had the best worldwide safety record of any energy industry.[29]

Later the Central Committee of the WCC added its endorsement to the action of the conference, thus making that action the policy of the WCC. Still later a small conference of the Working Committee on Church and Society, meeting in Africa with a group of African scientists, criticized the moratorium. The reason was not that the African participants advocated nuclear energy for their own countries, but that they wished the industrialized nations would substitute some nuclear energy for imports of oil, thus releasing the oil for the developing countries.[30] This development is a comment on, but not a change of the position of the WCC.[31]

This lengthy process, still incomplete, and the divided opinions are a good example of the mixture of issues that arise when a religious community makes ethical decisions in an area of high technology. Some of the debates are basically about technology, not ethics; for example, comparisons of the efficiency and safety of different methods of energy production, or estimates of the known reserves of existing forms of nonrenewable energy. On such issues religious conviction, as such, has little to say, but must draw upon the best available scientific evidence. Other debates are about the nature of human life and the necessity of high energy consumption for human values. Here technology, as such, has little to say. Fundamental faith becomes determinative. Social situation is also important. Americans, for example, may point out that a lower consumption of energy may well go with a higher quality of life; the people of India, however, may still see the need for greater energy consumption. Still other debates are about the ways of realizing some kind of justice in the face of great inequalities of resources and political-economic, technological power.

I shall return to these issues in the third part of this paper.

Bioethics

Medical treatment is the aspect of biological ethics that affects the largest number of people most directly.[32] It is also an area where science and technology have made spectacular advances in this century. In the eight decades following 1900 average life expectancy in the United States increased from forty-seven to seventy-three years—a truly impressive change.[33] In India, despite its great poverty, the average life expectancy of fifty-three years is, according to reports, "higher than that of nineteenth-century European nobility."[34] The change is due primarily to science and technology, which have increased food production, improved sanitation and found preventatives or cures for many diseases. Christians, who since New Testament times have rejoiced in healing, can only welcome this change. Despite the hazards that accompany modern technologies—acid rain, atmospheric pollution, the perils of the automobile, industrial accidents, etc.—science and technology have brought a net gain to human health.

But there have been problems. Some of these are connected with costs. Happily some of the most effective medical technologies are not very expensive. Vaccination against smallpox, leading to the apparent elimination of this centuries-old scourge of human life, was cheap enough for worldwide application. It was a democratic technological achievement; it benefited the whole human race.

Along with other beneficial technologies, it brought its side effects, including the major effect of the population explosion. Here Protestant ethics does not regret the technological gain; it looks to other technologies to meet the new problem. Technologies of food production mean that the planet can support a larger population. Technologies of contraception make possible a measure of "birth control" to match the measure of "death control" achieved by medical gains. Although many Protestant churches once opposed contraception, the virtually unanimous opinion now endorses a "responsible" use of contraception as a means of enhancing marital relations and the freedom to procreate or not procreate. There are many arguments about what constitutes "responsible" contraceptive practices.

Vaccination and contraception are relatively inexpensive and can—with conceivable changes in the structure of society—become available to the whole world. But that is not the case with all medical technologies. The "intensive care" typical of American hospitals is not available to most people in most of the world. The rising costs of health care trouble even this affluent society. In 1982 the expenditures on health care in the United States were probably above $300 billion, more than 10 percent of the Gross National Product.[35] Perhaps that is not too much to spend, especially by comparison with many things that this society pays for. But somewhere the rapidly rising costs of health care must meet a limit. Some of the GNP must go for food, housing, clothing, education, transportation, government, and (in this imperfect world) national defense.

One method of thinking about expense is the use of cost-benefit analysis, which is obviously helpful but ethically troubling. Clearly there is good sense in spending resources where they will do the most good. A given sum might be spent in purifying water, preventing auto accidents, giving shots to children, building hospitals, prolonging the lives of patients in terminal comas. Conceivably all of these can be expanded. But when funds are limited—as always they are—where shall they be assigned? Cost-benefit analysis gives useful guidance. Yet in disturbing ways it has the effect of quantifying the value of human life, a procedure that is offensive, in some respects necessary, yet delusive. Fred Hapgood charges that the National Highway Traffic Safety Administration puts the value of a human life at $287,175.[36] Anybody asking the value of a life will—at least unconsciously—ask, "whose life?" Is it *my* life— and if so, is it my life *now* or when I am ninety? Is it my spouse's life, my child's life? Or is it the abstract life that statisticians and actuaries reckon about? It is easy to talk about "the infinite value of every human life." But since every life is finite and no life is riskless, communities are always deciding that they will not pay the costs (in money or inconvenience) to eliminate some risks.

Furthermore, some medical treatments are *inherently* scarce. Even if money were unlimited, heart transplants would not be unlimited. So society is painfully trying to decide who shall get limited resources. Various methods are proposed: medical criteria (the severity of need and the probabilities of recovery), some kind of lottery, price-rationing or other forms of rationing,[37] selection by committees using criteria that are themselves subject to controversy. I expect that one consequence of scarce medical technologies will be the increasing bureaucratization of decisions about their use—and that will itself represent an increase of social technology.

Meanwhile the structure of the economy and society are largely determinative. For example, in the United States typical patients for coronary artery bypass grafting (CABG) are reported to be "middle-class, white, and male." The predominance of men over women is 79 to 21 percent. A *partial* but not complete reason is the higher susceptibility of males to heart troubles. Apparently about 97 percent of CABG patients are white, despite the fact that hypertension and heart problems are more prevalent among black people.[38] The reasons run deep through the nature of our society. They remind us that science and technology are not simply objective, abstract processes; they always operate in a social setting that has much to do with their direction and effectiveness.

A different ethical issue is the discontent that many people feel with the depersonalization that they experience in medical care. This depersonalization has two aspects, both related to science and technology. (1) Science almost inevitably means specialization; the patient must encounter many specialists who deal with a particular ailment or a particular aspect of that ailment rather than with the patient as a person. (2) Technology means elaborate equipment, with the result that treatment does not move to the patient but the patient moves to the treatment. The phrase "health delivery system" becomes a misnomer, as people increasingly must be delivered to the site of the equipment. Both the beginning and the end of life are more likely now than in a less technological past to be in the hospital rather than the home. There are sound reasons of efficiency for the change, which is part of the general improvement in health and life expectancy. But, like many medical treatments, it has its side effects.

When the Working Committee on Church and Society of the World Council of Churches met in Nigeria in 1981, it heard many testimonies from Africans on this issue. African scientists and physicians, themselves trained in "advanced" methods of treatment, told of patients unhelped by modern hospitals who then, returning to home and tribal doctors, found improvement in their health. They gave two reasons for the experience: (1) traditional methods and folk wisdom often have scientific efficacy that has been disdained because it was not discovered in laboratories; (2) the human support of a friendly community sometimes does what the depersonalized medical institution cannot do.[39]

None of the Africans at this meeting wanted to abandon the achievements of modern scientific medicine. They wanted to incorporate those gains into a context of human community.

One further ethical issue in medical treatment has to do with the effect of means on ends. Supposedly means serve ends; medical technologies serve the goals of human health and well-being. But as means become more impressive and comprehensive, they begin to modify and even prescribe ends. The most obvious and controversial case is the prolongation of life.

We begin with the assumption that death is biologically normal. Without death the human race would not know how to cope with rising and aging populations. Yet life is a very great value, and most people want to delay death for themselves and for others. I have already pointed with approval to the extension of life expectancy in the twentieth century. But when do the means of sustaining life go beyond any ethically justifiable purpose?

Suppose, to take the extreme case, it should become possible to sustain life on a virtually infinite scale. It may be that extreme cases make for bad ethics, just as "hard cases make bad law." But the extreme case, however improbable, sometimes raises issues that require rethinking of cases that are probable and even commonplace. So suppose that a combination of intravenous feeding, respirator, renal dialysis, and artificial heart should make it possible to keep the protoplasm of a human body in some sense "alive" indefinitely. Is it, to take an actual case, ethically good that Karen Quinlan should have been kept alive though comatose from April 11, 1975 until her eventual death more than ten years later.[40]

Protestant ethics has always assumed that life is a divine gift to be treasured and sustained, yet that life is never just biological existence. Encountering the new possibilities of extending life, the increasing (but not unanimous) Protestant consensus is (1) that, because human life is precious, health care should be extended to those who now often do not get it, but (2) that in times of severe terminal illness there is ethical justification for withholding extraordinary life-support systems. Debates continue on the details: how much voice does the patient (who may be unconscious) have in the decision, what economic resources should go to prolonging the lives of terminally ill people as compared with other neglected health needs of society, and so on? A minority of Protestant thinkers endorse euthanasia or suicide in some cases. A larger number make a distinction, admittedly imprecise, between acts that actually hasten death and acts that stop the prolongation of life. Continued discussion of these issues can be expected.

One other aspect of biological science, less commonplace but even more spectacular than medical treatment, is genetics. The discoveries of the contemporary generation of scientists raise profound ethical questions, for which ethical traditions have no precise answers because the questions were not real or plausible until our own time.

Ethical discussions of genetics center on three practices, actual or projected. The first follows from prenatal diagnosis of fetuses. A small but increasing number of genetic disorders, some of them very serious, can be discovered *in utero*. The diagnosis is usually made when the family history indicates risk of specific ailments or when the age of the mother increases the probability of a chromosomal disorder, such as Down's syndrome. If the abnormality is discovered, abortion is possible. Just as there is no Protestant consensus on the ethics of abortion, there is no common ethical opinion on the abortion of a defective fetus. For those who oppose all abortions or for those who have no objection to abortion, the answer may be simple. Between these two positions are many people who say that the strongest of all reasons for abortions is the diagnosis of a disease that dooms the fetus, if born, to a life that must suffer intense pain and can never mature. The same reasoning might say that since such an abortion comes later in fetal development—usually the eighteenth to twentieth week—than most abortions, it requires a graver justification.

The second practice is the deliberate choice of genetic ancestry of children. The simplest form is artificial insemination by donor, with the donor of the sperm chosen for genetic reasons. Geneticist Herman J. Muller proposed the establishment of banks of frozen semen, taken from biologically distinguished males, to be made available for insemination of women in order to improve the heredity of their children.[41] Some years after his death a sperm bank, appropriately named after Muller, was established in California, to make available the sperm of five Nobel laureates for the sake of "increasing the people at the top of the population."[42] The initial rules permitted insemination only of married women, unable to have children naturally by their husbands, with the consent of the husbands. Those limitations are, of course, not scientifically necessary, and the procedure might be extended far beyond its initial practices.

The achievement of *in vitro* fertilization and of surrogate motherhood extends the possibilities beyond the earlier proposals. It is technologically feasible for a woman to give birth to a child who is the genetic offspring of another female and a male, both chosen solely for their genetic qualifications.

Such possibilities are recent enough that there is no authoritative moral tradition speaking directly to them. Protestant responses, however, put the practices on a scale ranging from problematic to outrageous. The principal objections are two: (1) Christian faith and ethics usually advocate procreation as an outcome of the intimate sharing and sexual relation of husband and wife; (2) The new proposals embody conceptions of human excellence that are dubious and perhaps, as evidenced by the prejudices operating in past eugenics movements, pernicious. As one group convened by the WCC said, "Programmes of 'positive eugenics' attempted earlier in this century have invariably caused trauma and tragedy for people of certain ethnic identities."[43]

The third development is the new ability to manipulate DNA, the macromolecules that are the basic carriers of human heredity. Experimentation has proceeded a long way on bacteria; it has begun on some animals, including the injection of some rabbit DNA into the zygote of a mouse. Some scientists hope to modify human inheritance so as to (1) eliminate some hereditary ailments ("negative eugenics") and (2) increase human physical and mental abilities ("positive eugenics"). Nobody knows what may become possible. But the discussion of what is desirable is under way, as it should be if ethical evaluation is not going to trail behind *faits accomplis.*

Christian thinking on this issue usually starts with the assumption that healing is a good. If some diseases, universally recognized as destructive of life and health, can be healed by genetic therapy, that may be an extension of therapies already practiced with medicine and surgery. But there are two great warnings to be sounded. The first concerns experimental risks. Scientists have long experimented with the heredity of plants and of fruit flies. To experiment on human beings and perhaps to destroy or ruin some persons in the hope—real or imagined—of helping others is a different enterprise. The second warning concerns judgments as to what constitutes good or bad heredity. Should scientists modify, perhaps in irrevocable ways, the heredity of generations yet to be born, according to existing ideas and prejudices about what constitutes good heredity?

An international team of biologists, social scientists, and theologians, called together by the WCC in 1981, gave attention to these issues. It said: "Although medicine is often thought of as being objective, definitions of 'disease' and 'health' are individual and social as much as they are scientific determinations."[44] It recognized some ailments as so clearly harmful that a failure to remedy them—unless at risk of doing more harm—would be wrong. But, granting that there is "no absolute distinction between eliminating 'defects' and 'improving' heredity,"[45] it questioned the attempt of "positive" eugenics to improve human heredity. At that point the group divided in its opinion, some urging legal prohibition of "positive eugenic measures" and others rejecting such action.[46]

RECURRING ISSUES OF CONTENT AND METHOD IN ETHICS

The specific problems I have been addressing throw into high visibility some fundamental issues that run through all the concrete demands for decision. They have to do with both the content and the method of an ethic grounded in historic traditions but meeting technological issues that are new. I shall look at three such issues.

Power and Justice

Technology is a form of power and, as such, shares in the ambivalence of all power. Power surely is not evil; nobody wants to be powerless. But power is not an unqualified good; it hurts too many people.

There is some truth in the common opinion that technologies are ethically neutral; they can be used for good or bad. Automobiles and airplanes have saved lives and have, by intent or accident, destroyed lives. Radio and television transmit truth and lies. The machinery serves the purposes, good or bad, of those who run it.

But that common opinion is too simple. Some technologies are inherently beneficial. I have given the example of vaccination for smallpox. It *could* be used for bad purposes—to manipulate people or to make a profit at the expense of the needy. But basically it is good.

Other technologies are inherently harmful. It is not very helpful to say that biological warfare is good or bad, depending on the uses made of it.

But behind both biological healing and biological warfare is a scientific research that may be directed either way. In pursuing this question once with an eminent scientist experienced in governmental research projects, I got the opinion that three-quarters of the research once done at Fort Detrick on biological weapons was interchangeable with research sponsored by the National Institutes of Health for the sake of healing. The uses of science are unknowable and unpredictable; the uses of technology are more knowable and predictable, but not entirely so.

The ambivalence of power is made clear in a saying by C.S. Lewis that has become famous: "Each new power won *by* man is a power *over* man as well."[47] If there are a few possible exceptions (like vaccination against smallpox), most evidence supports the rule.

It is the ambivalence of power that worries many people about the new discoveries in genetics. Throughout history families and races have gone to great efforts to impose their ideals, usually inadequate and sometimes vicious, on the next generation. The young, often fortunately, have an ability to resist the manipulations of the old. But if the old learn methods of genetic manipulation that the young cannot resist, the results can be frightening. As biologist Robert S. Morison once put it, "The thing that has saved man from his limited visions in the past has been the difficulty of devising suitable means for reaching them."[48] Yet it would be defeatism—and probably an impossibility—to renounce new knowledge because it will be misused. Most of it will also be used for good. The point is to heighten the ethical awareness of persons and societies about the uses of science and technology.

One unhappy consequence of technology is that it usually increases the difference between the powerful and the weak, the rich and the poor. Technological power means the power to get more technology and to increase the advantage over the less powerful. This is true within societies and, on an international scale, between societies. So every issue of ethics connected with technology is in large part, although not solely, an issue of justice in the social structures that surround technology. It is not enough to appeal to the technologically powerful to use their power responsibly; at best they will use it in ways that seem to them responsible. The real problem, which our world is far from solving, concerns the distribution of power, methods of checks and balances, ways of enabling people and societies to participate in the decisions that affect their welfare.

The Relation of Humanity to Nature

Every ethic and every religion must pay some attention to the relation of human beings to the rest of nature—or, in biblical terms, of the human creation to the whole of creation. All objects in nature—the sun, microbes, gypsy moths, squirrels, and people—affect their environment. People affect their environments less than the sun but more than most objects in nature. And people, unlike other objects, even the sun, affect their environments deliberately and purposefully. They use objects in nature for their own purposes. They manipulate nature. They have some modest success in controlling nature.

In so doing, they separate themselves in some degree from their environment. They build a partially artificial environment. In the process they may forget their dependence on nature. They may lose their sense of mystery before the gift of creation and may gloat in a false sense of mastery over the nature that sustains them.

There are philosophies that make an ethical norm of nature. Ancient Stoicism and some versions of Christianity have done this. Some modern ecologists do it in a different way. Barry Commoner has revived the proverb "Nature knows best," and has interpreted it to mean, "Any man-made change in a natural system is likely to be *detrimental* to that system."[49]

The Christian ethical tradition offers a different possibility. It is that man and woman are intended to modify natural systems, to "till and keep" the garden of creation (Gen. 2:15), to exercise a reverent dominion combined with a responsible stewardship. The elimination of smallpox, the very considerable reduction of infant mortality, the moderation of birthrates by contraception are changes in the natural system, beneficial to human beings and not detrimental to the system.

But Margaret Mead once asked the thoughtful question: "Was it possible that modern man might forget his relationship with the rest of the natural world to such a degree that he separated himself from his own pulse-beat, wrote poetry only in tune with machines, and was irrevocably cut off from his own heart? In their new found preoccupation with power over the natural world, might men so forget God that they would build a barrier against the wisdom of the past that no one could penetrate?"[50] That is a wise warning against the arrogance of technological power, whether in the consumption of resources or in medical and genetic manipulation. It is not a demand that persons abdicate their power to act purposefully upon nature or that they sink themselves into the nonpurposive rhythms of nature.

The Responsibility of Making an Ethic

The attainments of science and technology mean that the present generation can do some things that no past generation could do. Therefore this generation must make some decisions that no past generation had to make. It cannot simply coast on the momentum of ethical tradition. It has to do some new and hard deciding.

Christianity, like all religious traditions, has had some experience of adapting to change, even while maintaining some continuity with its source and history. It has lived in many areas of the globe and many cultural climates. It has lived through cataclysmic changes. Today, once again, it must summon its insights and skills to meet new situations.

One example of an effort to do that comes from the 1979 Conference on Faith, Science and the Future, where one of the ten sections of the conference had the assignment of working "Towards a New Christian Social Ethic and New Social Policies for the Churches." Its conclusions, like most composite documents, lack the sharp clarity that an individual or a group of like-minded individuals might produce, but are the more interesting because they embody the thought of people from many areas of the globe and many Protestant and Orthodox traditions.

The group candidly acknowledged the insufficiency (not necessarily the invalidity) of old ethical codes. It stated: "The Bible and Christian tradition are silent on many decisions that Christians must make today, e.g. about the ethical evaluation of specific discoveries in genetics."[51] But it quickly added that new possibilities are not self-validating and, in fact, sometimes call for new appreciation of biblical and traditional insights.

Quoting an earlier WCC study on "Genetics and the Quality of Life" (1975), the group said: "Churchmen cannot expect precedents from the past to provide answers to questions never asked in the past. On the other hand, new scientific advances do not determine what are worthy human goals. Ethical decisions in uncharted areas require that scientific capabilities be understood and used by persons and communities sensitive to their own deepest convictions about human nature and destiny. There is no sound ethical judgment in these matters independent of scientific knowledge, but science does not itself prescribe the good."[52]

If there is no commandment "Thou shalt (or shalt not) rearrange DNA," there is likewise no assurance that the possibility of modifying human heredity is any sign that it is good to do so. Facts and technical possibilities will bear upon the ethical decisions that people must make today. But no pile of facts, however high, dictates the value of those facts. No technological achievement is the criterion of its own ethical validity, just as no nuclear weapon is the justification for its use.

The task of our time is, in some important senses, to make an ethic adequate for this time. The ethic must be developed with an acute sensitivity to the meaning and possibilities of science and technology. Among those contributing to the ethic in this pluralistic world will be some who have met their fellow human beings and God in biblical history and in the history of our age.

Notes

1. The Conference Report has been published in *Faith and Science in an Unjust World*, vol. 1, *Plenary Presentations*, ed. Roger L. Shinn, vol. 2, *Reports and Recommendations*, ed. Paul Abrecht (Philadelphia: Fortress Press, 1980), hereafter cited as *Faith and Science.*

2. Alfred North Whitehead, *Science and the Modern World* (New York: Macmillan, 1947), p. 18.

3. Hero's dates are unknown. He is usually placed between the first century B.C.E. and the third century C.E. For his achievements see Sir William Cecil Dampier, *A History of Science and Its Relations with Philosophy and Religion* (New York: Macmillan, 1949), p. 48; and Langdon Winner, *Autonomous Technology* (Cambridge, Mass.: MIT Press, 1977), pp. 73–74.

4. "And on the seventh day God finished his work which he had done, and he rested on the seventh day from all his work which he had done" (Gen. 1:2). "My Father is working still, and I am working" (John 5:17).

5. "The monk was the first intellectual to get dirt under his fingernails." Lynn White, Jr., *Machina ex Deo* (Cambridge, Mass.: MIT Press, 1968), p. 65.

6. Max Weber, *From Max Weber*, trans. and ed. by H.H. Gerth and C. Wright Mills (New York: Oxford University Press, 1958), pp. 148, 155, 350, 357.

7. Arend van Leeuwen, *Christianity in World History* (New York: Charles Scribner's Sons, 1965), pp. 419–420 (1st Dutch ed., 1954).

8. Harvey Cox, *The Secular City* (New York: Macmillan, 1965), p. 82. Cox modified this view in *The Feast of Fools* (New York: Harper & Row, 1969).

9. Reinhold Niebuhr, *The Nature and Destiny of Man*, 2 vols. (New York: Charles Scribner's Sons, 1941, 1943); *Faith and History* (New York: Charles Scribner's Sons, 1949).

10. Karl Marx and Friedrich Engels, *The Communist Manifesto*, many editions, pt. II.

11. Jacques Ellul, *The Technological Society* (New York: Vintage Books, 1964), p. xxv.

12. Ibid., p. 128.

13. Ibid., p. 80.

14. Lynn White, Jr., "The Historical Roots of Our Ecologic Crisis," *Science* 155 (March 10, 1967): 1205. The address has been reprinted in many places.

15. Arnold Toynbee, "The Religious Background of the Present Environmental Crisis," in *Ecology and Religion in History*, ed. David and Eileen Spring (New York: Harper & Row, 1974), pp. 145, 147. (This book also includes White's address.)

16. White, "Historical Roots of Our Ecologic Crisis," pp. 1206–1207.

17. René Dubos, *A God Within* (New York: Charles Scribner's Sons, 1972), p. 161.

18. Joseph Sittler, "Called to Unity," *Ecumenical Review* 14, no. 2 (January, 1962): 175]187.

19. H. Richard Niebuhr, *Radical Monotheism and Western Culture* (New York: Harper & Row, 1960).

20. James Gustafson, *Ethics from a Theocentric Perspective*, vol. 1, *Theology and Ethics* (Chicago: University of Chicago Press, 1981).

21. See *World Conference on Church and Society: Official Report* (Geneva: World Council of Churches, 1967).

22. Donella H. Meadows, Dennis L. Meadows, Jørgen Randers, and William W. Behrens III, *The Limits to Growth* (New York: Universe Books, 1972).

23. For the report on the conference see *Anticipation*, no. 19 (November, 1974).

24. For the papers presented at the hearing and the findings, see John Francis and Paul Abrecht, eds., *Facing Up to Nuclear Power* (Philadelphia: Westminster Press, 1976).

25. See *Anticipation*, no. 24 (November, 1977).

26. See *Anticipation*, no. 26 (June, 1979).

27. *Faith and Science*, 2: 96.

28. *Faith and Science*, 1: 261.

29. *Faith and Science*, 2: 103.

30. See *Faith, Science and the Future—the African Context* (Geneva: World Council of Churches, 1981).

31. I have here reported the process as accurately as I know how. I have given my more personal opinions on the issues in my book *Forced Options: Social Decisions for the 21st Century* (San Francisco: Harper & Row, 1982), chaps. 3 and 11.

32. As one evidence of the importance of this new field of ethics, see Warren T. Reich, ed., *Encyclopedia of Bioethics*, 4 vols. (New York: Free Press, 1978).

33. United Press International dispatch in the *New York Times*, (July 18, 1980), p. A6, reporting on a study by Dr. James F. Fries of Stanford University in the *New England Journal of Medicine*.

34. Nick Eberstadt, "Myths of the Food Crisis," *New York Review of Books*, (February 19, 1976).

35. Harry Schwartz, "We Need to Ration Medicine," *Newsweek*, (February 8, 1982), p. 13.

36. Fred Hapgood, "Risk-Benefit Analysis: Putting a Price on Life," *The Atlantic* (January 1979), pp. 33–38.

37. See Schwartz, "We Need to Ration Medicine."

38. Judith Randal, "Coronary Artery Bypass Surgery," *Hastings Center Report* 12: no. 1 (February 1982): 13–18.

39. *Faith, Science and the Future—the African Context*.

40. See Joseph and Julia Quinlan with Phyllis Battelle, *Karen Ann* (Garden City, N.Y.: Doubleday, 1977).

41. Herman J. Muller, "What Genetic Course Will Man Steer?" in *Proceedings of the Third International Congress of Human Genetics*, ed. James F. Crow and James V. Neel (Baltimore: Johns Hopkins Press, 1967), pp. 521–543.

42. Harold M. Schmeck, Jr., "Nobel Winner Says He Gave Sperm for Women to Bear Gifted Babies," *New York Times*, (March 1, 1980), p. 6.

43. *Faith and Science*, 2: 52.

44. Report of a Working Group on *Ethical and Social Issues in Genetic Engineering and the Ownership of Life Forms* (Geneva: World Council of Churches, 1981), p. 11.

45. Ibid., p. 12.

46. Ibid., p. 17.

47. C.S. Lewis, *The Abolition of Man* (New York: Macmillan, 1955), p. 71.

48. Robert S. Morison, "Comments on Genetic Evolution," in *Evolution and Man's Progress*, ed. Hudson Hoagland and Ralph W. Burhoe (New York: Columbia University Press, 1962), p. 41.

49. Barry Commoner, *The Closing Circle* (New York: Alfred A. Knopf, 1971), p. 41.

50. Margaret Mead, *Male and Female: A Study of the Sexes in a Changing World* (New York: New American Library, 1955), p. 19.

51. *Faith and Science*, 2: 153.

52. Ibid., p. 152.

Part II
Sexuality

Of all the social changes in recent years, few have attracted such broad interest as the so-called sexual revolution, which is frequently credited with having rejected the classical "Judeo-Christian ethic." In fact, what has been rejected may not be the authentic ethic of either Judaism or Christianity.

To begin to clarify this point, Timothy O'Connell demonstrates the importance of definitions, which can affect one's conclusions almost as much as the values at stake.

Having phrased the question, those engaged in ethical discussion must gather the necessary facts. New information thus forces a reevaluation of our ethical conclusions from time to time in order to determine whether or not they best embody these values. James Nelson describes this process, suggesting that modern experience has indeed produced new data which must be taken into account. Finally, David Novak searches a specific tradition, seeking in its narratives and norms a central value which can be applied to ethical discussions.

Running throughout these presentations is the affirmation of sexuality as God-given and hence good. The common assumption of a puritanical Judeo-Christian ethic is thus simplistic. That is not to say that any of these traditions would endorse the kind of free-floating hedonism so prevalent in contemporary society. Rather, all seek a proper setting for sexuality so that its meaning as a divine gift can be maximized rather than abused.

Sexuality and the Procreative Norm

Timothy E. O'Connell

In pursuing the Catholic understanding of sexuality, one might anticipate a common format: scripture, history, current understandings, suggestions. In this paper, I shall not spend any time on the first category, scripture. And in that decision of mine lies a tale worth telling.

If we take it as given that the function of religion is to put us in contact with the divine transcendent,[1] then we cannot avoid the key question: *how* do we contact, experience, discover the will of God? The answer, at least as usually formulated in the older Catholic theology, was: we contact God through scripture and tradition. That is, we encounter the divine through that document which functions as the charter of the Church, but we also experience God in the ongoing history and life of the Church itself. In more recent Catholic documents there has been an attempt to avoid a dichotomizing of the "two fonts" of revelation by integrating scripture and historical tradition. But inasmuch as the two are different, they cannot be completely unified.

So there are further questions. How are scripture and tradition to be related? What priority obtains between them? Of the various points that comprised the Protestant Reformation of the sixteenth century, certainly a key theme was the extent to which the Church had ignored scripture and had appropriate to itself such relevatory power as to be blasphemous. In reaction to this, then, Luther and the other reformers developed various religious visions characterized by *sola scriptura,* by the conviction that it is solely (or at least primarily) through scripture that we encounter God and are instructed and commanded by Him.

This is surely not the place for a thorough analysis of the Reformation and its descendants. But two points should be made. First, there is no doubt that much of the Lutheran critique was accurate. There was surely much in the life of the Church at that time that was morally and theologically reprehensible. Second, in highlighting the tendency of the Church to elevate tradition (or, if you will, the actual life of the community) and to downplay scripture as a source for authentic revelation, the reformers were accurately describing a quality of the Church at that time. Indeed, they were accurately describing an aspect of the Catholic vision throughout the centuries and even to this day.

Here, then, is my point. The Catholic religious vision is that the fundamental arena for the encounter with God is the community. Personal prayer is important, but it finds its real identity in the context of common and liturgical prayer. Grace is a matter of free divine initiative which comes to us undeserved, but that grace is manifested and so received particularly in the Church and her sacraments. The discernment of God's will is the key to the life of discipleship, but that will is to be discovered in the reflections of the community and in the teachings of its leaders. And finally, the scriptures have a very unique importance, and they are truly inspired. But inasmuch as oral traditions existed before the formulations of the written scriptures, inasmuch as the scriptures were formulated and accepted within the community, inasmuch as the scriptures represent precisely the experience of the community in its primeval encounter with God, and inasmuch as the scriptures even today are proclaimed within a community of faith—inasmuch as all this is true, it follows that the scriptures have their power precisely as a privileged and inspired document of and in the Church.[2]

In justifying its overall self-understanding, the Catholic Church has often referred to Matthew 16:19 and 18:18 ("Whatsoever you bind on earth shall be bound in heaven"). But, if one can overlook the irony of rooting a nonbiblical approach in a biblical text, the real font of the Catholic vision is a few verses later, in Matthew 18:20: "Where two or three are gathered in my name, there am I in the midst of them." It is in the community that the Lord is to be found.

From a Catholic perspective, then, the God of Jesus Christ, the God in whom they believe and whom they seek to follow, is indeed the God of the Book. But he is previously and preeminently the God of the Gathering.[3] And that is why this paper will not focus on the biblical data on sexuality. Those data are important. But, first, they will surely be dealt with by my Protestant and Jewish colleagues. Second, the Catholic presumption is that the biblical data have already and continually been incorporated into the ongoing teachings of the Church and thus will be included here by indirection. And third, an emphasis upon human insights and communal history will more accurately present the Catholic vision and, indeed, exemplify that vision in the telling.

In light of the above remarks, it should be clear that my task here will be to present the living tradition of the Catholic Christian community about the meaning of human sexuality, to evaluate and critique that tradition, and to take note of current developments in that tradition. Specifically, I will begin with a synthetic summary of what could be called the "received tradition." I will then discuss that tradition by looking at its pivotal proponents and its deeper roots. In a second major part, I will look at the contemporary scene. I will suggest that there are two points of view on the meaning of human sexuality within the Catholic Church today. I will try to characterize, exemplify, and analyze those two points of view. Finally, I will offer some reflections about the future agenda of sexual ethics.

RECEIVED TRADITION

Essence

What is human sexuality? The answer which traditional Catholic morality gave to that question was simple and unequivocal: human sexuality refers to that aspect of personhood by which persons are capable of and inclined to genital acts, acts suited to procreation and to the preservation of the species. What makes for right sexual behavior? Sexual behavior is right if it conforms to this reality, if it respects the procreative potential. It is wrong if it attacks that potential. (This I will call the procreative norm.)[4]

What is said here may sound simplistic and insignificant. Actually, for purposes of developing a sexual ethic, it was very useful. Indeed, its simplicity was not that of naivete, but rather that of ultimate elegance. Let me demonstrate.

Sex and its acts are for procreation. It follows that these acts should be pursued—

— with another person (so masturbation is wrong);
— of the opposite sex (so homosexual acts are wrong);
— within a stable marital union (so fornication is wrong);
— with one's partner (so adultery is wrong);
— in a complete genital act (so anal and oral sex are wrong);
— which is open to its procreative potential (so artificial contraception is wrong).

So this simple definition of sexuality led inexorably to very specific and exceptionless ethical norms. Criteria were present, in terms of which virtually all the variety of human sexual behavior might be evaluated. And consistent and clear grounds could be offered for approving or disapproving of each. Needless to say, in the vast majority of cases the response was one of disapproval; but at least the reasons for the objection were clear and straightforward.

This, then, is the received tradition in Catholic theology. And until quite recently it was a quite universal and unchallenged tradition. On the one hand, it was universally supported both by the official magisterium of the Church, the Pope and bishops, and the theologians of the Church. And on the other hand, it has survived with very little change for at least seven hundred years.

Sources

But how was this understanding justified? What were its sources? In an excellent summary article, theologian Margaret Farley points out that Thomas Aquinas

offered two grounds for the procreative norm of reason, which the tradition has so far affirmed. One was the Augustinian argument that sexual pleasure always, in the fallen human person, hinders the best working of the mind. It must, then, be brought into some accord with reason by having an overriding value as its goal. No less an end than procreation can serve to justify it. But secondly, reason does not merely provide a good purpose for sexual pleasure. It discovers that purpose through the very facts of the biological function of sexual organs.[5]

Fear of Pleasure Both of these perspectives have been maintained through the centuries. Let me demonstrate. The first, that only a limitation of sexuality to procreative contexts can control the human urge for pleasure, is at least implicitly affirmed in much of traditional Catholic writing. For example, many of the older textbooks worked out the specific norms of sexual morality precisely around the question of the "licit pursuit of sexual pleasure." That is, pleasure was the key principle of interpretation. And in much other writing, both ethical and ascetic, considerable emphasis was placed upon the need for mortification of the senses, a spirit of self-denial, a suspicion of sensuality, and the like.

As Farley points out, this perspective can be traced as far back as Augustine. Indeed, it could be argued that through Augustine it can be traced to the Stoic philosophers, with their emphasis on imperturbability, and to the Manichean religionists, with their disgust for the body and for all things fleshly. But for all its ambiguity and disreputable associations, this perspective still survives. Let me offer one example of this.

The textbook of Henry Davis defines the virtue of chastity not as the right use of the sexual faculty, but as "the moral virtue that controls in the married and altogether excludes in the unmarried all voluntary expression of the sensitive appetite for venereal pleasure."[6] In his discussion of specific moral issues, moreover, Davis begins by asserting that "all sexual pleasure, outside wedlock, that is directly voluntary is grievously sinful."[7] He further defends this position:

It is contrary to nature's purpose, and seriously so, if this pleasure is sought or accepted outside legitimate sexual intercourse, for the pleasure is annexed to an act that must be employed socially in legitimate wedlock, and not for the individual's gratification outside wedlock, since the obvious and only purpose in nature's, that is, God's, intention is that this pleasure should be experienced in and should attract to, that mutual act between man and wife, designed by nature for the propagation of the race, whether or not the effect ensues.[8]

In this defense, of course, Davis refers the limiting of pleasure to the proper and "natural" use of the sexual faculty. But that he considers the issue of pleasure to be significant in its own right becomes clear when he goes on:

A valid argument may also be derived from consequences, namely, that if it were permissible to procure or accept sexual pleasure outside wedlock, there would be little or no inducement to many men and women to undertake the burdens of married life. Solitary defilements and fornications, as well as other sexual irregularities would take the place of marriage in a vast number of cases....It may be admitted that some love marriages, as they are called, might take place, but the number would be negligible.[9]

Obsession with Nature   But this is not the only perspective within Catholic tradition. As Farley indicates, there is another line of argument often pursued in support of the procreative norm. And that is the argument from the nature of the sexual faculty and of the genital organs. This line of argument seeks to achieve a reasoned understanding of human sexuality and, on the basis of that understanding, to distinguish proper and improper behaviors.

This line of argument can be found in a wide variety of sources. For example, in *Casti Connubii*, the encyclical letter on Christian marriage issued by Pope Pius XI in 1930, one senses this approach. When, in the course of a discussion of various modern errors regarding marriage and its activities, the Pope comes to discuss artificial contraception, he declares that

no reason, however grave, may be put forward by which anything intrinsically against nature may become conformable to nature and morally good. Since, therefore, the conjugal act is destined primarily by nature for the begetting of children, those who in exercising it deliberately frustrate its natural power and purpose sin against nature and commit a deed which is shameful and intrinsically vicious.[10]

(par. 54)

Similarly, one of the standard textbooks, Noldin-Schmitt, despite some attention to the arguments regarding the propriety of pleasure, ultimately offers the definition that "the use-of-matrimony consists in that conjugal act which has been instituted by nature for the conservation and propagation of the human species, that is in carnal copulation."[11]

But in a particular way this second argument is associated with Thomas Aquinas and with those theologians who carefully studied and followed him. As Farley indicated, one can find texts in Aquinas to support the antipleasure argument. But the argument from human nature is far more typical of this author. Indeed, his use of Aristotle rather than Plato in much of his writing can be viewed precisely as an attempt to ground theology, on the one hand, in an appreciation of all that is real, both the physical and the spiritual, and on the other hand, in a respect for the power of human reason to discern the truths on whose basis life should be lived.

Nowhere is this approach more evident that when Thomas argues that one of the results of concupiscence (that lack of inner integration which resulted from the fall and is transmitted with original sin), is precisely a lessening of pleasure, "for rather sensible delectation was the greater in proportion to the greater purity of nature and the greater sensibility of the body" (I-93-2 and 3). Indeed, with his usual discretion, Aquinas in this context quotes a statement of Augustine that seems to reflect a very clear bias against sensual pleasure and then attempts to reinterpret it to say just the opposite.[12]

This Thomistic perspective is much in evidence in twentieth-century theology. Perhaps the best example is Josef Fuchs, a German theologian teaching at Rome's Gregorian University. In 1949 Fuchs published a landmark study of Aquinas' theology of human sexuality.[13] And when in the late fifties he developed a textbook of sexual ethics, this more positive perspective was obvious. Here we have a thoroughly Thomistic definition of sexuality: "The sexual faculty, and therefore its natural actualization, is of itself ordained to the generation of children; the generation of children is therefore—in a way to be specified here—its natural end."[14] Here also we have a reordering of the entire topic in a more Thomistic fashion. Fuchs does not organize his presentation around pleasure and its legitimate and illegitimate pursuit. Rather he builds on his definition, given above, and systematically reflects on the rectitude (not legality or permissibility, but rather intrinsic rectitude) of various forms of genital behavior.

In summary, then, the vision of sexuality presented by the Catholic tradition asserted that the meaning of human sexuality and of its acts resided in the fact of procreative potential. Hence, acts were morally acceptable if they contributed to, or at least did not attack, that value. This assertion, moreover, was defended, on the one hand, by reflections upon the natural finality of the sexual organs and the overall sexual faculty and, on the other hand, by arguments on the necessity of controlling and channeling the energies of the sexual appetite for venereal pleasure.[15]

RECENT DEVELOPMENTS

In this second major part of the paper I want to trace a number of recent developments. This I will do in three steps. First I will summarize the statements of two recent Church documents. Then I will discuss some contemporary theological presentations that reinforce this magisterial understanding. Finally, I will share some interesting theological revisions of that perspective.

Church Documents

Gaudium et Spes Perhaps a first step in the development of these newer understandings may be found in the documents of the Second Vatican Council, and in particular, the Pastoral Constitution on the Church in the Modern World (*Gaudium et Spes*).[16] For there one finds a discussion of human marriage that is notably different from anything we have so far encountered. It is different in style, format, and specific formulations.

First, as to style. It is well known that this document has a unique character among proclamations of the Catholic Church. Its very title, as a *pastoral* constitution, is unprecedented. And the way in which its opening words replace a defensive posture with one of sincere concern is obvious:

> The joys and the hopes, the griefs and the anxieties of the men of this age, especially those who are poor or in any way afflicted, these too are the joys and hopes, the griefs and anxieties of the followers of Christ. Indeed, nothing genuinely human fails to raise an echo in their hearts.
>
> (par. 1)

This style, moreover, incarnates itself in *format* when the document comes to discuss the issues of marriage and sexuality. There are many parallels between this document and the encyclical *Casti Connubii* to which we referred earlier. But there are many differences, too. And particular mention should be made of the place accorded to the human reality of love. In *Casti Connubii* marriage was seen as essentially a contract "by which each party hands over and accepts those rights proper to the state of marriage" (par. 6). Love, in contrast, is merely a desideratum, subsidiary and nonessential. "This conjugal faith [fidelity]...blooms more freely, more beautifully and more nobly, when it is rooted in that more excellent soil, the love of husband and wife" (par. 23).

But in *Gaudium et Spes*, love is viewed as central to marriage. In its very first statement, that marriage comes from God, the document characterizes marriage as "the intimate partnership of married life and love." It goes on, in marked contrast to *Casti Connubii*, to say that the permanence of marriage arises from their consent, which is "that act whereby spouses mutually bestow and accept each other," and not just "those rights proper to the state of marriage," as the encyclical had said. Instead of discussing the marriage contract, *Gaudium et Spes* has in view an intimate and interpersonal covenant. "Thus a man and a woman, who by the marriage covenant of conjugal love 'are no longer two, but one flesh' (Matt. 19:6) render mutual help and service to each other through an intimate union of their persons and of their actions" (par. 48).

When it explicitly speaks of genital relationships, it characterizes them as expressions of love. For "this love is uniquely expressed and perfected through the marital act" (par. 49). And finally, when the document comes to reassert the importance of procreation, this traditional point is given a new context by seeing it as the fruit of love. For "marriage and conjugal love are by their nature ordained toward the begetting and education of children" (par. 50). So in a very clear way love becomes the focus and the format for the council's reflections on the nature of human sexuality.

This leads us to the third point: specific formulations. You will recall that the Catholic tradition had spoken of the primary purpose of marriage and sexuality as being the procreation of children. This assertion, however, is significantly absent from the documents of Vatican II.

There is no doubt that the council fathers considered procreation important. The quotation from paragraph 50, mentioned above, would make that clear. But they do not see it as central. They do not see it as *the* preeminent purpose of marriage or sexuality, from which all other blessings flow. Indeed, their rejection of this vision is made explicit.

> While not making the other purposes of matrimony of less account, the true practice of conjugal love, and the whole meaning of the family life which results from it, have this aim: that the couple be ready with stout hearts to cooperate with the love of the Creator and the Savior, who through them will enlarge and enrich His own family day by day.
> (par. 50)

So procreation is one of the aims of marriage, coexisting with and complementary to its other aims. Indeed, inasmuch as love is always mentioned in these pivotal statements, it would not be unjustified to interpret the council as viewing love as the central aim and end of marriage and procreation as a necessary and quite special consequence.

In effect, then, through these gentle and carefully phrased statements, *Gaudium et Spes* turns the older tradition on its head, shifting the focus and in so doing changing the vision. What is sex? It is the capacity for mutual selfgiving in love. And what is one of the consequences of this love? It is the generous openness to and acceptance of procreation.

Apostolic Exhortation A second church document often considered when one is discussing sexual morality, and indeed almost identified with that topic, is *Humanae Vitae*, the encyclical letter issued by Pope Paul IV in 1968. And thus, when I began preparing this paper, I presumed that I would need to deal with that document. But on December 15, 1981, Pope John Paul II issued an Apostolic Exhortation on the Family, which addresses many of the same issues as *Humanae Vitae*, and with almost identical conclusions. So I will give my attention now to this very recent pronouncement.[17]

By way of background I should call to your mind that in 1980 there was held in Rome a Synod of Bishops, the most recent of a series of such meetings to be held since the end of the Vatican Council. At the 1980 synod the topic was family life, and at its conclusion the bishops submitted to Pope John Paul II a series of reflections and recommendations. This apostolic exhortation, then, is the Pope's response to the synod. Indeed, it is a proclamation of his vision of family life, articulated in large part by reference to the very words that the bishops had used in their reflections. Thus the apostolic exhortation is partly the pope's thoughts, partly the bishops'—or perhaps wholly the thoughts of both.

And what does the Exhortation say? Much like *Gaudium et Spes*, it begins with an expression of concern for the pressures experienced by the contemporary family. It then goes on to give a general description of marriage, the family, and human sexuality, as viewed from a Christian perspective:

Christian revelation recognizes two specific ways of realizing the vocation of the human person, in its entirety, to love: marriage and virginity or celibacy. Either one is in its own proper form an actuation of the most profound truth of man, in his being created in the image of God.

Consequently sexuality, by means of which man and woman give of themselves to one another through the acts which are proper and exclusive to spouses, is by no means something purely biological, but concerns the innermost

being of the human person as such. It is realized in a truly
human way only if it is an integral part of the love by which a
man and a woman commit themselves totally to one another
until death....

This totality which is required by conjugal love also
corresponds to the demands of responsible fertility....

(par. 11)

According to the plan of God, marriage is the foundation
of the wider community of the family, since the very institution of marriage and conjugal love is ordained to the procreation and education of children, in whom it finds its crowning.
(par. 14—here there appears a footnote to *Gaudium et Spes*)

The Exhortation then proceeds to describe in detail the
roles which the family exercises: namely, forming a permanent
community, serving life, participating in society, and sharing in
the mission of the Church. It is the second of these, serving life,
that concerns us here.

"Fecundity," says the Exhortation, "is the fruit and the sign
of conjugal love, the living testimony of the full reciprocal
self-giving of the spouses" (par. 28). And as if these words were
not sufficiently reminiscent of the new format of *Gaudium et
Spes*, the exhortation immediately proceeds to quote paragraph
50 of that document: "While not making the other purposes of
matrimony of less account, the true practice of conjugal love
...have this aim: that the couple be ready with stout hearts to
cooperate with the love of the creator and the savior, who
through them will enlarge and enrich his own family day by
day."

But what, specifically, does this attitude require? The document is quite clear and methodical in answering this question.
First it asserts that the Church teaching on the specific implications of this attitude is "always old yet always new," and exemplifies it by quoting the synod.

For this reason the synod fathers made the following declaration at their last assembly:

"This sacred synod, gathered together with the successor
of Peter in true unity of faith, firmly holds what has been set
forth in the Second Vatican Council (cf. *Gaudium et Spes*,
50) and afterward in the encyclical *Humanae Vitae*, particu-

larly that love between husband and wife must be fully human, exclusive, and open to new life (HV 11; cf 9, 12)."

(par. 29)

And on this basis, then, the Exhortation goes on to repeat that teaching in all its specificity:

> Paul VI affirmed that the teaching of the church "is founded upon the inseparable connection willed by God and unable to be broken by man on his own initiative between the two meanings of the conjugal act: the unitive meaning and the procreative meaning." And he concluded by reemphasizing that there must be excluded as intrinsically immoral "every action which, either in anticipation of the conjugal act, or in its accomplishment, or in the development of its natural consequences, proposes, whether as an end or as a means, to render procreation impossible."
> (par.32)

Finally, lest this teaching appear to be a surreptitious return to the old idea of procreation as the primary end of marriage or of sexual activity, the exhortation asserts that contraception "leads not only to a positive refusal to be open to life, but also to a falsification of the inner truth of conjugal love, which is called upon to give itself in personal totality." (par. 32)

So the argument is clear and consistent. The essential inner meaning of sexual activity is conjugal love. But that love involves, as a necessary and inevitable consequence, an openness to the procreative potential of the acts. Hence artificial interventions which would frustrate and foreclose that potential constitute a sort of existential untruth that ends up giving the lie to the love that is claimed. Not that the partners are, in conscious choice, refusing to love. Rather their behavior is incoherent with the life-oriented and life-accepting dynamic which that love necessarily entails.

These two documents, then, *Gaudium et Spes* and the Apostolic Exhortation (with its reaffirmation of *Humanae Vitae*), are the first step in our study of recent developments in the Catholic understanding of sexuality. And in this first step we find a refocused and modified overall vision, but we also find the same specific conclusions as were common in the earlier tradition.

Theological Reinforcements

The second step in our study leads us to several Catholic philosophers who have developed a theory of sexuality, and indeed of all morality, which reinforces this magisterial understanding. I have in mind here the work of Germain Grisez, John Finnis, William May, and others. For purposes of our discussion I will focus on the presentation of Dr. Grisez as representative of the group.[18]

Dr. Grisez's position is that in the conduct of human life we encounter a multiplicity of "basic goods." These realities, such as friendship and beauty, are good because they are aspects of being, and they are basic because they do not exist in service to any other reality but, on the contrary, are self-justifying and self-authenticating. In Grisez's view all of these goods are important, and because each is different they are incommensurable. This is to say, one cannot calculate how much friendship is equal to how much beauty. They are different and important, each in its own way.

It follows from this that the pursuit of any one of these goods is an admirable and ethically upright action. An insufficiency of any of these goods is truly regrettable. And a direct attack upon any of these goods is morally reprehensible.

In his developments of this theory, Grisez discusses eight different basic goods.[19] One of these, for our purposes the most significant, is procreation. This is the basic good of fertility, the capacity to make new beings like oneself, to share life, and to make love fruitful. In Grisez's judgment this fruitfulness is a basic good in human life. And like all the other basic goods, to pursue it is commendable, to attack it is reprehensible.

Of course, Grisez realizes that it is not always possible or desirable to have large numbers of children. Sometimes sterility makes procreation impossible. In such a case, however, sterility is obviously regrettable. Sometimes also a shortage of money or time or energy makes further procreation unrealistic, indeed, irresponsible. But this situation, too, is in some ways regrettable. So Grisez does not imagine that the maximum fertility is always required. He simply believes that direct attack upon fertility is always prohibited. Why? Because a direct attack upon fertility constitutes a direct attack upon a basic good, and that by implication involves a direct attack upon being itself, upon ourselves as human persons, and upon the source of human life, God.

This position, then, supports Vatican II's assertion that love is central to human sexuality. It also supports the magisterium's assertion that artificial contraception is always morally wrong. For while procreativity is not the central meaning of human sexuality, it is one of the basic goods regarding which human life should be conducted.

Theological Revisions

This position, however, is not the only one proposed in Roman Catholic theology today. Indeed, it would be fair to say that it does not even represent the majority position. So as the third step in our discussion of recent developments, I now want to present another position on the significance of procreation and, by implication, of human sexuality in general.

This position is exemplified not by philosophers but by theologians like Charles Curran, John Dedek, Richard McCormick, and Philip Keane. And while the following summary will not exhaustively report the position of any one of these authors, it is fundamentally representative of them all.[20]

According to this second perspective, there are indeed fundamental values in our world, values analogous to what Grisez would call "basic goods," values whose pursuit is always commendable, whose neglect is always morally reprehensible. But such values are not identified with specific external behaviors. On the contrary, they are identified with internal attitudes and personal styles of moral agents.

What this means, for example, is that it is always moral and obligatory to respect private property. It is always immoral and prohibited to abuse or violate private property. But it may be moral or immoral to give a particular person a loaded gun. That is, in the particular instance the concrete external act of passing the gun may be an incarnation of respect or abuse of private property. Thus, the proponents of this perspective would agree with Grisez that friendship and beauty are basic goods never to be attacked. But they would point out that it is precisely friendship that is the basic good, not a specific instance of shaking hands. It is precisely beauty that is the basic good, not the playing of a Mozart sonata at just this moment.

Therefore, in the case which concerns us here, this perspective would find Grisez guilty of an improper analogy. The proper way to formulate the matter would be as follows: Fruitfulness, the attitude of life involving an ability and willingness to transcend one's own needs, bring about a growing richness of life around one, and generously share one's life and resources— fruitfulness is a basic value. Concretely fertile behavior, on the other hand, may or may not be a real value, depending on the context and the alternatives that are really present.

But even if, concretely, fertility is undesirable at a particular moment, does that justify the implementation of an act rendered consciously infertile? In answering this question, the proponents of this second perspective develop an important insight.

The human world is a finite world. We can so often overlook this fact. We can pretend that all things are possible, that all goods can be achieved, all evil avoided. But it is not so. We live in a finite world. And an implication of our finitude is that values compete for our attention and our allegiance.

Let me take a very simple example. Sleep is, as we all know, one of life's good gifts. A peaceful night's sleep of sufficient duration and of the proper quality is one of life's great pleasures. But sleep is not the only good thing. Parents with a sick child may go without sleep for a long time, intuitively judging that care for their child is more important. For those who are well rested, even the prospect of a good movie may be enough to keep them up late. And the desire to earn a living motivates many people to arise early and go to work. Sleep is clearly a good thing, but whether it is a good to be embraced and actualized at a particular moment depends upon the other values which compete with it. There is an exquisitely subtle balance that must be achieved among the various values, the various goods which compete for one's attention.

This is the insight of the theologians we are considering. We live in a finite world. We, therefore, live in a world of competing values. Morally right behavior is constituted not when all good is done and no evil, but when as much good is done as possible, and as little evil as necessary.

It is never right to do an immoral act, of course. But an act is immoral precisely because and when it is more harmful than necessary. And whether a particular action is moral in a specific

instance depends upon whether it is the best, the most constructive or least destructive, of the available options. The key to
moral judging and moral living, then, is proportionality. It is the
virtue of prudence, of good judgment made in the negotiation
and reconciliation of competing values.

The relevance of this insight to the case at hand is obvious.
It has already been agreed that in the case we are considering
further procreation would be inappropriate. Fertility is not, all
things considered, desirable. The question is whether one can
nonetheless justify indulging in genital acts. The answer
according to this perspective is that it can be justified if and
when it serves other sufficiently important values. Is the act an
expression and renewal of conjugal love? Is it rooted in genuine
Christian commitment and concern? Is it a legitimate response
to sexual tension? Would forgoing the act be destructive in
some way or other? The answer to these questions, according to
this second perspective, might well lead to the conclusion that
the act is morally right and commendable. To put this another
way, there is no doubt that frustrating the procreative potential
of genital acts is a disvalue. But is it always the greatest of the
alternative disvalues? Is it the most harmful of the available
options? Or on the contrary, is it in some circumstances a
justifiable evil in view of other advantages to be gained, other
values to be served?

This second perspective, then, does not see the procreative
potential as a basic good. It sees it simply as a genuine human
good, demanding our attention and interest but competing for
our concrete actualization. Because it is a real value, so the
proponents of this perspective would assert, there need be no
fear that the overall vision of human sexuality will be dis-
mantled. On the other hand, because it is not a basic good or
nonnegotiable value, the absolute prohibitions of the older syn-
thesis must be reevaluated. Those prohibitions, in this perspective, are not absolutes but rather presumptive judgments.

REFLECTIONS

The current situation within Catholic theology regarding the
understanding of human sexuality is complex, and in some

ways the diversity of opinions is frustrating. Certainly it would be helpful if, on a matter of this importance, people of goodwill could achieve some unanimity. It would be nice if we could know for sure what counts for good, humane, fulfilling, appropriately Christian sexual living. To some extent, however, it is impossible.

But that does not mean that we are reduced to silence. It does not mean that Catholic theology and its tradition of reflecting on sexual behavior has nothing to offer. In the third part of this paper, I wish to offer a series of reflections, comments, and observations.

Shift from Procreation to Love

The change in focus from procreation to love was neither inappropriate nor unexpected. In a fascinating article, sociologist Teresa Sullivan has collected a number of statistics demonstrating the degree to which the human need for procreation has recently diminished.[21] As recently as the mid-nineteenth century in the United States, the modest goal of simply maintaining the size of the human community required married couples to rear and raise approximately six children. The situation was, as Sullivan describes it, a high-fertility, high-mortality culture. The advent of the sophisticated techniques of modern medicine, however, has changed all that. Infant mortality has been drastically reduced, life expectancy has been greatly expanded. The result is that at the present time maintenance of the population requires from each married couple only slightly more than two children.

It seems to me that the implications of these data are substantial. When the Catholic tradition focused upon the importance of procreation, it was not merely proposing a pious ideal. It was stating a fact. The essence of marriage, its primary purpose, clearly was the procreation and education of children, the production of the next generation. Now, however, the actual function of marriage has drastically shifted. Marriage is no longer primarily an institution for the production of the next generation. Rather, marriage is the locale for a primary relationship, a place of conjugal love.[22] Similarly, in earlier eras the high priority of procreation in combination with the absence of viable contraceptive options made it not at all surprising that the essence of sexuality should be understood as procreation. Now, however, options exist and the procreative need is greatly reduced. It is not surprising that sexuality is now understood primarily as a mode for the expression of love.

Sullivan's data do not negotiate between the two perspectives presented above. They do not settle the question of whether, granted that sex and marriage are fundamentally about love, genital acts ought *also* to remain open to the procreative potential. But the data do help us understand why the shift of focus took place and why at the present time there is a good deal of disagreement regarding the details of our sexual ethic. The simple fact is that in terms of the actual function of sex, the human community is in a new situation. And new situations take a while to achieve clarity.

Shift from Law to Values

The recent focus upon values as opposed to rules is commendable. The history of Catholic moral theology is intricate and extensive, and this is not the place to pursue it in detail. But it ought to be said in this context that the occasional temptation toward arbitrary rule-making was not helpful. There is a tendency even today for people to understand morality as a set of rules and to understand Christian living as an exercise in obedience. The best of the Catholic tradition, understood as "natural law," viewed morality otherwise. Morality is the project of serving the human community well, of doing that which is helpful and avoiding that which is hurtful. Rules, when they are valid, derive their justification from the fact that they accurately articulate and transmit insight into values.[23]

In light of this appreciation of the best of the Catholic tradition, it is noteworthy that both of the perspectives described above focus on values. When Grisez reaches the conclusion that contraceptive intercourse is immoral, he does so on the grounds that attacking the basic good of procreation is attacking oneself. It is a self-destructive act, and therefore a great and fundamental human disvalue. He is not indulging in legal positivism but in metaphysical humanism. When the proportionalists assert that contraceptive intercourse, though sometimes inappropriate and always regrettable, is also sometimes justifiable, they reach this conclusion on the grounds that they judge it to be the least of the available evils. They see their task as protecting human values to the extent possible within a conflicted and finite world. And on this basis they draw the conclusion that these acts may be morally right. In both cases our authors are concerned about values. They are concerned about human life as it exists. And in this they are like the best of the Catholic moral tradition.

Areas of Agreement

Areas of disagreement are outweighed by areas of agreement. I believe that this point is extremely important and is often overlooked. There is a tendency in Catholic morality, perhaps in all schools of moral thought, to emphasize disputed points to the extent that areas of agreement are overlooked. In the case of sexual morality, however, if the consensus is ignored, people will be hurt. For the matters discussed here are substantial. The human sexual power has a significant capacity to be either creative or destructive; it either enriches people's lives or it wounds them. And when a body of wisdom such as the Catholic community and Catholic tradition possesses is not made available to the wider community, a serious loss occurs.

But what does this tradition say upon which all would agree?

First, it says that sexuality is good. The Christian and Catholic tradition obviously has been ambivalent on this question. The focus upon things spiritual, upon the life to come, has at times led to a denigration of the human. Augustine did have his day. But always the fact of incarnation stood against this dualism. God became human and in so doing symbolized the goodness of the human. Sexuality may be problematic, but it is fundamentally good. One would think that a society so filled with sex as our own would be well convinced of this fact. But I am not so sure. Are the purveyor of pornography, the client of the peep show, the pursuer of promiscuous escapades really pursuing the goodness of sex? Or doth he or she protest too much? Does not behavior such as this really symbolize a profound distrust of sex, a sense that it is evil or at least suspicious?[24] In response, the Christian and Catholic tradition declares unequivocally: sex is good.

Secondly, this good thing needs a home. Sex, as understood by the Catholic tradition, depends upon commitment. It needs a place to reside. It needs a yesterday and a tomorrow within which to live in order to fulfill its own promise. This emphasis upon commitment, upon the fact that sex belongs in marriage, is not in this view a killjoy's attempt to discourage fun. It is, if anything, the attempt to protect fun, to guarantee its deepening, its continuing, its flourishing into joy. Masters and Johnson, in one of their more fascinating studies, *The Pleasure Bond*, discovered that pleasure and commitment are not opponents but rather correlates.[25] People who are committed to each other have more fun in their sexual behavior. And this surely makes sense. For they have an environment of security, of confidence, of trust within which to "play at sex." And so there is, it seems to me, wisdom in the assertion of a Catholic tradition that sex needs a home.

Thirdly, sex should be self-transcending. Should all couples have children? Clearly not. Even Pope Pius XII recognized the propriety of postponing procreation, indeed even postponing it permanently in certain cases.[26] So the issue is not whether everyone should bear children, but whether every act of sexual intercourse should remain open to procreative potential, at least to the extent of not artificially excluding it. As we have seen, the honest fact is that the Catholic community is divided on this question. The best wisdom of the leadership of the Church, as expressed in formal statements, is that it should. Many members of the Church find it otherwise. But it is clear that procreation is a value, that fruitfulness is an even more fundamental value, and that the going out from oneself and even from one's partner into a vital concern for all of life is the most profound value of all. Sexuality, as the drive toward another, toward union with that other, toward pleasure with that other, is the drive from the person into the world. As such, it should lead to a concern for, and joy in, all the world.

So at least in some particulars, there is a real consensus among Catholic Christian thinkers. At least when it comes to the fact that sex is good, that it has the goal of committed fidelity, and that it challenges us to a self-transcending fruitfulness, we can achieve a common voice. And, as I have said, it is a voice that needs to be heard.

Remaining Questions

But there is a diversity, too. In fact, there is contradictory disagreement. It will not be quickly eliminated; it certainly will not be squelched by authoritarian commands. So perhaps the best we can do at this moment is to list the differences and disagreements clearly. I will name four.

First, there is the question of the significance of the body. Hidden in the debate about the morality of artificial contraception is an abiding question about the proper way for human persons to relate to their bodies. Should we view our bodies as ourselves in the sense of accepting the limitations of body, of conforming ourselves to the demands of the body? Indeed, would anything else, would the "use" of our bodies and the mechanical manipulation of body rhythms, really amount to a sort of dualism, where we view ourselves as essentially spirits only accidentally connected to bodies which are mere tools for the achievement of chosen ends?[27]

Or is this single-minded call to conformity really nothing but a new version of that passive sense of natural law for which the Greeks were famous? After all, we utilize technology and science to cure disease. Can we not also use the human sciences to form and shape and control the human capacity for procreation? Indeed, is it not true that the refusal to make use of human intelligence in this enterprise is the real dualism—isolating the human spirit from the more mundane realities of the body, dividing the human person into "human" spirit and "animal" body?[28]

I don't know the answer to this question. And I don't know anybody who does. It is clear that total passivity before the bodily "facts of life" is inhumane and, ultimately, stupid. If I collapse with a heart attack, you will, rightly, rush to employ all the technological skill at your command. But at the same time, I am aware that the human penchant for technocracy, for the attempt facilely to dominate all of life by endless tinkering, is hardly without fault.[29] Our record as solvers of human problems is not good. It was, I think, Justice Holmes who said that science is that field of knowledge that makes a major contribution to minor needs.[30]

And so I am not prepared to support the technological imperative with complete confidence. It is just possible that the more humane and humanizing way to respond to the challenge of controlling human fertility is through intelligent cooperation with natural rhythms. We do not know; and that is one of today's insoluble problems.

Second, there is the question of sexual norms in general. I will take it as given that sexual activity, while not by any means the central issue of human life, is a real concern. People do in fact hurt one another by some of the ways in which they sexually relate. So the enterprise called sexual ethics is not inappropriate. But if that is true, then what shall be our criterion to distinguish appropriate, humane, respectful, and respectable sexual behavior from inappropriate, destructive, and reprehensible aberration? The procreative norm, as I have indicated, at least had the virtue of clarity and coherence. For the moment we have nothing so helpful.

I mentioned early on the systematic way in which various aberrant behaviors could be adjudged immoral by the procreative norm. If one votes down that norm, if one asserts that sexual acts may be morally commendable despite the absence of any immediate reference to or openness to procreation, then how does one judge any behavior as wrong? What about homosexual acts between consenting adults? What about masturbation? Many are prepared to support these acts, and with quite impressive argumentation. But what about marital infidelity? What about sexual intercourse with no reference to permanent commitment? What about bestiality, indeed?

I do not mean to suggest that the elimination of the procreative norm immediately leads to normless antinomianism. It does not. But I do mean to suggest that the development of appropriate and really helpful norms is no small task. And it is a problem which has not yet been fully resolved.

Both of these items, the question of the significance of body and the search for norms, lead to my third point: what is the significance of gender? A large and significant literature is developing around this issue,[31] but my judgment is that we are presently confronted with more questions than answers. Certainly one component of the issue is homosexuality. It was, as we saw, easy to condemn homosexual genital acts under the force of the procreative norm. In the absence of that norm, can they be critiqued? Or what should be the ethical evaluation of them? If, for example, they are judged to be morally proper, at least for those of a confirmed homosexual orientation, then should they be viewed as in any way inferior to heterosexual acts? Is it appropriate and meaningful to describe the latter as more fully or satisfactorily human?[32] And if not, if one chooses to make no distinction,[33] then has not the entire reality of gender become irrelevant to human life? And then, at least, are we not guilty of a body-distancing sort of dualism? On the other hand, if we take body seriously and gender seriously, then we are again confronted by the innate, if you will, orientation of genitality to procreation.

So, as I say, the issue of gender reveals itself in the current ethical discussions of homosexuality, discussions that occupy the attention of Catholic scholars as much as anyone else's.[34] But it also arises in other discussions. For example, the discussions of roles for men and women in society, the efforts to avoid sexism, the profound and challenging discussions of the role of women in ministry—all these raise the question of the significance of gender. I, for one, sense that we ought to assert a genuine and irreducible difference between males and females. But how to describe it? I do not want to reduce it to their relationships in bed. But I also do not want to universalize the cultural roles that I happen to have experienced. So I am forced to ask myself: is there a proper way to formulate a "dual anthropology," an anthropology that says there really is no such thing as a "human person," pure and simple. There are males and females, period. Or am I forced to a unitary anthropology? And if I accept that, how do I avoid that dualism that views our bodies as accidental accretions to the process of human being?[35]

These are troubling questions, these three. How shall we ever answer them? And how shall we deal with the fact that we presently do have answers to at least some of them, but answers which many people find thoroughly unsatisfactory? This is my fourth and last question. My question revolves around the significance of the community for ethical learning.

I have referred to the Synod of Bishops held in Rome in 1980. At that synod Archbishop John Quinn of San Francisco gave a speech frankly admitting the fact that the current teaching of the Catholic magisterium on sexual behavior and especially on contraception, the teaching I have called the procreative norm, is not accepted by a majority of the Catholic faithful. In light of that fact, said Archbishop Quinn, it is the responsibility of the Church to take a fresh look at that teaching, not necessarily to change it, but at least to deepen and enrich its presentation so that it might be found plausible, if not immediately convincing, to the millions of faithful people.[36]

By way of response to Archbishop Quinn, another bishop spoke at the synod. He reminded his audience that the Church is not a democracy, that ethics is not developed through counting noses, and that, in the end, the data of public opinion polls are utterly irrelevant to the enterprise in which the bishops were engaged.[37]

I want to say that this second speaker was wrong. More than that, I want to say that his comments are ultimately contradictory to the traditional Catholic vision of morality and of the Christian life. I spoke of this at the very beginning of this paper, and I want to return to it at the end. The Catholic tradition believes not only in the Lord of the Book but also, and especially, in the Lord of the Gathering. And that means that the prudent judgment of believing persons is relevant to the enterprise of Christian ethics.

If the polls taken by George Gallup tallied the opinions of all human persons, without any reference to their religious convictions and practices, to their commitment to discipleship and their desire to live with justice, respect, and love, then perhaps it would be fair to call their opinions irrelevant. But that is not the case here. The opinions being tallied are those of believers, of followers of the Lord. Within my communion it should be said that they are the opinions of good, churchgoing, faith-following, God-fearing, praying, and acting Catholics. They are not the opinions of ciphers on a computer printout; they are the opinions of the People of God, the Mystical Body of

Christ. Therefore, somehow or other they must be seen to embody the fidelity and love and wisdom of the divinity.

I do not say that polls can finally resolve the questions I have spelled out here. No, there are too many cases in the history of the Church of the deception of communities by popular movements and trendy styles of the moment. But I do say that those opinions must be taken seriously. And they must be responded to. The data of the polls force us to the conclusion that the magisterial judgment incarnated in the procreative norm is either wrong or has only been articulated in the most deficient form. And in either case, this means that study must occur. And that, after all, is just what Archbishop Quinn said.

I hope that study will take place, within the Catholic Church, between the various churches of the Christian tradition, and among all men and women of goodwill. For, as I have said, these are truly important questions.

There is much about the American culture that is narcissistic and involuted. There is much that is static and stagnant. We are, in certain frightening ways, already an old society. In this regard, I believe, we contradict our sexuality and its promise. And so, when the best of our various traditions stands up and speaks for the beauty and the goodness of sexuality, for the promise and the challenge of sexuality, for the depth and the mystery of sexuality, it does a good and noble task. And when it leads us in addressing the questions that still remain, when it dares us not to flee those questions but to confront them with honesty and humility and hope, then it speaks to us, I believe, with the voice of God.

Notes

1. This concept of religion and its implications are brilliantly developed by J. Danielou, "Christianity and Non-Christian Religions," in The Word in History, ed. T. P. Burke (New York: Sheed & Ward, 1966), pp. 86–101.

2. This very point is made in one of the more unusual and significant observations of the Roman Catholic magisterium. In 1977 a volume entitled Human Sexuality was published by the Catholic Theological Society of America. The volume, a report of a committee of CTSA, received a significant amount of criticism. One example of this was a statement issued by the Committee on Doctrine of the

National Conference of Catholic Bishops. One of the committee's objections, it turns out, was the way the report had dealt with scripture. But was the bishops' problem a slipshod approach to exegesis? Was their problem a tendency to underestimate the biblical prohibitions in the area of sexuality? This is what they say: "The Committee on Doctrine regrets to find in the report a rather impoverished concept of the role the word of God must play as a foundation for theology. While critical exegesis *contributes* to the church's understanding of the sacred texts, it cannot be considered the *ultimate source* of their meaning. God's word is proclaimed in the living reality of the church which by its teaching, its liturgy and the witness of its saints continues to reveal the riches of this word" (emphasis added). "Bishops' Doctrinal Committee Responds to Book on Sexuality," Origins 7 (1977): 376.

    3. This characteristically Catholic approach is noted by Birch and Rasmussan, The Bible and Ethics in Christian Life (Minneapolis: Augsburg, 1976).

    4. This term I take from Margaret Farley, "Sexual Ethics," in Encyclopedia of Bioethics, ed. W. T. Reich (New York: Free Press, 1978), 4:1580.

    5. Ibid. Farley cites, as an example of Aquinas' use of the first line of argument, S. T. I–II, 34, 1 ad 1; as an example of his use of the second approach she cites S. T. II–II, 154, 11 and Summa Contra Gentiles III, 122, 4 and 5.

    6. H. Davis, Moral and Pastoral Theolgy (New York: Sheed & Ward, 1935), 2:172.

    7. Ibid., p. 177.

    8. Ibid., pp. 177 f.

    9. Ibid., p. 179.

    10. Five Great Encyclicals (New York: Paulist Press, 1939). While my quotations are from this version, I will simply include, with the text, an indication of the paragraph number. This will be the procedure for all ecclesiastical documents.

    11. H. Noldin and A. Schmitt, Summa Theologiae Moralis, Complementum: De Castitate, ed. H. Heinzel, 36th ed. (Oeniponte: Rauch, 1958), p. 59 (translation).

    12. D. Doherty, however, believes that this argument can indeed be traced to Augustine: "The Tradition in History," in Dimensions of Human Sexuality, ed. D. Doherty (Garden City: Doubleday, 1979), p. 48. In any case, this idea that concupiscence lessens the capacity for pleasure is discussed and beautifully developed by Karl Rahner, "The Theological Concept of Concupiscentia," in Theological Investigations (Baltimore: Helicon, 1961), 1:347–382, esp. pp. 372 f.

    13. Die Sexualethik des. hl. Thomas von Aquin (Koln, 1949).

14. *De Castitate et Ordine Sexuali*, 3d ed. (Rome: Pont. Univ. Greg., 1963), p. 40 (translation).

15. Another excellent discussion of the history of Roman Catholic Sexual ethics is Doherty, "The Tradition in History," which also provides additional bibliography.

16. *The Documents of Vatican II*, ed. W. H. Abbott (New York: Herder & Herder, 1966).

17. "The Apostolic Exhortation on the Family," *Origins* 11 (1981): 437–468.

18. G. Grisez (with R. Shaw), *Behond the New Morality* (Notre Dame: University of Notre Dame Press, 1974), and G. Grisez, *Contraception and the Natural Law* (Milwaukee: Bruce, 1964). Cf. also J. Finnis, *Natural Law and Natural Rights* (Oxford: Clarendon Press, 1980), and J. Connery, "Morality of Consequences: A Critical Appraisal," *Theological Studies* 34 (1973): 396–414.

19. E.g., *Beyond the New Morality*, pp. 64–74.

20. E.g., C. Curran, "Utilitarianism, Consequentialism, and Moral Theology," in *Themes in Fundamental Moral Theology* (Notre Dame: University of Notre Dame Press, 1977) pp. 121–144; and "Sin and Sexuality," in ibid., pp. 165–190. J. Dedek, *Contemporary Medical Ethics* (New York: Sheed & Ward, 1975), esp. pp. 57–76. R. McCormick, "Ambiguity in Moral Choice," in *Doing Evil to Achieve Good* (Chicago: Loyola University Press, 1978) pp. 7–53; and "A Commentary on the Commentaries," in ibid., pp. 193–265. P. Keane, *Sexual Morality: A Catholic Perspective* (New York: Paulist Press, 1977), esp. pp. 35–56 and 121–133. Cf. also my *Principles for a Catholic Morality* (New York: Seabury Press, 1978), esp. pp. 144–173.

21. "Numbering Our Days Aright: Human Longevity and the Problem of Intimacy," *Toward Vatican III: The Work That Needs to Be Done*, ed. D. Tracy, with H. Kung and J. Metz (New York: Seabury Press, 1978), pp. 282–294.

22. A public furor arose when, on Jan. 26, 1982, an Associated Press story reported that an impotent paraplegic was being refused permission to marry in the diocese of Joliet, Illinois. Subsequently, Bishop Joseph Imesch gave permission for the marriage. What strikes me as significant is neither the legal question of whether this man can marry nor the pastoral solution achieved by Bishop Imesch. Rather, I am struck by the nearly unanimously negative reaction when the first story appeared. Conservatives and liberals, clergy and laity, Catholics and Protestants and Jews all seemed offended. Why? I would suggest that the reason is that we have all already agreed that in fact marriage is primarily a locus for relationship and only secondarily an institution for the production of the next generation. The Catholic tradition, of

course, thought just the opposite. Rather the tradition would have us say to this man: "You are capable of a wonderful, lifelong, faithful friendship with this woman. And we would support you in this friendship. The one thing you are not capable of is marriage." No one seems to be saying that today (except one unrenewed pastor)!

23. Cf. my Principles for a Catholic Morality, p. 145.

24. This pessimistic interpretation of current mores is cogently urged by E. Becker, The Denial of Death (New York: Free Press, 1975).

25. W. Masters and V. Johnson, The Pleasure Bond (New York: Bantam Books, 1976), esp. "Commitment: The Pleasure Bond," pp. 267–285.

26. Address of Pope Pius XII to the Italian Catholic Union of Midwives, Oct. 29, 1951, as quoted in E. Healy, Medical Ethics (Chicago: Loyola University Press, 1956), p. 165.

27. The point of view espoused by W. May, "An Integrist Understanding," in Dimensions of Human Sexuality, ed. D. Doherty (Garden City: Doubleday, 1979), esp. p. 105.

28. The position of J. Nelson, "Sexual Alienation: the Dualist Nemesis," in Embodiment (Minneapolis: Augsburg, 1978), pp. 37–69, as well as throughout the book.

29. A point discussed by Time magazine (April 2, 1973) under the interesting title "Second Thoughts About Man" (pp. 78–81).

30. As quoted by D. Maguire, The Moral Choice (Garden City: Doubleday, 1978), p. 455.

31. Most recently an entire issue, entitled "On the Relations Between the Sexes," of Communio 8 (1981): 198–304.

32. The position of P. Keane, Sexual Morality: A Catholic Perspective (New York: Paulist, 1978), pp. 84–90; also C. Curran, "Dialogue with the Homophile Movement: The Morality of Homosexuality," in Catholic Moral Theology in Dialogue (Notre Dame: University of Notre Dame Press, 1972), pp. 184–219, and "Sin and Sexuality," in Themes in Fundamental Moral Theology (Notre Dame: University of Notre Dame Press, 1977), pp. 165–190, esp. 181 f.

33. As urged by Nelson, Embodiment, pp. 197–199. Or so it seems. Nelson does not say so explicitly. But he presents this viewpoint as the fourth and last of the alternative interpretations he is aware of and it is the only one of which he does not point out underlying flaws. This position is also held by J. McNeill, The Church and the Homosexual (Kansas City: Sheed, Andrews & McMeel, 1976).

34. The most recent additions to the literature include an historical study: J. Boswell, Christianity, Social Tolerance, and Homosexuality (Chicago: University of Chicago Press, 1980), and an excellently diverse set of theological essays: E. Batchelor, ed., Homosexuality and

Ethics (New York: Pilgrim Press, 1980). A rather different but illuminating approach to the whole question is E. Malloy, *Homosexuality and the Christian Way of Life* (Washington, D.C.: University Press of America, 1981).

35. The term "dual anthropology" comes from, and this issue was focused for me by, S. Butler, ed., *Research Report: Women in Church and Society* (Bronx, N.Y.: Catholic Theological Society of America, 1978).

36. The text appears in "'New Context' for Contraception Teaching," *Origins* 10 (1980): 263–267.

37. As reported in *Origins* 10 (1980): 279.

Sexuality in Protestant Interpretations

James B. Nelson

WHAT PROTESTANTS HAVE IN COMMON

Sexuality in Protestantism is a fascinating and confusing picture.[1] While in Jewish and Roman Catholic traditions there are divergent views and emphases, within Protestantism this is multiplied many-fold. With an enormous denominational diversity, with the absence of a central ecclesiastical teaching authority, with differing convictions on biblical interpretation and on the weight to be given to contemporary sources, it is even more difficult to speak meaningfully of a "Protestant position" on sexuality than with the other major faith groups. Nevertheless, there are several commonalities which might characterize the majority of Protestants.

One is the affirmation that sexuality is a good gift of the Creator which has been marred and distorted by human sin. Our sexuality is a basic dimension of our humanness. It includes but is not limited to genital feelings and expressions. Sexuality is our way of being in the world as male or female persons, involving our varied and unique self-understandings of masculinity and femininity, our sexual-affectional orientations, our perceptions of our embodiedness, and our capacities for sensuousness and emotional depth. All of this is God's good gift to human beings, God's way of drawing us out of isolation and into communication and communion. But Protestants believe that sexuality, like every other dimension of human life, has been marred and distorted by "the fall." Our alienation from God, from neighbor, and from ourselves is experienced sexually as well as in other ways.

A second commonality is that the two alienating dualisms regarding sexuality are part of all Protestant history. The first, "spiritualistic" or "Hellenistic" dualism, is one shared with Roman Catholics. It has its roots in the body-spirit split which pervaded Greek philosophy and culture at the beginning of the Christian era. Spirit and body were believed essentially separate and only temporarily linked in uneasy alliance. Spirit was eternal, immortal, and good, while the body was temporal, mortal, and viewed with suspicion. Whatever else salvation might mean, it meant release from the confines of bodily limitation and corruption into the life of "spirit." And, since sexuality was viewed as essentially bodily, it was suspect.

While the Jewish tradition is significantly free of spiritualistic dualism, it has been heavily marked by "sexist" or "patriarchal" dualism, and Christians—both Roman Catholic and Protestant alike—share this distortion. This is the systematic subordination of women in social, institutional, and interpersonal life. The two dualisms came together as men assumed to themselves spiritual and rational superiority, and identified women with body, emotion, and sensuality. Hence, it was assumed that the superior part (spirit, male) was destined to lead and discipline the inferior part (body, female).

The third Protestant commonality, in distinction from Roman Catholic, is the lack of a history which exalted virginity and celibacy as superior to married sexual life. This break with the Catholic tradition came when the sixteenth-century Reformation theologically undercut salvation by good works (including virginity and celibacy) and, at the same time, elevated the doctrine of Christian marriage.

Fourth, Protestantism rather early abandoned procreation as the primary purpose of marriage and sexual expression. Instead of procreation, the fundamental aim became the expression of faithful love.

Fifth, "mainstream Protestantism" (as distinguished from ultraconservative and fundamentalistic groups) has showed considerable openness in recent years to new empirical knowledge about sexuality, to the historically and culturally relative nature of sexual norms, and to the feminist consciousness of the pervasive conditioning of male sexism upon the church's understandings.

Finally, there has emerged within mainstream Protestantism the desire to move from an essentially negative approach to a more positive one, from a physically oriented focus on categories of sexual acts to a more interpersonal focus upon the meanings of sexual expressions.

PROTESTANTS AND SEXUALITY: THE SIXTEENTH THROUGH THE NINETEENTH CENTURIES

The Protestant Reformation of the sixteenth century brought with it some important shifts from the Catholic tradition on certain, if not all, sexuality issues. The two pervasive dualisms—spirit-over-body and man-over-woman—underwent important theoretical modifications, even though their tenacious hold continued in other ways.

Two doctrinal emphases of the Reformers were directed at spiritualistic dualism. First, they regarded as quite unbiblical the Catholic medieval distinction between the lower realm of nature and the higher realm of grace. The medievalists tended to see sex itself as inherently tainted and sinful, part of the lower realm of nature which must be transcended through the church's means of grace—even while the married couple were obligated to propagate the race. The Reformers could not view nature (and, with it, sex) as in itself evil. Rather, the evil lay in the corruption of the human will and in the ways that fallen people expressed themselves in the natural (and sexual) realms.

The second doctrinal distinction was the Reformers' strong insistence upon justification by grace rather than by works of the law. If no human achievement could merit divine favor, then there could be no special merit to sexual celibacy. The cult of virginity was thus undercut both by the affirmation of the essential goodness of nature and by the emphasis upon salvation by grace. Marriage was lifted to a new level of Christian affirmation, and Martin Luther advised monks and nuns to abandon celibacy for the married state.

Nevertheless, the Protestant Reformers had considerable ambivalence about sexuality. Luther himself was both a radical and a conservative in this regard. On the one hand, he treated sex with an earthy frankness and honesty seldom seen in theological writings. He believed that in most persons (especially males) sexual desire had an urgency and compulsion which could not be denied. Hence, while God had ordained marriage as a great gift, a "school of heavenly love" for the spouses and their offspring, at the same time marriage was "a hospital for the sick," an emergency arrangement for the illness of human drives. In the *fallen* human being, sexuality was always pervaded by lust and corrupted. Yet, God's strange work was to take a couple's corrupted sexual desire, and through divine pardon and permission make of it a vehicle for propagating the race and restraining human sin.

John Calvin was somewhat less pessimistic. If Luther's main concern was to confine sex's raging power within marriage, Calvin believed that sex could have constructive effects for the couple, provided that there was mutual consent between the spouses, and provided that any sexual activity was moderate and within the appropriate bounds of "delicacy and propriety." If self-control and modesty were to characterize all sexual expression in marriage, then there followed an immediate gain for the wife's position. While Luther had believed that the husband's powers of instinct were felt so strongly that the wife must submit, it was not so with the Geneva Reformer. There must be mutual discipline and respect. If to Calvin the woman's status was still subordinate to the man's, still there was a notable development taking place. He began to believe that it was companionship rather than procreation and the restraint of lust which was God's chief design for marriage. This was to have major consequences for later Protestant thought.

Nevertheless, neither Reformer could break cleanly with certain medieval assumptions. If in theory sex as such was natural and not sinful, still in practice sexual acts were viewed with suspicion. Further, like their Catholic predecessors, Luther and Calvin did not look upon sexuality as a fundamental dimension of human nature, but rather dealt more narrowly with sexual acts.[2]

While, particularly in the Calvinistic emphasis upon companionship, there was a chipping away at sexist dualism, the

Reformation also resulted in some backward steps concerning sexual equality. Within the Catholic tradition, women had the church's blessing to live independently of men and to make their own contributions to the church—through the female religious orders. Now, however, these orders were abolished for Protestants, and the housewifely ideal for women was given divine blessing. Further, the Protestant Reformers turned to the Old Testament patriarchs for models of what the Christian family should be. Even Calvin, who saw the woman more positively than did most earlier male theologians, saw her as the man's subordinate helper and support. In addition, certain ecclesiastical practices implicitly reinforced traditional masculinism. Reacting against serious churchly abuses, some notable Reformers, such as Ulrich Zwingli, attacked the use of physical representations in churches—stained glass, crucifixes, images of the Virgin, even church organs. Such things were emotional and stirred up fleshly feelings, whereas "true worship" was disciplined and controlled. But the iconoclastic attack upon the physical and the emotional was also a buttress to traditional male control over the so-called female impulses.[3]

The most significant Protestant developments in the two centuries following the Reformation took place among the heirs of Calvin: the Puritans, the Quakers, and some of the Anglicans. In these groups developed an increasing conviction that procreation was not the major purpose of sexuality. Rather, love and companionship were. Thus, Richard Baxter could speak of mutual comfort and nurture as the chief end of sexuality, and his fellow Anglican Jeremy Taylor could speak of the value of sexual intercourse "to lighten and ease the cares and sadnesses of household affairs" and "to endear each other."[4] And the great English Puritan poet John Milton (in spite of his subordinationism regarding women) was convinced that the sexual union of spouses could prefigure the heavenly realm. Indeed, so convinced was Milton that companionship (not procreation) was the chief end of marriage that in his tract *The Doctrine and Discipline of Divorce* he made a brief for accepting divorce on the grounds of incompatibility, a remarkable departure from previous Christian teaching.

Contrary to some unfair stereotypes which have branded Puritans as simply sex-negative, the picture was not that simple. True, their emphasis upon discipline led to frequent legalisms, and they were often harsh in punishment of fornication and adultery. Yet their writings concerning the positive joys and gifts of marital sex attest to the other side. In addition to the companionate over the procreative emphasis on sexuality, the Puritans were noteworthy for one other development: their understanding of marriage. For the sixteenth-century Reformers, the church's role in marriage was purely instrumental, pronouncing God's blessing upon a sexual union which was a matter primarily between the couple and God. With the Puritans, however, the church's role increased. Now marriage became an act in which the church as a social institution gave its approval and permission to a couple to live in sexual covenant. The shift at this point was away from sexuality as a natural (if distorted) good of life and toward a belief that sexuality itself was something which expressly required the church's approval for its exercise.

Nineteenth-century Protestantism on the whole provided few new developments in sexual understanding. In England and America, the century was largely marked by the Victorian retrogression—a strong suspicion of sexuality, including marital sexual excess, horror over masturbation and homosexuality, and the Comstock laws to erase sexual obscenity. Victorianism also brought with it a strong tendency toward "spiritual femininity"—the placing of women (especially of the middle and upper classes) on a pedestal, characterizing them as delicate and above the animality of sex. Thus was the Victorian mother's advice to her daughter for the latter's wedding night: "Just close your eyes, dear, and think of England." One other development in late nineteenth-century Protestantism, however, was different: the social justice emphasis. Both the women's suffrage movement and the Protestant Social Gospel movement lifted up women's rights as a major concern for church and society.

TWENTIETH-CENTURY DEVELOPMENTS

Early-twentieth-century American Protestantism was marked by an internal tension of values over the issue of contraception. Particularly in its first two decades, the exclusivistic vision of a Protestant America was still strong. This vision included a strong emphasis upon the duty of Protestant families to procreate abundantly in order to stem the dilution of this religious dominance by the increasing waves of Catholic immigration. By the century's third decade, however, both the sinfulness and futility of this vision were largely recognized. Furthermore, Protestants, with their inveterate individualistic strain coupled with their openness to science and technology, became the religious supporters of individual procreative decisions and the use of contraception for family planning.

Toward the middle of this century, Protestant academic theology was moving decisively away from a law-centered and act-focused ethics and toward an attempt to base sexual morality more fully upon interpersonal considerations. This shift went hand-in-hand with a new recognition that sexuality is a fundamental dimension of human life, an appreciation owed in no small measure to developments in modern psychology. The decades of the 1960s and 1970s saw Protestant theologians and church bodies attempting to respond to the rising movements of feminist women and gay men and lesbians, both outside and within the churches. The pluralism typical of Protestants on so many theological, ecclesiastical, and social issues became increasingly a fact of life in matters sexual.

To characterize Protestant attitudes in the early years of the 1980s requires a distinction (a rough one but perhaps defensible) between evangelicals and mainline denominations.[5] The former emphasize personal religious experience, conversion, evangelism, and the centrality of the Bible in doctrine and morals. Many of them remain highly traditional about sexual ethics, and yet two developments in Evangelical Protestantism are significant.

One development is the shift of numerous fundamentalist evangelicals into right-wing political activism. The Moral Majority and similar groups of the New Right in religion and politics have centered considerable attention on sexuality issues, condemning homosexuality, pornography, abortion, and the Equal Rights Amendment, and exalting the male-dominated nuclear family as the normative family style and only valid sexual unit. Other paramount New Right concerns, such as prayer in public schools, resistance to further racial integration, support of military superiority and a politics of international confrontation, may not, on first glance, appear to be sexual issues. Yet each suggests an ideology which is both highly masculinist and suspicious of sexuality as such.

Quite different are left-wing evangelicals. Here the familiar emphases upon personal religious experience and scriptural authority are mated with liberal, even radical, social justice concerns, including a fresh look at numerous sexuality issues. Feminist concerns are taken seriously. In contrast to the New Right's strident condemnation of homosexuality, left-wing evangelicals support social justice for lesbians and gays, and exhibit some movement toward affirming the committed homosexual relationship as valid and analogous to heterosexual marriage.

"Mainline denominational Protestantism" shows considerable sexual ferment. No comparable outpouring of books and articles, ecclesiastical studies, debates, and churchly pronouncements on the subject can be found in earlier years. No earlier period saw the emergence of so many caucuses and movements intending either the reform of certain sexual views or the protecting of churches from unwanted sexual change. Moving away from a dominant focus upon rules and categories of action, mainline Protestant sexual ethics now characteristically gives greater attention to relationships, motivations, and concrete situations, convinced that ethics must be oriented fundamentally toward persons rather than toward abstract concepts. These emphases, together with an openness to clinical and social sciences, have led Protestants to reevaluate a variety of sexual expressions and to begin to rethink the meanings of sexuality as such.

A CONSTRUCTIVE STATEMENT

Paul Ricoeur has identified three major stages of Western evolution in the relation of sexuality to religion.[6] The earliest stage identified the two realms. Through the patterns of myth, ritual, and symbol, sexuality was incorporated into the believer's total understanding of reality. Then, however, came the second stage, wherein the great religions arose, separating sexuality from the religious experience. The sacred now was believed transcendent and untouchable, heavenly and not earthly. Sexuality was demythologized and limited to only a small part of the total order, particularly that of procreation within the institution of marriage. Discipline was to restrain sexual expression, and when it threatened to break out of its prescribed order its power was feared and condemned.

The third period, which Ricoeur believes is now emerging, is marked by the concern to release once again "the lyricism of life" in uniting sexuality with the experience of the sacred. This concern is prompted by more wholistic understandings of the person and of ways in which human sexuality is present in the entire range of human experience. Unlike the second period, in which sexuality (especially sexual desire) was believed a distraction to the life of mind and spirit, now there is a growing recognition that sexuality is so involved in the center of one's life that the powers of creativity are thwarted by its repression. Sexual expression still needs ordering and discipline, indeed. But that is quite different from the denial of sexuality's spiritual power.

The following list suggests what I believe to be a slowly emerging paradigmatic shift in at least some Protestant (and other religious) thinking about sexuality.

From the Old Paradigm	To a New Paradigm
1. Theologies about human sexuality	1. Sexual theologies
2. Sexuality as either incidental to or detrimental to the divine-human relationship	2. Sexuality as intrinsic to the divine-human relationship
3. Sin as essentially wrong sexual acts, violations of sexual norms	3. Sin as alienation from our divinely intended sexuality
4. Salvation as antithetical to sexuality	4. Salvation as including the recovery of sexual wholeness
5. Sexuality as incidental to the life of the church	5. Sexuality as fundamental to and pervasive in the life of the church

Some comment on each item is in order.

Sexual Theology

The vast majority of religious statements on sexuality in the past have assumed essentially a one-way question: what does Christian theology (or the Bible, or the church's tradition) say about human sexuality? It is important now that we recognize another question as well. The clue comes from those Christians writing liberation theologies from feminist, black, and Third World perspectives. They are insisting that their own experience, in those instances the experience of oppression, affords extraordinarily important insights into the meanings of Christian faith itself. Thus, for sexuality as well, the concern becomes two-directional, dialogical and not monological. In addition to the still-important question, "What does our religious tradition say about human sexuality?" is the question, "What does our experience as sexual human beings say about the ways in which we experience God, interpret our religious tradition, and attempt to live the life of faith?"

Sexuality and the Divine-Human Relationship

How does God make the divine presence and meaning known and real to human life? Christian faith makes the bold claim that the most decisive experience of God occurs not fundamentally or primarily in doctrine, creed, ideas, or in mystical otherworldly experience. Rather, it happens in flesh. "And the Word became flesh and dwelt among us, full of grace and truth" (John 1:14a). Christian faith is one of incarnation. And while Christians confess that they have seen God with greatest clarity and focus in and through one human being—Jesus, whom we call the Christ—it is an error to limit God's incarnation to that one figure, as decisive and central as he is for the faith community. By limiting God's incarnation to him alone we both deny his genuine humanity and treat him as an anomalous exception to the general human condition. Further, we close ourselves off from the richness of the incarnationalist faith itself: the realization that God continues to be experienced fundamentally in the embodied touching of human life with human life. Our sexuality, in its full sense, is both the physiological and the psychological grounding of our capacity to love. It expresses God's intention that we find our authentic humanness not in isolation but in communion—an intention which applies equally to the genitally active and to the celibate, to the aged and to the youthful, to the able-bodied and to the disabled.

Sexual Sin

It has been commonplace in Christian understanding to think of sexual sin in terms of certain acts—sexual acts done with the wrong person, against divine or natural law, or harmful to others and the self. While there is, indeed, truth in the assumption that sin will be *expressed* in acts, it is a mistake to equate the two. In its better moments, theology has long known that sin basically is the experience and condition of alienation. And alienation is inevitably experienced simultaneously in three dimensions—alienation from God, from the neighbor, and from the self.

This is true of sexual sin. More basic than any particular acts, sexual sin is alienation from our divinely intended sexuality. It is experienced as alienation within and from the sexual self. The sexual body becomes object—either that which is to be constrained out of fear or that which is a pleasure machine but essentially other than the self. It is spiritualistic dualism. But it is also sexist dualism, for it is alienation from the neglected half of one's intended humanness, with males fearful of tenderness, emotion, and vulnerability, and females fearful of or kept from claiming their strength, assertiveness, and intellect.

Sexual sin is also sexual alienation from the neighbor. Emotions and bodies are distanced, and relationships are truncated. Sexual distortions contribute to dehumanizing uses of power and manipulation, to social violence, to persisting expressions of racism, and to ecological abuse. Sexual sin, most basically, is alienation from God. Thus in Christian history both spiritualistic and sexist dualisms helped mightily to shape the notion of a hierarchical, ladder type of spirituality. As one "progressed upward" in spirituality, one loved God quite apart from any creaturely love—and both neighbor and self became incidental to, if not inimical to, the love of God. The soul was envisioned as a solitary, uncontaminated virgin contemplating a similar deity. But such spirituality cannot in the end nurture and express the intimate relationship of God, neighbor, and self, for it is inherently an invitation to division and distance.

Sexual Salvation

Unfortunately, throughout the greater part of Christian history, spiritualistic dualism has so marked Christian thought and experience that salvation has been associated with disembodiment and release from the realm of the flesh into the "higher" life of the spirit. Yet, more authentic to the heart of both Christian and Jewish faith is the claim that the experience of salvation in this life, incomplete though it may be, involves the greater realization of our sexual wholeness. If sin is basically alienation, salvation is reconciliation. If sexual sin is fundamentally alienation from the divinely intended sexuality, sexual salvation involves reconciliation and reintegration of the sexual self. It is "resurrection of the body."

Two classic words from the Christian tradition deserve reinterpretation in this light. The process of salvation traditionally (and quite rightly) has been understood to involve the polar experiences of justification by grace and sanctification by grace. Justification refers to God's activity directed toward the self from "outside." It is the Cosmic Lover's radical, unconditional, unearned acceptance of the person. When we experience this radical acceptance as directed toward the total body-self (and not toward some discarnate spirit), there begins a reclaiming of sexual dimensions of the self which had been lost. One's body feelings, one's fantasies, one's masculinity and femininity, one's heterosexuality and homosexuality, one's sexual irresponsibility as well as one's yearning for sexual integrity—all are graciously accepted by the divine Love. And, in the moment of that realization, everything is transformed and different. If the old fears, dualisms, and alienations return—as they will—still the self is not the same as before.

Sanctification, the second dynamic of salvation, refers to God's activity *within* the self. Traditionally, it frequently has been understood as growth toward a spiritualized, antibody, antisexual "holiness." More adequately, sanctification might be seen as God's gracious empowerment within, which both includes and enables the self's increasing sexual wholeness and fulfillment.

This might mean several things. It might mean growth in self-acceptance and positive self-love, the kind which "personalizes" the body, making me more vitally aware that I can celebrate the body which I am and thus affirm the ways in which my body-self relates to the world. Sanctification can mean growth in the capacity for sensuousness, wherein the body becomes a means of grace and the graceful expressions of the body a vehicle of love. It can mean renewal of the capacity for play. It can involve the diffusion of the erotic throughout the entire body rather than the narrow focus of sexual feeling in the genitals only. With such resexualization of the body might come an eroticization of the world, wherein our experienced environment reclaims the sensuous qualities which we had forgotten or failed to recognize. Sexual sanctification can mean growth in the possibility of androgyny, wherein each individual finds freedom to lay claim to his or her own unique personality configuration and expression, not coerced into rigid sex-role stereotypes which make us half-human. And, supremely, sexual sanctification means the awakening of the self to its destiny as an embodiment of love, the reintegration of our sexual dimensions around love's meanings.

If any human experience of salvation is partial, incomplete, and fragmentary (as it is), surely this is true of that salvation which involves our sexuality. But its partiality does not negate its reality. The Word is made flesh, and our flesh is confirmed.

The Church as a Sexual Community

Throughout most of Protestant history, sexuality has been seen as incidental to the life of the church or even inimical to the church's purposes. It is time that this community of faith, worship, and service be understood also as a sexual community. This is so not only because its members are sexual beings, but also because sexual meanings and feelings pervade all dimensions of the community's life, both for good and for ill. Such has always been the case, and conscious recognition of the fact can assist the church to reform the distorted sexual aspects of its life.

The church is a sexual community in its theological expressions, as the feminist movement forcefully reminds us. Stereotypically masculine language and images have pervaded Christian understandings of God and hence have given rise to a masculinized spirituality. A more androgynous theology and language can nurture a more androgynous spirituality, and both will be truer to the best in the tradition.

Reclaiming positive dimensions of sexuality in liturgy and sacramental life can enhance the connections of those experiences with the lives of the worshippers. Mainline Protestant worship has been marked, on the whole, by a masculinized emphasis upon the spoken word and a suspicion of body feelings—touch, movement, color, play, and imagination. To the extent that worship patterns reflect the alienating sexual dualisms, they only reinforce and do not assuage those dualisms in the lives of the worshippers. Further, recapturing an awareness of the rich sexual imagery in the two Protestant sacraments—baptism (the womb of new birth) and the Lord's Supper ("This is my body, given for you")—might assist the participant's understanding of the ways in which the total human sexual experience itself has sacramental potentialities. Sexual love, at its best, does have the capacity to break the self open not only to deep communion with the partner but also to the life-giving communion with God.

In education and social witness, consciousness of the church as sexual community can also expand our awareness. Beyond the neglected but important role of the church in positive and effective sexuality education for its members of all ages, there can arise sensitivity to the sexual dimensions of a vast variety of social justice issues which the church is called to address. Some justice issues are quite obviously sexual: justice for women, gays, and lesbians; the abortion issue; sexual abuse of women and children; prostitution; pornography; family-planning and overpopulation, to mention just a few. Beyond these are large social issues which are not apparently sexuality-related, but in fact are. In social violence and militarism, in stubbornly persisting white racism, in the ecological dilemma and abuse of the natural environment, patterns of distorted sexuality contribute enormously. When the church can more fully realize the ways in which it is also a sexual community, when it can affirm more celebratively the potential sacramentality of human sexuality, then it might also more fully grasp the vision of an erotic sensibility toward the whole human community in a sacramental world.

FOUNDATIONS FOR A PROTESTANT SEXUAL ETHICS

While there are different nuances and emphases within Roman Catholic sexual ethics, the presence of a strong natural-law tradition within that communion together with a clearly defined teaching authority, the magisterium, has resulted in a more coherent body of teachings than is found in Protestantism. Protestants have largely attempted to formulate a sexual ethics from biblical grounds. The resultant ethical approaches show a considerably greater variety, coming as they do from a diversity of faith communities with looser patterns of authority in doctrine and morals.

Historically, Catholic ethics has its strengths, particularly in universality of application, objectivity of norms, and in the attempt to be specific in application. But those strengths have been matched by certain weaknesses: a rigid insistence upon absolute moral judgments about specific acts and a strong tendency to evaluate sexual acts in terms of their physical contours.

Protestant sexual ethics has been strong in its attempt to be faithful to scriptural sources, in its openness to change, uniqueness, and particularity, and in its attempt to take motives and dispositions as seriously as the physical acts themselves. But Protestant ethics has perennially had difficulty in finding a firm grounding for sexual values and norms and in finding ways of adjudicating conflicting norms. Protestants, moreover, have been less methodologically clear. Attempting to affirm the Bible as primary authority within a plurality of other sources, mainstream Protestants have discovered that the relativity of biblical texts and themes has made it difficult to specify particular rules of sexual conduct and to demonstrate the primacy of the Bible's authority.[7]

Protestant ethics has thus struggled to find a course between legalism on one side and normlessness on the other. Legalism is the attempt to apply precise laws and rules to actions regardless of the unique features of that context. It assumes that objective standards can be applied in the same way to whole classes of actions without regard to the particular meanings those actions have to particular persons. And, it might be noted, the tendency toward legalism seems stronger in sexual morality than in virtually any other arena of human behavior.

The antidote to legalism is an ethics which finds its center and direction in *love* rather than in a series of specific absolute injunctions. Such an ethics takes the Bible seriously, but understands the need for critical awareness of how its sexual teachings and practices not only reflected the biblical community's perception of God's intentions, but also reflected sexual mores common to those historical circumstances. A love-centered ethics understands human nature as grounded in the will to communion. We are thoroughly social beings, nurtured into our humanness in community and destined for ultimate communion. This means that the positive ethical claim is to become what we essentially *are*. We are to realize through our actions a responsiveness to the divine loving. Negatively, sin is not fundamentally the breaking of moral codes or disobeying of moral laws (though it may involve that). More basically, it is the failure to become who we are, the failure of our responsiveness to the Cosmic Lover. It is the estrangement and alienation which distort fulfillment and destroy communion.

Our sexuality itself is a dramatic sign of our destiny to communion, for its dynamism presses us toward intimacy and community. Even in its distortions, our sexuality negatively witnesses to its power to oppress and destroy persons and their fulfillment.

If love is the central (albeit not only) norm for Christian ethics, it is the central meaning of our sexuality and the measuring standard and justification for any particular sexual act. Nevertheless, the word is dangerously slippery, and countless dehumanizing acts have been done in the name of love. So, further comment is necessary.

Love's source is God, our Creator, Redeemer, and Sustainer. Love takes its content from the Christian community's historic perceptions—both in scripture and in tradition—of God's ways with humankind. Sexual acts which respond to the loving of God will be marked by qualities which mirror and reflect God's own creativity, reconciling activity, and sustaining, fulfilling purposes.

Love is multidimensional. Christian ethics long has utilized the four classic distinctions in speaking of love: *epithymia* or *libido* (the desire for sexual fulfillment); *eros* (desire and aspiration for the beloved); *philia* (mutuality and friendship); and agape (freely offered self-giving). These are different dimensions of love's unity—not different or opposing kinds of love. Each needs the other. Thus, sexual desire (epithymia) without the desire for communion with and fulfillment in the other (eros), without a strong element of mutuality and friendship (philia), and without the transformative quality of self-giving abandonment (agape) becomes distorted.

Love is indivisible and nonquantifiable also in regard to other-love and self-love. Self-love has been a perennial problem in Protestant ethics, and the confusion here has spawned enormous sexual confusions. Self-love has been mistakenly confused with egocentrism and selfishness, hence condemned. Thus, Protestantism has had a difficult time dealing positively with sexual pleasure in general and with certain issues, such as masturbation, in particular. Without positive self-love, however, authentic intimacy is impossible, for the possibility of intimacy rests in considerable measure upon each individual's own sense of worth as a person. Without such self-affirmation, we elevate the other person into the center of our lives, hoping that the partner will assure us of our own reality. But that is too large an order for the other; it idolizes the partner. Self-love and other-love are not antagonists, but are mutually complementary.

Further, love, Christianly understood, expresses itself in a variety of values. These can become criteria by which specific sexual acts might be measured in a nonlegalistic manner.[8] Love is self-liberating. In a sexual act, it expresses one's own authentic self-affirmation and also the desire for further growth. Love is also other-enriching, displaying a genuine concern for the well-being and growth of the partner. Sexual love is honest, expressing as truthfully as possible the meaning of the relationship which actually exists between the partners. Love is faithful, expressing an ongoing commitment to this relationship, yet without crippling possessiveness. Sexual love is socially responsible, concerned that sexual acts reflect values which enhance the larger community. Love is life-serving; the power of renewed life is shared by the partners when sexual expression has been appropriate. And authentic sexual love is joyous, exuberant in its appreciation of love's mystery, life's gift, and sex's playfulness.

Does such a perception of love involve any principles and

rules for sexual ethics? Yes, it can give structure to ethics without the rigidity of legalistic absolutes. It can provide general principles. For example, love presses us toward a single standard and not a double standard for sexual morality. That is, the same considerations apply equally to males and females, to the young and the aged, to the able-bodied and the disabled, to the homosexual and the heterosexual. Another of love's principles is that the physical expression of one's sexuality with another person ought to be appropriate to the level of shared commitment. Such principles as these do not give exact prescriptions about specific acts, but rather provide a direction for making such decisions.

An ethics centered in love can also have specific sexual rules. It will most likely understand the authority of the rules, however, in a certain way. Such rules will not likely be understood as exceptionless absolutes (a new invitation to legalism). Nor will they be understood simply as guidelines which can be dismissed rather lightly if they do not seem to fit. Rather, love's sexual rules will have weight without absolutism. They will express the wisdom of the moral community and serve as a check upon our own finitude and sin, our limitations in both knowledge and virtue. We take such prima facie rules seriously and presume in their favor. But given the rich complexity of human situations and God's freedom to intend the new expression of love, these moral rules are not exceptionless. Yet, having presumed in favor of the rule, the burden of proof then is upon the one who would depart from it. The question now is: given this particular situation, will an exception to the rule actually express greater loyalty to the divine loving experienced in the neighbor and in the self?

An ethics centered in this kind of love will be neither legalistic nor antinomian. It will not guarantee freedom from mistakes in the sexual life. It will place considerable responsibility upon the individual. It will be sensitive to relationships, motivations, concrete situations, and it will be more oriented toward persons than toward abstract concepts. It will be more concerned about the authentic fulfillment of persons than the stringencies of unyielding laws or the neat cataloging of types of sexual acts. It can serve our human becoming and our maturation as lovers in the image of the Cosmic Lover by whom and in whom we are continually being created.

SOME SPECIFIC SEXUAL ISSUES

Marriage, Family, and Divorce

Protestantism early elevated the institution of marriage by rejecting meritorious celibacy and insisting that marriage was one of God's natural orders, an "order of creation." Especially in the Puritan experience, the family was viewed as an indispensable moral unit of society and as the church's crucial subcommunity for Christian nurture. For all of the religious attention given to the family by the church, however, several theological problems have persisted.

One has been the overly sharp distinction between nature and grace, between marriage as an order of creation and marriage as a sacrament or order of redemption. Protestantism early insisted upon the former, holding marriage to be a worldly and not a sacramental institution. It has no redemptive significance. No one is saved through it. God has established it for all persons, and its validity does not depend upon the church's rites or upon the couple's faith. All of this distinguished Protestant from prevailing Roman Catholic views. However, this tends to establish a sharp disjunction between nature and grace, a dualism of lower and higher orders. Such a disjunction undercuts a fully incarnationalist theology wherein we might see that the whole creation and its embodied, fleshly relationships are potential media of God's healing and life-giving salvation.

Protestants, appropriately I believe, sensed the unwarranted imperialism of the medieval church's claim that marriage was an official sacrament, for that implied that only those whom the church officially blessed were truly married. They appropriately insisted that it was the covenant of the two parties that was crucial. The covenant was blessed by God and the church, to be sure, but it was the covenant which was primary. What Protestant theology has less adequately expressed is the manner in which marriage can have sacramental and redemptive qualities. It is not the only sort of human relationship through which the healing and humanizing love of God can be vividly encountered, but surely it is a primary arena for many people. Among Protestants, perhaps Anglicans have more fully recognized this than most others.[9]

A second Protestant problem is its tendency to interpret the notion of cohumanity in a way that makes heterosexual marriage the only means through which persons can truly recognize their divinely intended humanity. What theologians have wanted to affirm is that the "image of God" is not something possessed by the solitary individual. Rather, we are created as relational beings, destined for communion, with a sexuality which is intrinsic and not peripheral to our capacity for cohumanity. This admirable emphasis, however, has frequently led to two major problems.

One is the suggestion that fully human existence is possibly only in marriage—an imperious claim which unfairly leaves the permanently single, the separated and divorced, the widowed, and the gay or lesbian person in a second-class human status. In fact, Jesus himself would not qualify for full humanity. Far better it is to say that we are created for communion and relationship, of which heterosexual marriage is one important form through which this might be realized.

The other related issue is the tendency of some Protestant theologians to give certain sex-role characteristics an ontological status. This overlooks both their historical relativity and the dehumanizing features of many masculine and feminine images. If I assume that as a man I am incomplete without a woman because I am by nature cognitive and she by nature intuitive, I strong and assertive, she vulnerable and nurturing, and because of these differences the two halves need each other to make one whole, then we have a marriage built on truncated and alienating sex-role assumptions. Far better it is to insist that marriage is not the union of two "natures" but of two unique persons, a personal relationship whose meaning is love.[10]

A third problem is the ascription of normative religious status to the nuclear family. Thus, it is assumed that God's intended form for the family is a husband (working outside the home), a wife (who is the homemaker), and their immediate offspring living together under one roof, with the husband considered head of the household. But such an understanding, for all of its unfairness to other family forms, does not even take history seriously. Actually, it was not until the nineteenth century that the present form of nuclear family arose, for only then did mobility undercut the extended family, and not until then was mothering seen as full-time occupation or childhood viewed as a separate era of life. Those who insist that there has been one normative family form do not have Christian history on their side.

The antidote for this problem is a time-honored Protestant emphasis—the "Protestant principle." This is the insistence that nothing finite ever be absolutized. It is a reflection of the Decalogue's first commandment. It is the realization that when Jesus said that the Sabbath was made for persons, and not vice versa, he was teaching us that every human institution is relative.

In spite of each of these problems, Protestant understandings of marriage and family have struck important positive notes. Marriage is essentially a covenant relationship for which mutuality and companionship are primary values. Thus, love is central to its meaning, and procreation of children may be an "added blessing." Valid marriage is not the sole possession of the church, but is open to all. And the building of that small community of intimate support and nurture through which our destiny to communion may be significantly experienced is of inestimable importance for our humanness, though particular family forms themselves are historically relative and changeable.

Protestants generally have upheld the monogamous marriage as the appropriate place for total sexual intimacy. Nevertheless, there is growing recognition that not all premarital sex acts are equally irresponsible. Indeed, if the reality of marriage itself is constituted by the covenanting of the couple, we may need to distinguish between "preceremonial sex" and that sex which takes place outside of any meaningful covenant. Adultery is generally condemned by Protestant spokespersons not only because of the significance of intercourse itself and what it symbolizes of God's faithfulness, but also because of predictable damage to the marital relationship through deception and the adulteration of love's bonding. Again, however, some Protestants argue that while sexual exclusiveness in marriage is a strong presumptive rule, it is not an absolute one, for there may be unusual exceptions. What of extramarital sex with the knowledge and consent of the spouse? Though this receives little support, a few Protestant writers argue that fidelity is the key issue here, and fidelity is best understood as the bonding of honesty, trust, and primary commitment—which may or may not include genital exclusivity. In all of these issues, however, mainline Protestants, while they vary in emphasis, commonly stress the Christian's responsibility to use God's good gift of sexuality in ways which maximize interpersonal fulfillment and faithful intimacy, and which take responsibility for the consequences of our sexual acts.

Regarding divorce, Protestants have attempted to take seriously both Jesus' teaching concerning the permanence of marriage and the evidence that lifelong unions generally best serve the needs of the marriage partners, their children, and society. Thus, divorce is never to be taken lightly.

Yet Protestants early broke with the medieval Catholic doctrine of the metaphysical indissolubility of marriage, the notion that once the bond between wife and husband had been established, it was absolutely incapable of dissolution except by death. Neither the vows spoken nor the church's blessing nor sexual intercourse automatically establishes such indissolubility. Jesus' teaching does not imply that what God has joined in principle *cannot* be dissolved. Rather his teaching lays upon the couple and upon society the moral obligation not to frustrate God's purpose of permanent union. Protestants have recognized that marriage breakdown sadly does occur and must be dealt with. If the central meaning of marriage is the covenant of love, then the irreparable breakdown of that covenant—the failure of love—essentially constitutes divorce. If marriage is essentially a moral and not simply a legal union, a personal relation and not a metaphysical construct, then the disintegration of such a relationship must be recognized to prevent further destructiveness to persons.

Successful remarriage to another after divorce, however, is heavily contingent upon a creative process wherein persons and their supportive communities honestly face the earlier failures and, through mutual forgiveness, find themselves genuinely divorced from the first union and ready for the second. Without this, the first marriage has not fully been dissolved, but persists as a negative bonding of guilt and resentment, which can only impair the next relationship.[11]

Contraception

If in the last two generations Protestants have been champions of family planning and birth control, such was not always the case. The Reformers were as adamant about the obligations of the married to procreate as were their Catholic predecessors. In fact, the religious rivalry which emerged in the sixteenth and seventeenth centuries led Protestant leaders to place a new premium upon the reproduction of the faithful. Late-nineteenth-century American Protestants supported numerous laws forbidding commerce in contraceptives, and the vision of a Protestant America continued the large-family and anticontraceptive ideologies.

By 1930, however, medical opinion had shifted from disapproval of contraception to acceptance, and in that year the bishops of the Anglican church, at the Lambeth Conference, made the first major Protestant statement of endorsement. Not long after, virtually all major Protestant church bodies and theologians publicly supported responsible family planning through artificial contraception.[12]

The view that procreation is secondary to love and companionship in the purposes of marriage and sex undergirded Protestantism's gradual acceptance of contraception. Openness to modern technology and an emphasis upon the nurture of children also helped. Like Roman Catholics, Protestants have argued that each sexual act ought to be "open to the transmission of life," but in distinction from them Protestants have interpreted "life" not in a physical, procreative sense but in the sense of interpersonal life-giving qualities.

Singleness

Historically, the Christian tradition has given its official approval to only two life-styles, monogamous marriage and celibacy. Since Reformation doctrine undercut the notion of meritorious celibacy, Protestants have given comparatively little theoretical attention to the single state. However, there has been widespread agreement on two counts. First, celibacy is to be embraced prior to marriage. Second, when lifelong celibacy is chosen because of vocational reasons or personal circumstances and not as a matter of sexual self-rejection or as a quest for special merit, it is to be affirmed. In such cases, the individual is still a sexual being, though choosing abstinence from genital relations.

In recent years, Protestant insistence upon complete premarital genital abstinence has become less rigid in many quarters. Part of this is undoubtedly due to changes in cultural attitudes, part of it due to the greater possibilities of pregnancy and disease control, and part of it due to increased knowledge of psychosexual development. Protestant ethics on this matter now lacks a unified voice, though those who admit the possibility of morally responsible acts of intercourse before marriage typically reserve this to the committed relationship, vastly different from an endorsement of unfettered recreational sex.

What of the single adult who does not intend marriage (or remarriage) and who does not choose celibacy? Churches have been notably uncomfortable with adult singles, not only because they raise the sex-outside-marriage issue but also because by their very presence they seem to question marriage as the normative assumption for the Christian life. Further, since so much of the Protestant church's congregational life and education is based upon the image of the nuclear family, single adults do not quite seem to fit.

Many Protestants are beginning to recognize, however, that, while a single adult's choice to be fully expressive sexually will involve risks, it can be compatible with responsible Christian living. Love's evaluative standards apply here as elsewhere. The relationship should be marked by honesty, genuine commitment, deep respect for the other as a person, caring, and concern for the consequences of intimacy.

Masturbation

Though masturbation is one of the most widely practiced genital expressions of all ages and types of persons, it is still one of the least understood, most guilt-ridden, and least illuminated by Christian reflection. There is no biblical teaching on the subject, though cultural attitudes present in biblical times emphasized the importance of procreative sex, on the one hand, and, on the other, attributed to the male semen the presence of life itself. Hence, for the male, masturbation involved the deliberate destruction of human life and the refusal to be procreative.

Churchly condemnation persisted throughout the centuries and was gradually joined by medical opinion, which for several centuries attributed dire physical consequences to the act. Now, however, contemporary medical opinion has changed dramatically and attributes no harmful physical effects to masturbation. Since Protestants have not had the Catholic emphasis upon the "procreative finality" that must be present or possible in every valid genital act, they are now either silent or divided on the subject.

Some still find it an intrinsically disordered act, simply because genital expression is divinely intended for interpersonal union. Others find it normal in adolescents and the lesser of evils for single adults or for the married in absence of the spouse. Still others find it of little cause for concern unless it becomes a persisting self-centered choice or sign of pathological disturbance.

Some Protestants, however, give positive endorsement to masturbation. While it does not have the relational-emotional possibilities of intercourse with the beloved, nevertheless it can be a positive experience of sexual self-exploration and knowledge, of self-affirmation and intrapersonal communion. Like other sexual acts, masturbation is susceptible of a whole range of meanings, and its ethical evaluation depends less upon the physical act itself than upon the constructiveness or destructiveness of its meanings to the person.

Homosexuality

The range of theological and ethical opinion about homosexuality is enormous. Inasmuch as Protestants have considered themselves a "people of the Book," careful biblical interpretation on this issue is imperative. While biblical literalists find in scripture unqualified condemnation of both homosexuality as such and all homosexual genital acts, other Protestants find other interpretations more persuasive. Many scholars now agree that there is no clear scriptural message about homosexuality as a psychosexual orientation, for sexual orientation is a distinctly modern concept, foreign to the biblical writers. They also insist that those several passages which clearly refer to homosexual acts must be carefully interpreted in their particular literary, religious, and historical contexts. There appears to be no definitive biblical judgment about same-sex genital expres-

sions of committed love. What we find are various condemna-
tions of homosexual acts in the contexts of idolatry, rape, lust,
and promiscuity. Further, in a patriarchal society, male homosexual acts appeared to involve the fruitless loss of the revered
semen and also were interpreted as a threat to the status of the
male, one of whom presumably was "womanized" in such an
act.

Nevertheless, even after careful biblical interpretation there
remain differences of Protestant conviction. Many argue for a
rejecting but nonpunitive position. They believe that homosexuality is unnatural, contrary to God's design for creation, and
cannot be Christianly affirmed, yet hold that lesbians and gays
ought not to be treated punitively by the church, but rather with
a pastoral sensitivity which hopes for their sexual reorientation
if such be possible and for their chastity if it is not. Other
Protestant groups and writers argue for qualified acceptance.
They agree with the former stance that homosexual orientation
falls short of God's intent, but acknowledge on the basis of
current evidence that such orientation is irreversible in many
persons. In those instances, gay men and lesbians should be
supported to live out their lives responsibly—in chastity if that
is possible, but, if not, in a permanent, monogamous, same-sex
relationship.

There is, however, a growing minority Protestant opinion
which presses for the full Christian acceptance of homosexuality.
This position sees the biblical evidence as inconclusive on the
subject itself, but not on the wider issue of sexuality. Though
homosexual expression is not biologically procreative and thus
cannot realize the secondary intent of sexuality, it is fully capable
of realizing sexuality's primary and central purpose: love and
responsible intimacy. Thus, love's same standards and ethical
discernments should apply to all persons regardless of sexual
orientation. But, further, the church needs to give particular
understanding and support to lesbians and gays who must live
in a society still pervaded by homophobia and oppression.

While in the past decade several ordinations of avowed
homosexual candidates have been performed in mainline Protestantism (in the Protestant Episcopal Church and in the United
Church of Christ), the ordination question remains a heated

issue. The majority of Protestant ecclesiastical bodies have either refused to reconsider the issue or have decided it in the negative.

Women and the Church

The ordination of women in mainline Protestantism has increased dramatically during the past decade, as has the number of women seminarians. Here the effects of feminism on theological and ecclesiastical patterns has been much more pronounced than in either Roman Catholicism or Judaism. Such effects include the press toward sexually inclusive language, the use of feminine as well as masculine images and metaphors for the divine, and expanded use of the varied senses in worship, the reform of hierarchical male leadership patterns, and support for social justice and equality regardless of sex. Indeed, such feminist-initiated changes are potentially more far-reaching in their implications than any church reform in several centuries. Many feminists believe, and I agree, that we are on the edge of a basic paradigm shift in our ways of viewing the world.

Conclusion

In all of these varied ethical considerations, Protestants find themselves with many differences of conviction. That is inevitable in such a pluralistic religious body. But an increasing number—as witnessed by denominational sexual pronouncements within the past decade—are committed to finding sexual understandings which are at once faithful to the biblical witness and faithful to human experience, sexual understandings which place gospel at the center and law at the boundary, understandings which celebrate the mystery of sexuality as a language of love and see in it a fundamental dimension of God's invitation to our humanness.

Notes

1. I have treated many of the issues in a different form in the following: *Embodiment: An Approach to Sexuality and Christian Theology* (Minneapolis: Augsburg, 1978); "Toward a Theology of

Human Sexuality," in *Religion and Sexuality: Judaic-Christian View-points in the U.S.A.*, ed. John M. Holland (San Francisco: Association of Sexologists, 1981); "Between Two Gardens: Reflections on Spirituality and Sexuality," *Studies in Formative Spirituality* 2, no. 1 (February, 1981); and "Sexuality Issues in American Religious Groups: An Update," *Marriage and Family Review* 6, nos. 3–4 (Fall–Winter 1983): 35–46.

2. For interpretations of the Reformation on sexuality, see chap. 4 of William Graham Cole's *Sex in Christianity and Psychoanalysis* (New York: Oxford University Press, 1955), chap. 2 of Derrick Sherwin Bailey's *Common Sense About Sexual Ethics: A Christian View* (New York: Macmillan, 1962), and chap. 2 of Otto A. Piper's *The Christian Interpretation of Sex* (London: Nisbet, 1942).

3. See Eleanor L. McLaughlin, "Male and Female in Christian Tradition: Was There a Reformation in the Sixteenth Century?" in *Male and Female: Christian Approaches to Sexuality*, ed. Ruth Tiffany Barnhouse and Urban T. Holmes III (New York: Seabury Press, 1976).

4. Bailey, *Common Sense About Sexual Ethics*, p. 57.

5. See Letha Scanzoni, "Protestant Views of Sexuality," in *Religion and Sexuality: Judaic-Christian Viewpoints in the U.S.A.*, ed. John M. Holland (San Francisco: Association of Sexologists, 1981), pp. 32 ff.

6. See Paul Ricoeur, "Wonder Eroticism, and Enigma," in *Sexuality and Identity*, ed. Hendrick M. Ruitenbeck (New York: Dell, 1970), pp. 13 ff.

7. For a good overview of tendencies in recent Christian sexual ethics, see Lisa Sowle Cahill, "Sexual Issues in Christian Theological Ethics," *Religious Studies Review* 4, no. 1 (January, 1978).

8. For this listing of love's values I am indebted to Anthony M. Kosnick et al., *Human Sexuality: New Directions in American Catholic Thought* (New York: Paulist Press, 1977), pp. 92 ff.

9. On this issue, Norman Pittenger (*Making Sexuality Human* [Philadelphia: Pilgrim Press, 1970]) provides a good corrective to the view of Helmut Thielicke (*The Ethics of Sex*, trans. John V. Doberstein [New York: Harper & Row, 1964]).

10. On this issue, D.S. Bailey (*Common Sense About Sexual Ethics*) provides a good corrective to the view of Karl Barth (*Church Dogmatics* III/4 [Edinburgh: T. & T. Clark, 1960]).

11. I find Bailey's interpretation of divorce particularly helpful (*Common Sense About Sexual Ethics*, pp. 155 ff.).

12. For a history of contraception, see John T. Noonan, "Contraception," in *Encyclopedia of Bioethics*, ed. Warren T. Reich (New York: Free Press, 1978), pp. 204 ff.

13. On the varied treatments of homosexuality, see John Boswell, *Christianity, Social Tolerance, and Homosexuality* (Chicago: University of Chicago Press, 1980); Edward Batchelor, Jr., ed., *Homosexuality and Ethics* (New York: Pilgrim Press, 1980); and John J. McNeill, *The Church and the Homosexual* (Kansas City: Sheed, Andrews & McMeel, 1976).

Some Aspects of the Relationship of Sex, Society, and God in Judaism

David Novak

INTRODUCTION

In approaching the topic of sexuality in Jewish tradition, it seems to me that the wisest methodological principle is expressed in the talmudic maxim, "Whoever grasps too much grasps nothing; whoever grasps much less grasps something."[1] The topic is too vast and too complex to be treated intelligently within the limits of time and space allotted me. Furthermore, because human sexuality is a topic of such frequently prurient interest and such contemporary verbosity, an intelligent inquiry must stipulate the specific questions to which it will address itself if it is not simply to be entertaining. For these reasons and more, I limit myself to "Some Aspects of the Relationship of Sex, Society, and God in Judaism."

Let me propose a thesis about this topic and then raise two questions which arise directly out of this thesis. In exploring how these questions are dealt with in Jewish tradition, I hope that helpful insights will emerge, for they call for rational reflection on the part of all moral and religious persons.[2] The thesis I propose is that Judaism teaches that the human person is essentially (1) a sexual being; (2) a social being; (3) the image of God. From this thesis I now ask two questions: (1) What is the relation between human sexuality and human sociality? (2) How are human sexuality and sociality related to God?

In looking for answers to such weighty questions in Jewish tradition, one should be aware that this tradition, especially as

140

manifested in rabbinic literature, its most comprehensive and influential historical product, expresses itself in two forms: (1) halachah—law, and (2) aggadah—what might be loosely termed theological speculation. Precisely because halachah is the norm of the historical Jewish community, it is here that one should first look for answers to questions having normative significance. Aggadah, on the other hand, can be employed most helpfully in illuminating the theoretical issues which have informed the halachic process in its ongoing development.[3] As one of the greatest rabbinic scholars of this century, the late Professor Louis Ginzberg (d. 1953), wrote:

> It is only in the Halakah that we find the mind and character of the Jewish people exactly and adequately expressed. Laws which govern the daily life of man must be such as suit and express his wishes, being in harmony with his feelings and fitted to satisfy his religious ideals and ethical aspirations.[4]

HUMAN SEXUALITY

The first part of the thesis stated that the human person is an essentially sexual being. This is brought out in the following halachic text:

> One who was half-slave and half-free is to serve his master one day and himself the other, in the opinion of the School of Hillel. The School of Shammai said to them...he may not marry a slave woman because he is already half-free; and he may not marry a free woman because he is still half-slave. Shall he do nothing [yibbatel]?! Was not the world created [nibra' ha'olam] for procreation? For Scripture states, "He did not create it as a void, but formed it for dwelling" [Isa. 45:18].[5]

The case here seems to involve a slave owned by two partners when only one of them emancipated him.[6] The solution to the sexual dilemma of this slave in the above-quoted text is that he be fully emancipated and that he sign a note for his emancipation price. By being emancipated, he then became a full member of the community.[7]

Concerning this text, my late revered teacher, Professor Boaz Cohen (d. 1968), wrote:

> The phrase *nibra' ha'olam* (the world was created) is the nearest the rabbis came to the term *Natura*, which literally means to be born. Since the Beth Shammai invoke natural law as their reason, they cite Isa. 45:18, and not Gen. 1:28 which lays down the religious law from which the slave was exempt.[8]

Sex is considered a natural right precisely because its legitimacy is based on a description of a state of affairs rather than a specific precept or admonition. This also comes out in a later talmudic treatment of the dispute between the School of Shammai and the School of Hillel concerning how one fulfills the commandment "be fruitful and multiply" (Gen. 1:28, 9:1). The Shammaites require that one have at least two sons; the Hillelites require a son and a daughter, as Scripture states, "male and female He created them" (Gen. 5:2). The Talmud states that the reasoning of the Hillelites is based on "the creation of the world" (*me-briyato shel olam*).[9] This is important because the seeming admonition "be fruitful and multiply" is taken in the descriptive rather than the prescriptive sense. In other words, society in its law confirms and implements nature.

It should be emphasized that this text does not deal with specifically Jewish sexuality but rather with human sexuality. The theory behind it is a reflection on the essential character of human life. The question here is that a legal difficulty has prevented a human being from exercising his sexuality. Sexuality is rooted in the natural order created by God. Although the Law itself is also a creation of God, legal difficulties come from the social order created by man.[10] Here the halachah is indicating that the social order may not obliterate the natural order, that society is to fulfill natural human needs, not deny them.[11] This is why celibacy is so roundly condemned.[12] Along these same lines the rabbis went to unusual legal lengths to alleviate the plight of the *agunah*, a woman who, because it is uncertain whether her husband is dead, is unable to live with any other man as his wife.[13] Moreover, in the aggadah the denial of sexuality is considered destructive of human life.[14] Human sexuality cannot be overcome, but only channeled.[15]

HUMAN SOCIALITY

The indispensability of sociality in human life is seen, for example, in the legal attempts of the rabbis to alleviate the plight of the *mamzer*. According to scriptural law, as tradition-ally expounded, a person born of an adulterous or an incestuous union "may not enter the congregation of the Lord" (Deut. 23:3), which precludes marriage with any fully pedigreed member of the community.[16] The problem of the *mamzer* is social, not sexual. He may marry virtually any member of the community who is less than fully pedigreed—and there seem to have been many of them in talmudic times.[17] The *mamzer*'s frustration is the social stigma he carries, a stigma which prevents his full participation in society and is perpetuated in his descendants. The following halachic text shows a solution to this problem:

> R. Tarfon says that *mamzerim* are able to be cleared [*lee-taher*]. How is it so? Let a *mamzer* marry a female slave [*shifha*] and the offspring will then have the status of a slave [*ebed*]. Let the offspring be emancipated and have the status of a freeman [*ben horeen*].[18]

This ingenious legal solution of R. Tarfon is accepted as valid by later authorities.[19] Also, there was a tendency among the rabbis not to delve very carefully into family pedigree.[20] Furthermore, the offspring of a union between a Jewish woman, even a married one, and either a gentile or a slave was not a *mamzer*.[21] This was probably an attempt to remove any social stigma from rape victims and their offspring.[22] There is also the striking rabbinic ruling that a *mamzer* who is a scholar of the Torah takes social precedence over an ignorant high priest—the most pedigreed member of the community.[23] Finally, an aggadic text reports the complaint of one Daniel the tailor against the legal authorities who have it in their power to alleviate the social stigma of the *mamzer* totally and yet do not act as boldly as they could.[24] All of this reflects the notion that no innocent person is to be denied the fulfillment of his or her sociality. The plight of Honi Ha-Me 'agel, the rabbinic forerunner of Rip Van Winkle, as expressed in aggadic language, shows the motivating idea behind the attempts to remove legal barriers to full sociality. Honi says, "either fellowship [*haberuta*] or death."[25] Even a criminal sentenced to death, and thereby permanently severed from human society (even denied burial in a regular cemetery), is allowed to publicly repent of his crime so as not to lose the fellowship of the world-to-come.[26]

THE SOCIALIZATION OF SEXUALITY

We have thus seen how both sexuality and sociality are considered to be natural needs which society as an institution is to help fulfill. As such they assume the status of "natural rights," namely, society's recognition that the fulfillment of the needs of its human participants is its authentic task.[27] However, because sociality is the immediate source of society's *raison d'être* and its guiding goal, society in its law and institutions channels sexuality in socially acceptable directions, thereby limiting its intentional range. As Maimonides succinctly put it, "What is natural is left according to nature, but measures are taken against excess."[28]

The following legal exegesis shows this social process of sexual limitation at work. Commenting on the scriptural verse "And a man shall leave his father and his mother and cleave to his wife and they shall be one flesh" (Gen. 2:24), the first-century C.E. sage R. Akiba states:

"His father" means his father's wife; "his mother" literally means his mother; "he shall cleave" means not with a male; "with his wife" means not with his neighbor's wife. "And they shall be one flesh" means with those whom he is capable of becoming one flesh, thus excluding an animal or beast with whom he cannot become one flesh.[29]

This text is the basis of the elimination of incestuous, homosexual, and nonhuman objects from socially legitimate sexuality. The socialization of sexuality is the constitution of the family. The family, then, is the institution which directs natural sexuality toward personalistic social goals.[30] Both the attempt to solve the sexual problem of the person half-slave and half-free and the attempt to solve the social problem of the *mamzer* involve removing the legal barriers to their living in a normal family.

In their aggadic speculations about human sexuality the rabbis see its primordial manifestation as incestuous. Incest is seen as the natural human state, which is only overcome in the interest of sociality. Note the following aggadic text:

> Scripture states, "If a man takes his sister, the daughter of his father, or the daughter of his mother, and she sees his nakedness, it is a reproach" [ḥesed—Lev. 20:17]. R. Abin said that one should not say that Cain's marrying his own sister and Abel's marrying his own sister are a reproach. Rather, "I [God] said that the world is built by kindness (ḥesed)" [Ps. 89:3].[31]

Here in the passage from Leviticus we see the word ḥesed, which usually means "kindness," used in its opposite sense of "reproach."[32] The text plays on this disparate double meaning and states that what is now a reproach was at the dawn of humanity a social necessity, namely, the outward extension of the human race, beginning with siblings. Thus in a parallel text we read:

> If you say, "Why did not Adam marry his daughter?" the answer is, in order that Cain might marry his sister so that "the world is built by kindness."[33]

These discussions are based on the older legend that Cain and Abel were each born with a twin sister, which explains how Scripture can all of a sudden say, "and Cain knew his wife" (Gen. 4:17).[34] The assumption behind all of these discussions seems to be that sibling incest at a very primitive level might well be motivated by a desire to build a human world—a society—a motive considered good.[35]

The same aggadic reasoning comes out in this discussion of the incest between Lot and his daughters.

> R. Johanan said that what does Scripture mean when it states, "The ways of the Lord are straight, and the righteous walk in them and the wicked stumble in them" [Hos. 14:10]?...for example, this refers to Lot and his two daughters. They, whose intent was good [le-shem mitzvah], are "the righteous [who] walk in them." He, whose intent was evil [le-shem aberah], is "the wicked [who] stumble in them."[36]

It will be recalled from the scriptural story of Lot and his daughters that they justify their incest by stating, "There is no man on earth to come upon us according to the way of all the earth. Come, let us give our father wine to drink, and we will lie with him, and we will then continue life from our father [uneḥayeh me'abinu zar'a]" (Gen. 19:31). About Lot it is stated, "he was unaware [ve-lo yada'] when she lay down and when she rose up" (Gen. 19:32, 35). Thus Lot acted out of immediate physical desire, unaware of the objects of his desire, much less justifying it by any human purpose.[37] It is this socialization which effects the sublimation of sexuality's most immediate objects.[38]

Philo of Alexandria, a first-century Hellenistic Jewish sage, sees the rationale for the prohibition of incest as follows:

> Why hamper the fellow-feeling [koinōnias] and intercommunion of men with men [pros tous allous anthrōpous] by compressing within the narrow space of each separate house the great and goodly plant which might extend and spread itself over continents and islands and the whole inhabited world [oikoumenēn]? For intermarriages with outsiders [othneious] create new kinships.
>
> On this principle he [Moses] prohibits many other unions...[39]

By "intermarriage with outsiders" Philo does not advocate marriages between Jews and non-Jews. In fact he explicitly condemns such marriages in an adjacent text.[40] Rather, he is advocating that each generation break out of the consanguineous circle of the immediate family when marrying.

The halachah recognizes the universal ban of incest.[41] It also eliminated a loophole in Jewish law which in effect would allow de facto incest. For according to Jewish law a convert is "born again" (ke-qatan she-nolad dami). If this juridical notion is carried to its furthest logical conclusion, then a convert could marry his own mother (who had also converted to Judaism), since they are both, de jure, no longer consanguineously related. Nevertheless, direct incest of this type was prohibited so that the converts might not say, "We have come from a higher level of sanctity to a lower one."[42] Incest is considered to be radically disruptive of society because it introduces regressive sexuality rather than sublimation. Thus the ninth-century theologian R. Saadyah Gaon sees the prohibition of incest as required by the integrity of the familial relationship. In presenting his rationale for the commandment to honor one's father and mother he writes:

> ...in order that men might not become like beasts with the result that no one would know his father so as to show him . reverence in return for having raised him.... A further reason was that a human being might know the rest of his relations ...and show them whatever tenderness he was capable of.[43]

The rationale for the ban of homosexuality is closely related to that for the ban of incest. Homosexuality is considered to be counterfamilial and, also, counterprocreative. Its intentionality is purely sensual.[44]

In the aggadah heterosexuality is seen as rooted in the essentially bisexual nature of man. "R. Jeremiah ben Eleazar said that the first man had two faces [duo partzuf panim]...as it is written, 'male and female He created them' [Gen. 5:2]."[45] This theme appears in a number of rabbinic texts. Another aggadah expresses it as follows, "R. Eliezer said that they were created as a hermaphrodite [androgynos]...R. Samuel said that He created him with two faces, front and back, and split him and sawed him in two."[46] This notion of the original bisexuality of man, which has been confirmed by modern embryology, was prevalent in the ancient world.[47] Its most famous enunciation was by Plato.[48] The idea here is that man's experience of himself as lacking his "missing other half" is the source of heterosexual desire.[49] Thus homosexuality is considered a regression in that it does not seek that "other side."[50] Only the successful consummation of this desire for the other side leads to the recognizable family unit and the possibility of procreation.

Concerning R. Akiba's exegesis of "he shall cleave [unto his wife]" (Gen. 2:24) as meaning "not to a male," the eleventh-century French exegete, Rashi, writes:

> For there is no cleaving [dibbuq], because the passive partner [ha-nishkab], not receiving pleasure, does not cleave with

him ['immo]. It is from the seed which goes forth from the mother and the father that "one flesh" is made.[51]

Here Rashi makes two important points. First, homosexual intercourse per anum is not the same as heterosexual vaginal intercourse.[52] It is not that the passive homosexual partner does not experience pleasure—homosexuals would surely dispute that—but, rather, the pleasure of male-female union is precluded. Secondly, such homosexual pairing totally preclude procreation.[53] In other words, Rashi understands "one flesh" (basar eḥad) on two levels: (1) the level of the union of the male and female bodies; (2) the possibility of a new body emerging from this union in conception and, ultimately, in birth.

Homosexuality is considered inconsistent with authentic human sociality, that is, it is considered inconsistent with human nature. In the aggadah it is seen as part of the overall degradation of human life and society in Sodom: "And they called to Lot and they said to him, 'Where are the men who came to you; bring them out to us that we might know them [ve-ned 'ah otam]'" (Gen. 19:5). In Targum Pseudo-Jonathan the last phrase is interpreted to mean "that we might have intercourse with them [u-neshamesh 'imehon]." Other aggadic texts present the same point.[54] Obviously, the aggadists took the verb "to know" (yado'a) in the sense of "carnal knowledge," as in "And the man knew [yada'] Eve, his wife, and she conceived" (Gen. 4:1). Since Scripture designated the Sodomites as "exceedingly wicked and sinful unto the Lord" (Gen. 13:13),[55] homosexual rape is seen as one of their foremost sins. The rabbis were clearly aware of the prevalence of homosexuality in the Greco-Roman world. Various halachic rulings reflect this awareness.[56] Indeed, their ostensive reflections about the sins of Sodom probably had a more contemporary situation in mind.[57] Furthermore, the concern of this aggadic source with homosexual rape might very well be the rabbis' reflection about the presence of sadistic elements in many homosexual acts, a view found in the halachah.[58] It does not imply that only homosexual rape, but not consensual homosexuality, is forbidden. Another aggadic text interprets homosexuality per se as a fundamental human error. "Bar Kappara said to R. Judah the Prince, 'What does "abomination" [to'evah—in the prohibition of homosexuality in Lev. 20:13] mean?'...R. Judah the Prince said God meant "abomination" means 'something in which you go astray' [to'eh attah bah]."⁵⁹ Female homosexuality, too, is considered by the rabbis as "lewdness" (peritzuta b'alma) because there is no explicit scriptural prohibition of it.⁶⁰

The rabbis were especially critical of any society which would formally legitimitize homosexual unions, undoubtedly because they are considered to be fundamentally antisocial in that they are a burlesque of heterosexual family life. Thus an aggadic text reads:

> R. Hiyya taught why is "I am the Lord" repeated twice [Lev. 18:3 and 4]?—I am He who punished the generation of the Flood and Sodom and Egypt; I will in the future punish whoever does according to their deeds. The generation of the Flood was blotted out from the world because they were steeped in immorality [sheṭufin be-zenut]...R. Huna said in the name of R. Jose that the generation of the Flood was only blotted out from the world because they wrote marriage contracts [gomasiyot] for male unions and for female unions.⁶¹

The rabbis seem to be making a distinction between a society where homosexuality is prevalent and one where there is an official sanction and recognition of it. This text might well be based on the report that the Roman emperor Nero went so far as to write a marriage contract for one of his favorite male lovers.⁶² Perhaps even in the Greco-Roman world, where individual homosexuality was quite common, Nero's elevating a homosexual relationship to the level of a "marriage" was considered shocking and a sign of extreme social decadence.

The prohibition of bestiality was also used by the rabbis to speculate about the development of human sexuality. The rabbis seem to have recognized that at the level of what psychoanalysts call "primary process," bestiality, or at least the motif of bestiality, is a human possibility. Thus when Scripture states about the animals, "He [God] brought them unto the man to see what he would call them" (Gen. 2:19), an aggadist speculated as follows:

> R. Eleazar said that why did Scripture state, "this time [zo't ha-pa'am] it is bone from my bone and flesh from my flesh"

> [Gen. 2:23]?—It teaches that Adam had sexual relations [she-ba'] with every animal and beast, but was not satisfied [ve-lo nitqarerah da'ato] until he had sexual relations with Eve.[63]

Eve satisfied him because with her he could once again— following the motif of primordial bisexuality—"become one flesh." Furthermore, it is emphasized that with Eve alone could Adam speak.[64] Whereas speech is not required by sexuality, it is required by sociality.[65] Thus heterosexuality between human partners is a restriction of biological primary process by human sociality. Satisfaction in the personal sense is even more social than it is physical.

The socialization of human sexuality in Judaism can be seen in the way the legal role of woman in the marital relationship developed into one of true mutuality. For if one reflects on heterosexuality as a physical phenomenon, it clearly requires male initiation and suggests male dominance. This is assumed by the halachah where marriage and divorce are initiated by the man.[66] Reflecting on this legal fact the Talmud records the following aggadic speculation:

> R. Simon says that why did the Torah state, "when a man takes [yiqah—a woman; Deut. 24:1]" and does not state "when a woman is taken to a man"? This is because it is the way [darko] of a man to go after a woman, but it is not the way of a woman to go after a man. It is like one who lost something. Who goes back after whom? The owner [ba'al] of the lost article goes back after the lost article.[67]

Thus at this level we see that the desire for the primordial bisexual union, which we discussed before, is initially male.

Nevertheless, the Talmud notes that in a key rabbinic text the woman, not the man, is made the subject of the initiation of marriage.[68] From this, among other texts, it is inferred that a woman may not be married against her will, that is, acquired like property.[69] Furthermore, even though according to scriptural law a female child may be married off by her father without her consent, and even rabbinic law had to accept such a marriage as valid ex post facto, this practice was subsequently prohibited ab initio, that is, a father was to wait until his daughter was mature enough to say, "It is him whom I want."⁷⁰ The following aggadic text shows how the lack of mutual consent in marriage was seen as socially disadvantageous.

> A Roman lady asked R. Jose bar Halfta, "Everyone agrees that God created the world in six days. From the sixth day on what has He been doing?"... R. Berakhyah said...he said to her that He arranges marriages in His world,... She said that she could make a thousand such marriages in one day... so she brought a thousand male slaves and a thousand female slaves and paired them off.... However, when night came, fighting broke out among them.⁷¹

The point that emerges from this is that slavery, that is, the subjugation of one person to another, is inimical to human fulfillment. One can see the entire development of Jewish matrimonial law as the steady emancipation of women from anything even resembling slavery.⁷²

Along these same lines, even though according to scriptural law only the man could divorce his wife, rabbinic law subsequently enabled the woman to sue for divorce based on certain objective grounds.⁷³ Moreover, in rabbinic law a woman was to be provided with a marriage contract (ketubah), which stipulated that in the event of divorce (or her husband's death) she was to be paid a considerable sum of money, the reason being "that she not be easy [qalah] to be sent out."⁷⁴ Later authorities ruled that under any circumstances a woman could not be divorced against her will.⁷⁵ Thus the mutuality which was eventually recognized as being required at the initiation of marriage was finally required at its termination as well.⁷⁶ Also, as early as the first century C.E. Rabban Johanan ben Zakkai eliminated the ordeal of the wife suspected of adultery. He argued that it presupposed mutual standards of virtue, something that could no longer be assumed.⁷⁷ As late as the sixteenth century, R. Moses Isserles made male unfaithfulness grounds for divorce, as female unfaithfulness had always been the grounds for divorce in the past.⁷⁸

The social requirement of true mutuality can only be achieved in monogamy. The introduction of monogamy as the only acceptable heterosexual union in Judaism ultimately required the elimination of concubinage, polygamy-polyandry never having been permitted.[79] It should be noted that concubinage and polygamy were taken for granted in Scripture as perfectly acceptable practices.[80]

It was Maimonides, the preeminent twelfth-century theologian and halachist, who banned concubinage:

> Before the giving of the Torah it was that a man would meet a woman in the marketplace and, if they mutually agreed, then he would give her her price, have relations with her along the way, and would then go on his way. Such a woman is what is called a qedeshah. When the Torah was given, the qedeshah was outlawed . . . therefore, anyone who has relations with a woman for purposes of fornication [le-shem zenut] without marriage [be-lo qiddushin] is to be lashed according to scriptural law because he has had relations with a qedeshah.[81]

Maimonides' scriptural proof-text is, "There shall not be any qedeshah among the daughters of Israel, nor any qadesh among the sons of Israel" (Deut. 23:18). Even though one might think that qedeshah/qadesh, coming as they do from the root qadosh, meaning "sacred," refer only to prostitutes associated with pagan shrines and temples, Maimonides makes no distinction between "sacred" and "secular" prostitution.[82] As one of the commentators on Maimonides notes, his reference concerning pre-Torah conditions is the story of Judah and Tamar recorded in Genesis 38.[83] There Tamar, posing as a prostitute in a clearly noncultic setting, is called a qedeshah (34:21). This term is used interchangeably with the term zonah (34:15), an ordinary prostitute. In other words, a concubine, for Maimonides, is, in essence, a prostitute, and the Torah outlawed all prostitution.

Now a number of subsequent halachists, although sympathetic with Maimonides' high moral standards and aspirations for the Jewish people, nevertheless argued that concubinage, as distinct from full marriage, is permitted by both Scripture and the Talmud.[84] It would seem, then, that Maimonides was making an explicit innovation in Jewish law, something he did in other areas as well.[85] He might very well have been repulsed by the use of women as concubines in the upper-class Muslim circles in which he worked as a physician. Indeed, the concubine is in essence a woman as a sexual object alone.[86]

SEX, SOCIETY, AND GOD IN JUDAISM / 153

It was the eleventh-century German halachist Rabbenu Gershom of Mainz who banned polygamy. Here too there is clearly no explicit precedent in either Scripture or the Talmud. Indeed, we do not even have the original text of this ban, much less Rabbenu Gershom's reasoning for it.[87] Nevertheless, one can see its effect at least as being one more step in the process of making true mutuality in the personal relationship of marriage a social reality. It is interesting to note the following aggadic speculation concerning the first polygamous marriage recorded in Scripture, namely the marriage of Lamech and his two wives Ada and Zillah (Gen. 4:19):

> R. Azariah said in the name of R. Judah that this was what the men of the generation of the Flood were doing. One would take two wives, one for procreation and one for sex [le-tashmish]. The one for procreation would be sitting like a widow during her lifetime; the one for sex would be given a sterilizing potion to drink, and she would sit before him like a prostitute.[88]

The important thing to note about this speculation is that neither woman is treated as a person. Both are used by the man. Now, of course, one could say that this speculation only concerns the generation of the Flood. However, it should be recalled that polygamy is often described in Scripture as a cause of human unhappiness.[89] Indeed, in Scripture the first marriage between Adam and Eve, which God Himself, according to the aggadah, celebrated, was monogamous.[90] In any polygamous marriage the man is necessarily divided in his heterosexual affection, whereas the woman becomes a particular functionary rather than a whole person relating to another whole person. It is only in a monogamous union that in effect *both* the man and the woman are exclusively sanctified to each other.[91]

SEXUALITY AND GOD

In classical Jewish thought all aspects of human life are ultimately related to God. Therefore, we should now examine how man as a sexual/social being is the image of God.

At the beginning of the talmudic tractate *Kiddushin,* which deals with Jewish marriage, the Palestinian version records the following statement:

> For we learn that the gentiles do not have religious marriage [*qiddushin*], so how can they possibly have religious divorce [*gerushin*]?! R. Judah ben Pazzi and R. Hanin said in the name of R. Honeh, elder of Sepphoris, that either they do not have religious divorce or they divorce each other.[92]

Undoubtedly basing himself on this text, Maimonides begins his discussion of Jewish marriage law as follows:

> Before the giving of the Torah a man would meet a woman in the marketplace. If they mutually agreed that he marry her, then he would bring her into his house and would have sexual relations with her privately and she would become his wife. When the Torah was given, Israel was commanded that if a man marry a woman he would acquire her [*yiqah otah*] initially in the presence of two witnesses and afterwards she would become his wife, as Scripture states, "when a man takes [*ki yiqah*] a woman and comes to her" [Deut. 24:1].[93]

Now at first glance these texts seem to indicate that the Torah removed an original mutuality from the initiation of marriage. Nevertheless, the subsequent factor of the woman's required consent clearly indicates that even when marriage is a state initiated by the man, it clearly requires mutuality to be valid.[94] Therefore, one must see the point being made that Jewish marriage is more than a civil contract but, rather, a covenant rooted in the covenant between God and His people, Israel. This explains why Maimonides emphasizes the presence of witnesses. Obviously, the initiation of pre-Toraitic marriage, taking place as it does "in the marketplace," is also a public matter. However, whereas this marriage is *consummated* as a *private sexual matter* between the man and the woman, Jewish marriage is consummated as a public nonsexual matter.[95] The witnesses represent the minimal presence of the sacred community, and as such, they do not simply confirm a legal fact but, rather, constitute its essential meaning.[96] Indeed, in order for the liturgical rite of marriage, with the full invocation of God's name, to be fully celebrated, a minimum worship quorum of ten is required.[97]

The presence of God in Jewish marriage is the subject of profound aggadic speculation.

> He [R. Simlai] said to them [his students] that originally Adam was created "from the dust of the earth" [Gen. 2:7], and Eve was created from the man. After Adam they were created "in Our image after Our likeness" [Gen. 1:26]. It is impossible for man to live without woman; it is impossible for woman to live without man; and it is impossible for both to live without God's presence [Shekhinah].[98]

This idea is further reflected in the talmudic statement that "There are three partners in a human being: God and the father and the mother."[99] In other words, God is present in Jewish marriage and in its fruits.

We have seen how human sexuality and human sociality are correlated in marriage. The idea of marriage as a sacred covenant correlates this relation with man's status as the image of God. Now we must ask: Does this acknowledgment of marriage as a sacred covenant add anything significantly new? Or, is the sacred dimension simply the deification of society as a whole greater than the mere sum of its individual participants, as Émile Durkheim, the founder of modern sociology, so consistently and powerfully argued?[100]

In answering this question, I would call attention to the analogy between marriage as the male-female relationship and God's relationship with His people, so often made in Scripture and rabbinic literature. The analogy is based on the idea of faithfulness (emunah) which is to be the foundation of both relationships.

> And it shall come to pass on that day, the Lord says, that you will call Me "my husband" [ishi] and you will no longer call Me "my master" [ba'ali].... And I will make a covenant [berit] with them on that day...and I will betroth you unto Me forever, and I will betroth you unto Me rightly and with

> justice and with kindness and with compassion. And I will
> betroth you unto Me in faithfulness [b'emunah], and you
> will know the Lord.
>
> Hos. 2:18–21

> And this second thing you do to cover the altar of the
> Lord with weeping and wailing....And you say "why?"—
> Because the Lord witnesses between you and the wife of
> your youth against whom you have been unfaithful [bagada-
> ta], and she is your companion, your covenanted wife [eshet
> beritekha].
>
> Mal. 2:13–14[101]

In rabbinic literature the most outstanding example of this line
of thought is the interpretation of Song of Songs, which uses the
image of a male-female love relationship to express God's love
for the people of Israel allegorically.[102]

This analogy is usually explained as being a comparison of
God's love for His people with the relationship of a man and a
woman in a loving marriage.[103] Nevertheless, I find such an
interpretation to be wide open to the critiques of religion by
Ludwig Feuerbach and, especially, Sigmund Freud, namely,
that religion projects onto an idealized realm what is a purely
human reality.[104] It seems to me to be more accurate and theologically more cogent to explain the analogy as a comparison of
male-female love with God's love for His people. In other words,
God's love is the primary reality into which human love becomes
a participation. This can mean one of two things.

For the kabbalists, the late medieval Jewish mystics, male-
female union is a symbolic participation in the union of the
male-female aspects of the Godhead itself. As the classic document of Jewish mysticism, the Zohar, puts it:

> Come and see that the desire of a male for a female and the
> desire of a female for a male and their union [v'itdabquta]
> produces a soul...and this earthly desire is included in
> heavenly desire [be-t'eubtah de-l'ela].[105]

The problem with this line of interpretation is that it is, as is all
kabbalistic theology, a compromise with strict monotheism—a
point not lost on the Jewish critics of Kabbalah.[106] Furthermore,

by making human sexuality only a symbol of a truly divine reality, it eclipses the factor of finite human embodiment, which seems to be such an essential factor in this human reality. As such it can be seen as countersexual.[107] Finally, it is a serious departure from the essential aspect of divine love emphasized in Scripture and rabbinic literature, namely, love as an act of God's self-transcendence, His recognition of a truly nondivine *other*. In Kabbalah all divine love is essentially a self-enclosed love into which creatures are ultimately incorporated.

I would, rather, emphasize that sexual love in the sacred covenant of marriage is a participation, a reflection of God's everlasting love for His people. This everlasting love was, perhaps, best expressed by Deutero-Isaiah in these words:

> ... with everlasting kindness have I loved you, says the Lord your Redeemer.... For the mountains will depart and the hills be moved, but My kindness will not depart from you, and My covenant of peace will not be moved, says the Lord who loves you.
>
> Isa. 54:8–10[108]

This connection comes out more clearly if we consider the phenomenology of sexual love. It is mistaken, it seems to me, to consider the essence of sexual love to be pleasure, although it is certainly a *conditio sine qua non* of it. For in all other bodily pleasures, such as eating, drinking, bathing, we seek a heightened sense of bodily awareness. Our pleasure is essentially a *taking-in*, that is, our desire is to make our world around us an extension of our own bodies. In heterosexual love, on the other hand, we seek ecstasy, which comes from two Greek words, *ex histēmi*, meaning to "stand out." In other words, our sexuality intends transcendence. Eros seeks spirit.[109] It seems that *we seek to go beyond our bodies through them*. For a moment we experience a going beyond the body, which is ordinarily the limit of the soul.[110] Nevertheless, sexual love in itself only lasts for a moment before the body, that everpresent, finite, mortal vessel, claims the soul once again. This comes out in the following aggadah:

> David said before God, "My father, Jesse, did not intend to sire me, but only intended his own pleasure. You know that

this is so because after the parents satisfied themselves, he turned his face away and she turned her face away and You joined the drops."[111]

Eros is not a function of the body, but, rather, the eroticized body ultimately intends that which is beyond limit, that which is beyond death. As embodied souls[112] we can only experience this by moving through the body beyond it. It cannot be done through any ascetic shortcuts; we cannot pretend to be angels when we are only flesh and blood.[113] And this is why the periodic monthly separation enjoined by the halachah on husband and wife is seen as a cultivation of eros which is more than bodily.[114] Indeed, even the most banal love lyrics sung today almost inevitably express "undying love." The intention of what is eternal seems to be essential to even the most crudely expressed sexual desire.

In Judaism such desire is seen as being grounded in God's everlasting love for His people. This grounding alone enables sexual love to be an expression of creative energy and the ultimate antithesis of all narcissism.[115] This comes out in the rabbinic interpretation of that most erotic of all Scripture, the Song of Songs. In conclusion let me cite one outstanding example. Scripture states, "For love is strong as death ['azah ke-mavet]; jealousy is harsh as the grave; its flashes are fiery flashes, the very torch of God" (Cant. 8:6). From the text it seems as though "death" is used as a superlative, namely, it is the strongest thing we experience, beyond which we know nothing. Love is considered equally strong and equally final. However, the rabbis seem to want to make love stronger than death. Thus they revocalized the word ke-mavet ("like death") and read it as ke-mot, that is, "it is like."—It is like what?

> For love is strong as [ke-mot] the love which God has for you, as it states, "I have loved you, says the Lord" [Mal. 1:2]. "Jealousy is harsh as the grave"—this refers to the times they made Him jealous with their idolatry [abodah zarah], as it says, "They made Him jealous with strange gods" [zarim— Deut. 32:16].... Another interpretation: "For love is strong as death"—this is the love of a man for his wife, as it says, "experience life with a woman you love" [Eccles. 9:9]..."Its

flashes are fiery flashes, the very torch of God."—R. Bera-
khyah said it is like the heavenly fire which does not consume
the water nor does the water extinguish it.[116]

In Judaism human sexuality, socialized and sanctified in the
covenant of marriage, becomes the way two mortal creatures
together existentially affirm God's love, which alone never dies.

Notes

1. *B. Rosh Hashanah* 4b.

2. For a treatment of the question of why Jewish tradition can be
of interest to ethicists, see D. Novak, "Judaism and Contemporary
Bio-Ethics," *Journal of Medicine and Philosophy* 4, no. 4 (December,
1979): 347–366.

3. See D. Novak, *Law and Theology in Judaism*, Vol. 1 (New
York, 1974), pp. 1–14; Vol. 2 (New York, 1976), pp. xiv–xvi.

4. "Jewish Thought as Reflected in the Halakah," *Students,
Scholars and Saints* (Philadelphia, 1928), p. 117. See his "The Signifi-
cance of the Halachah for Jewish History," trans. A. Hertzberg, in *On
Jewish Law and Lore* (Philadelphia, 1955), p. 78.

5. *M. Git.* 4:5 and *M. Eduyot* 1:13, see *B. Git.* 43b; *J. Git.* 4:5 (46a).

6. *B. Git.* 42a (top).

7. See *B. Shabb.* 135b, also *B. Ber.* 47b. This full integration into
the community was seen as entailing a limitation of the licentiousness
formerly enjoyed by a slave. See *B. Git.* 12b, *B. B. Mez.* 19a and Rashi,
s.v. *zekhut*; Maimonides, *Mishneh Torah, Hilkhot Abadim* 5:2 and 6:1;
Lev. Rab. 8:1.

8. *Jewish and Roman Law*, Vol. 1 (New York, 1966), p. 28, n. 97.

9. *B. Yebam.* 61b–62a.

10. See *Gen. Rab.*, beginning; Maimonides, *Guide for the Perplexed* 1:65 and 2:40. For the human source of legal difficulties, see *T.
Sotah* 14:9 and *B. Sanh.* 88b.

11. See D. Novak, *Suicide and Morality* (New York, 1975), pp.
63–65.

12. *M. Yebam.* 6:6 and *B. Yebam.* 63b (bottom). For the fulfilling
status of female sexuality, *B. Sanh.* 22b re Isa. 54:5.

13. See *M. Yebam.* 16:7; *M. Eduyot* 6:1 and 8:5; *B. Git.* 3a and
parallels; also, *B. Qid.* 7a and parallels.

14. *B. Yoma* 69b and *B. Sanh.* 64a. Cf. *B. Sotah* 47a and *B. Qid.*
81b. For a classic study, see D.M. Feldman, *Birth Control in Jewish
Law* (New York, 1968), p. 88. The dangers of denying sexuality are

brought out by the ancient Greek dramatist Euripides, who in his play *Hippolytus* has Aphrodite say: "Hippolytus, alone among the inhabitants of Troezen, calls me the most pernicious of the heavenly powers; he abhors the bed of love; marriage he renounces;...But Hippolytus has insulted me and shall suffer for it" (*Euripides: Three Plays*, trans. P. Vellacott [Baltimore, 1953], p. 28). Cf. Sigmund Freud, *The Origin and Development of Psychoanalysis* (Chicago, 1955), pp. 67–68. For a recent treatment of celibate suffering, I recommend the 1981 Australian film *The Devil's Playground*. The celibacy of the first-century C.E. sage Ben Azzai is considered his personal peculiarity. See *B. Yebam.* 63b (bottom), cf., however, Maimonides, *Mishneh Torah, Hilkhot Ishut* 15:3. For Ben Azzai's unhappy end, *B. Hag.* 14b; also *Midrash Tanhuma* (ed. Buber), *Aharay-Mot* 31b–32a, for the notion of celibacy as arrogance.

15.   For a rabbinic recognition of sublimation of other instincts besides sexuality, see *B. Shab.* 156a (bottom).

16.   *M. Yebam.* 4:13, *M. Qid.* 3:12.

17.   See *M. Qid.* 4:1 ff.

18.   Ibid., 3:13. Upon manumission a slave became a full member of the community. See *B. Ber.* 47b.

19.   *B. Qid.* 69a.

20.   Ibid., 71a (top).

21.   *B. Yebam.* 45b and parallels.

22.   See, for example, *M. Ket.* 2:5 and *B. Ket.* 23a; R. Moses Isserles, *Darkhay Mosheh* to *Tur: Eben Ha'Ezer* 7, n. 13.

23.   *M. Hor.* 3:8 and *J. Hor.* 3:5 (48c).

24.   *Lev. Rab.* 32:7. See *B. Ber.* 7a re Exod. 34:7 and Deut. 24:16. Cf. *B. Git.* 33a and Tosafot s.v. *v'afka'inu*. For another attempt to eliminate social exclusion, *B. Nazir* 23b re Prov. 18:1 and *M. Yad.* 4:4.

25.   *B. Ta'an.* 23. For separation from the discourse of the community as a cause of depression, see *B. Men.* 29b. For sympathy for those separated from the community because of disease (Lev. 13:45), see *B. Mo'ed Qat.* 5a.

26.   *M. Sanh.* 6:2 and *B. Sanh.* 47a.

27.   See R. Joseph Albo, *Sefer Ha'Iqqarim* 1:5.

28.   *The Guide for the Perplexed* 3:49, trans. S. Pines (Chicago, 1963), p. 611.

29.   *B. Sanh.* 58a. Sigmund Freud saw this verse as describing the normal course of psychosexual development. See "The Most Prevalent Form of Degradation in Erotic Life" (1912), in *Collected Papers*, trans. J. Strachey (London, 1950–52), 4:205–206.

30.   On the family as society's link with nature, note G.W.F. Hegel: "Just as the family thereby finds in the community its universal

substance and subsistence, conversely the community finds in the family the formal element of its own realization, and in the divine law its power and confirmation. Neither of the two is alone self-complete. Human law as a living and active principle proceeds from the divine, the law holding on earth from the nether world, the conscious from the unconscious, mediation from immediacy" (*Phenomenology of Mind*, trans. J.B. Baillie [London, 1931], pp. 478–479).

31. *J. Yebam.* 11:1 (11d). Cf. *J. Sanh.* 5:1 (22c). For "seeing" as a euphemism for possession, see, for example, *B. Pesaḥ.* 5b re Exod. 13:7.

32. See the commentary of Rashbam on Lev. 20:17.

33. *B. Sanh.* 58b.

34. *Gen. Rab.* 22:1.

35. For a certain tolerance of quasi-incest, see *B. Yebam.* 62b–63a; *B. Sanh.* 76b re Isa. 58:7.

36. *B. Hor.* 10b re Hos. 14:10.

37. See *B. Nazir* 23b re Prov. 18:1 and Tosafot, s.v. *le-ta'avah.*

38. See *B. Yoma* 69b.

39. *De Specialibus Legibus*, 3.25–26, in *Philo*, trans. F.H. Colson (Cambridge, Mass., 1937), 7:488–489. Cf. Augustine, *De Civitate Dei*, 15.16.

40. *De Specialibus Legibus*, 3.29.

41. See Maimonides, *Mishneh Torah, Hilkhot Melachim* 9:5.

42. *B. Yebam.* 22a. See Maimonides, *Mishneh Torah, Hilkhot Isuray Biah* 14:12.

43. *Book of Beliefs and Opinions* 3:2, trans. S. Rosenblatt (New Haven, 1948), p. 141. See Nahmanides' comment on Gen. 2:24.

44. See Maimonides, *Guide for the Perplexed* 3:49; D. Novak, "On Homosexuality," *Sh'ma* 11/201 (November 14, 1980): 3–5. Cf. Aristotle, *Nicomachean Ethics*, 1174b, 30ff.

45. *B. 'Erub.* 18a. See *B. Ber.* 61b re Ps. 139:5; *B. Meg.* 9a; *B. Ket.* 8a; *B. Sanh.* 38b (top); L. Ginzberg, *The Legends of the Jews* (Philadelphia, 1925), 5:88–89, n. 42.

46. *Midrash Tehillim* 139:5, ed. Buber, 265a. See *Gen. Rab.* 8:1 and Ginzberg, *Legends*, 5:90, n. 48.

47. See K.L. Moore, *The Developing Human*, 2d ed. (Philadelphia, 1977), pp. 228 ff.

48. *Symposium*, 191D–192B.

49. Cf. the use of the term *sitra aḥra* ("the other side") for the feminine aspect of being in Kabbalah. See Gershom Scholem, *Kabbalah and its Symbolism*, trans. R. Manheim (New York, 1965), p. 157.

50. See *Zohar* III (*Qedoshim*) 81a–b re Job 23:13.

51. *B. Sanh.* 58a, s.v. *ve-dabaq.*

52.   Even between heterosexual partners it is considered degrading; see, for example, *Gen. Rab.* 80:5 re Gen. 34:2.

53.   See *Sefer Ha-Ḥinukh,* no. 29.

54.   See *Gen. Rab.* 50:5; *Midrash Tanḥuma* (printed ed.), *Va-yere',* no. 12, Josephus, *Jewish Antiquities* 1.200.

55.   See *T. Sanh.* 13:8.

56.   See, for example, *M. Abod. Zar.* 2:1 and *T. Abod. Zar.* 3:2. Cf. *M. Qid.* 4:14, *B. Qid.* 82a, *J. Qid.* 4:11 (66c); also, R. Joseph Karo, *Shulḥan Aruch: Eben Ha'Ezer* 24:1.

57.   See *B. Git.* 57b. Thus, for example, when the rabbis mentioned Edom, they were referring to Rome. See, for example, *Lev. Rab.* 13:5.

58.   See *M. Sanh.* 8:7.

59.   *B. Ned.* 51a. See also *B. Sanh.* 82a re Mal. 2:11; *J. Ber.* 9:2(13c) re Jer. 25:30.

60.   *B. Yebam.* 76a; *B. Shab.* 65a, Rashi, s.v. *gane'an;* Maimonides' comment on *M. Sanh.* 7:4 and *Mishneh Torah, Isuray Biah* 21:8.

61.   *Lev. Rab.* 23:9 à la *Sifra: Aḥaray-Mot* (ed. Weiss), 86a. See *B. Sanh.* 54b re l Kings 14:24; *B. Ḥul.* 92a–b. Re the image of the generation of the Flood as a paradigm of future divine punishment, see *M. B. Mez.* 4:2.

62.   See Suetonius, *Lives of the Caesars,* 4.28.

63.   *B. Yebam.* 63a.

64.   See *Gen. Rab.* 18:4; Novak, *Law and Theology in Judaism,* 2:13–14.

65.   For speech as the essence of human sociality, note Aristotle: "And why is man a political animal in a greater measure than any bee or any gregarious animal is clear. For nature, as we declare, does nothing in vain; and man alone of the animals possesses speech [*logon echōn*]" (*Politics,* 1253a10, ed. H. Rackham [Cambridge, Mass. 1932], p. 10). For attempts to qualify the rabbinic maxim "Do not engage in much discourse with a woman, even one's own wife" (*M. Abot* 1:5), see *Abot De-Rabbi Nathan* A, chap. 7 (ed. Schechter) 18a; *B. Erub.* 53b (bottom); the sense of which is to ridicule the maxim. Cf., however, *Abot De-Rabbi Nathan* B, chap. 15, for the notion that all female speech is seductive; also *B. Ḥag.* 5b re Amos 4:13.

66.   *B. Qid.* 5b, *J. Qid.* 1:1 (58c), *B. Git.* 88b.

67.   *B. Qid.* 2b. See *Gen. Rab.* 17:8. For the use of the noun *derekh* ("way") as a euphemism for sexual intercourse, see Gen. 19:31 and Prov. 30:19.

68.   *M. Qid.* 1:1.

69.   *B. Qid.* 2b. See *B. Git.* 85b.

70.   *B. Qid.* 41a. Cf. ibid. 3b re Deut. 22:16.

71.   *Num. Rab.* 3:4. See *Lev. Rab.* 8:1, ed. M. Margoliot (Jerusalem, 1953), 1:166, n. 4.

72. See *Law and Theology in Judaism*, 2:140–142. Indeed, the fourteenth-century Provençal exegete R. Menahem Ha-Meiri noted that if Scripture had explicated the originally valid status of involuntary marriage and divorce, "there would not be any daughter left to Abraham our father!" (*Bet Ha-Behirah*, ed. A. Sofer [Jerusalem, 1963], p. 8), viz., no woman would want to remain a Jewess. (cf. *B. Ket.* 72b.)

73. *M. Ket.* 5:6 and *B. Ket.* 77a. See *Law and Theology in Judaism*, 1:31–33.

74. *B. Qam.* 89a. See *B. Ket.* 11a and 57a.

75. R. Moses Isserles, note to *Shulhan Arukh: Eben Ha'Ezer* 119:6.

76. For the essential analogy between divorce and marriage, see *B. Qid.* 5a and parallels.

77. *M. Sotah* 9:9 re Hos. 4:14 and *B. Sotah* 47b re Num. 5:31; *J. Sotah* 9:9 (24a).

78. Note to *Shulhan Arukh: Eben Ha'Ezer* 154:1. Cf. *M. Sotah* 6:1, *B. Git.* 46a.

79. See *B. Qid.* 2b and Tosafot, s.v. *d'asar*. Cf. *B. Meilah* 18a–b, Tosafot, s.v. *ayn* and *v'omer*; *J. Qid.* 3:1 (63c).

80. See, for example, Cant. 6:8.

81. *Mishneh Torah, Hilkhot Ishut* 1:4 à la *Sifre, Debarim*, no. 260 (ed. Finkelstein): 283; *Sifra: Qedoshim* (ed. Weiss) 90d; *T. Qid.* 1:4 re Lev. 20:14. See *B. Sanh.* 82a re Mal. 2:11 and Maimonides, *Guide for the Perplexed* 3:49:603.

82. See J. Reider, *Deuteronomy with Commentary* (Philadelphia, 1984), p. 217.

83. R. Vidal of Tolosa, *Maggid Mishneh* thereto.

84. See note of R. Abraham ben David of Posquières thereto; Nahmanides, *Teshubot Ha-Ramban*, ed. C.B. Chavel (Jerusalem, 1975), no. 105; R. Solomon ibn Adret, *Teshubot Ha-Rashba*, Vol. 4 (Jerusalem, 1960), no. 314.

85. See *Law and Theology in Judaism*, 2:121–122.

86. See *B. Sanh.* 21a re 2 Sam. 5:13; *J. Ket.* 5:2 (29d). Most concubines were captives in war. The Talmud considers the scriptural permission to take a warbride (Deut. 21:10–14) as a compromise with lust. (See *B. Qid.* 21b–22a and *B. Sanh.* 59a [bottom].) Indeed, the initial contact of the Jewish soldier with such a woman was premarital, i.e., her status was that of a concubine. See Maimonides, *Mishneh Torah, Hilkhot Melakhim* 8:5–6.

87. See Feldman, *Birth Control in Jewish Law*, pp. 38ff.

88. *Gen. Rab.* 23:2; cf., however, *B. Yoma* 15b.

89. See, for example, Gen. 16:5, 21:10, 30:15; also, *M. Sanh.* 2.4 re Deut. 17:17 and *B. Sanh.* 21b re 1 Kings 11:4.

90. *Gen. Rab.* 18:3 re Gen. 2:22.

91.　See B. Qid. 4b, Tosafot, s.v. haykha, and 7a bottom.

92.　J. Qid. 1:1 (58c). Cf. J. B. Batra 8:1 (15d–16a); Josephus, Jewish Antiquities, 15.7, 10 and 17.5, 4.

93.　Mishneh Torah, Hilkhot Ishut 1:1; cf. Hilkhot Melakhim 9:8.

94.　Mishneh Torah, Hilkhot Ishut 4:1. See B. Yebam. 110a and B. B. Batra 48b.

95.　Thus the original scriptural permission to initiate marriage by a publicly evident (although not seen—B. Git. 81b) act of sexual intercourse (M. Qid. 1:1; T. Qid. 1:3; Sifre, Debarim, no. 268, ed. Finkelstein, 287; J. Qid. 1:3; B. Qid. 9b re Deut. 24:1 and 22:22; J. Qid. 1:1 [58b]) was later removed in the interest of public propriety. See B. Qid. 12b; also B. Ket. 56a and Maimonides, Mishneh Torah, Hilkhot Ishut 10:2.

96.　This point was brilliantly expounded by the late Professor Samuel Atlas (d. 1977) in his posthumous work Netibim Be-Mishpat Ha'Ibri (New York, 1978), pp. 246–247. See also, D. Novak, "Annulment in Lieu of Divorce in Jewish Law," Jewish Law Annual, 4:188–206.

97.　B. Ket. 7b (bottom).

98.　J. Ber. 9:1 (12d).

99.　B. Niddah 31b and B. Qid. 30b.

100.　"In a general way, it is unquestionable that a society has all that is necessary to arouse a sensation of the divine in minds, merely by the power that it has over them; for to its members it is what a god is to his worshippers. In fact, a god is, first of all, a being whom men think of as superior to themselves, and upon whom they depend.... Now society also gives us the sensation of a perpetual dependence. Since it has a nature which is peculiar to itself and different from our individual nature, it pursues ends which are likewise special to it;...It requires that, forgetful of our own interest, we make ourselves its servitors, and it submits us to every sort of inconvenience, privation and sacrifice, without which social life would be impossible" (The Elementary Forms of the Religious Life, trans. J.W. Swain [New York, 1965], pp. 236–237). The most powerful antithesis to this approach with its reductionism is found in the work of Rudolf Otto (The Idea of the Holy) and Mircea Eliade (The Sacred and the Profane). For a theological critique of the equation of society and transcendence, see Novak, Law and Theology in Judaism, 2:19–20.

101.　See B. Git. 90b; Law and Theology in Judaism, 1:12–14.

102.　See Cant. Rab. 1:11; also S. Lieberman, appendix to G. Scholem, Jewish Gnosticism and Merkabah Mysticism (New York, 1960), pp. 118ff.

103.　See R. Gordis, The Song of Songs and Lamentations, rev. ed. (New York, 1974), pp. 1–3.

104. See *The Essence of Christianity*, trans. M. Evans (London, 1893), secs. 643–644; *The Future of an Illusion*, trans. W.D. Robson-Scott (Garden City, N.Y., 1964), pp. 48ff; Novak, "Judaism and Contemporary Bio-Ethics," pp. 361ff.

105. *Zohar* I (*Lekh Lekha*) 85b. See, also, the earlier kabbalistic work (of disputed authorship), *The Holy Letter*, chap. 2, trans. S.J. Cohen (New York, 1970), pp. 48–49 and 58–59.

106. See R. Isaac bar Sheshet Parfat, *Teshubot Ha-Ribash* (Constantinople, 1574), no. 159.

107. Thus an important scholar of Jewish mysticism, Professor R.J.Z. Werblowsky, writes, "The Jewish Kabbalist...performed his marital duties with mystico-theurgic intentions, but realized that he was not allowed to give himself up either to his partner or to his passion. Transformed, in theory, into a sacramental act, the 'holy union' of husband and wife was in practice an ascetic exercise which admitted of no genuine relationship between the partners because the kabbalist had to identify himself with the mystical intention of the act and not with its actuality" (*Joseph Karo: Lawyer and Mystic* [Oxford, 1962], p. 137).

108. See Isa. 40:6–8, Job 19:25–26, also 1 Sam. 13:15 and M. *Abot.* 5:16.

109. Thus the late-nineteenth-century poet Robert Bridges wrote in his poem "Eros":

Why hast thou nothing in thy face?
Thou idol of the human race,
Thou tyrant of the human heart,
The flower of lovely youth thou art;
Yea, and thou standest in thy youth
An image of eternal Truth...

(in *Seven Centuries of Verse*, ed. A.J.M. Smith, 2d rev. ed. [New York, 1957], pp. 543–544).

110. In classical Jewish thought an unembodied human life is inconceivable. See, for example, *Lev. Rab.* 4:5. For embodiment as limitation, see Maimonides, *Mishneh Torah, Hilkhot Yesoday Ha-Torah* 1:7; *Guide for the Perplexed* 1:49.

111. *Lev. Rab.* 14:5. See D. Novak, *Law and Theology in Judaism*, 2:82–86. This insight is somewhat similar to that of the medieval saying that *omna animal post coitum triste est* ("every animal is sad following intercourse").

112. See Maurice Merleau-Ponty, *Phenomenology of Perception*, trans. C. Smith (London, 1962), pp. 148ff.

113.   See B. Qid. 54a and parallels; Cant. Rab. 8:13 re Num. 19:14.

114.   See R. Moses Cordovero, Tomer Deborah, chap. 9. Cf. Plato, Symposium, 202E: "What then...can Love [erōs] be...A great spirit [daimōn]...for the whole of the spiritual is between divine and mortal" (trans. W.R.M. Lamb [Cambridge, Mass., 1925], pp. 178–179).

115.   Freud writes, "But towards the outer world at any rate the ego seems to keep itself clearly outlined and delimited. There is only one state of mind in which it fails to do this.... At its height the state of being in love threatens to obliterate the boundaries between ego and object" (Civilization and Its Discontents, trans. J. Riviere [Garden City, N.Y., 1958], p. 3). He then goes on, "Originally the ego includes everything, later it detaches from itself the external world. The ego feeling we are aware of now is thus only a shrunken vestige of a far more extensive feeling—a feeling which embraced the universe and expressed an inseparable connection of the ego with the external world" (ibid., p. 6). For Freud, sexual love is the experience of the strongest pleasure. Even more than other pleasures it is a taking-in of the external world, a narcissistic reduction. However, the phenomenology of sexual love seems to indicate that it is essentially the intention of an other, irreducible to the embodied ego or any of its functions. As such, sexual love is transcendent in essence; it is not enclosed in an immanently human (and, for Freud, individual) circle. In other words, there is an essential difference between sexual love and "pleasures," even though pleasure is certainly an indispensable component of sexual love without which it is impossible. Nevertheless, the difference between sexual love and all other pleasures is generic, not just specific, as it is for Freud.

116.   Cant. Rab. 8:6. It might be useful to compare this ancient Jewish statement about the essence of love with a modern one. In his 1927 novel The Bridge of San Luis Rey Thornton Wilder concludes with these words. "But soon we shall die and all memory...will have left, and we ourselves shall be loved for a while and forgotten. But the love will have been enough; all those impulses of love return to the love that made them. Even memory is not necessary for love. There is a land of the living and a land of the dead and the bridge is love, the only survival, the only meaning" (2d ed. [New York, 1955], p. 148). If love, as Wilder seems to be saying, is a state of being (as we say today, "I am in love"), then it is conceivable that it can transcend individual persons and individual memories. But if love is an act (indeed, actus purus in the medieval philosophical sense), then it is only a person who can consciously do it. If, then, we can love with an undying love, it is only because we have been loved by God.

Part III
Social Justice

Religious communities cannot and do not exist in a vacuum. Even purists are influenced by the culture which surrounds them, while often the most committed religious figures actively enmesh themselves in society so as to bring it into accordance with their own vision of God's will. As George Higgins points out, the economic system itself is subject to moral judgment, a judgment which may change as the religious community's own attitudes evolve—due in no small part to the influence of the very society which is being assessed.

Although some sociologists have gone so far as to suggest that religions do little more than provide supernatural endorsement for the existing social order, the relationship is, in fact, reciprocal. To what extent a religious community's ethical values can be socially and historically conditioned is the subject of Eugene Borowitz's observations. Finally, Orlando Costas proposes a different role for religious communities—suggesting that they forgo mere protest in favor of making themselves agents of change.

The question of social ethics thus brings us full circle back to the problem with which we began. No longer is the issue simply one of comparing various viewpoints on the question of social justice, but rather the far larger problem of religion's own place within and in relationship to the larger society in which it finds itself. When to endorse society, when to challenge it, when simply to ignore it, and, more fundamentally, how to make such decisions—these are the underlying issues which must govern the question of the role of ethics within a religious system.

The Present State
of Catholic Social Teaching

George G. Higgins

It is currently rather fashionable in neoconservative circles to denigrate recent encyclicals and related social documents emanating from official Church bodies. Several participants at a recent seminar on the social teaching of the churches repeatedly charged that the social encyclicals of Leo XIII and Pius XII and especially those of John XXIII and Paul VI betray a complete misunderstanding of contemporary capitalist economic theory and practice. Not all went so far in this respect as Professor P.T. Bauer of the London School of Economics, but none of them demurred when Bauer asserted that "the papal letters [on socio-economic problems]... can only confuse believers. They are political statements supported by bogus arguments.... [They] are immoral because they are incompetent" and also because they legitimize envy and spread confusion about the meaning of charity.[1]

Professor Bauer and several others complain in particular that these documents pay too much attention to the distribution of wealth and little if any to the need for greater productivity under a system of democratic capitalism. As one of them put it with specific reference to the social documents of the American bishops, "ethics seems to be confined to workers and their rights and to distribution, without ever considering how and why things are freely produced and distributed."[2]

Dr. Bauer is not the only one to have made this point in recent years. A number of other writers on both the Left and the Right have felt constrained during the past decade or so to demythologize the social encyclicals in the light of modern scholarship. A few examples will suffice.

Richard L. Camp's book-length study, *The Papal Ideology of Social Reform: A Study in Historical Development, 1878–1967* is perhaps the most detailed of all the recent reappraisals of encyclical teaching.[3] In it, as John M. Krumm describes:

> The papal teachings themselves are subjected to a fairly rigorous and searching analysis, and the weaknesses are unfailingly pointed out. Leo XIII's obsessive concern about the inviolability and divine sanction attaching to private property, for example, is shown to be a serious distortion of the Thomistic teaching and, in any case, to be justified in *Rerum Novarum* on grounds that socialists had a relatively easy time demolishing thoroughly. Failure to discriminate between moderate and extreme left-wing socialism led with calamitous results to a papal blindness to the dangers of fascism in the years between the two world wars. John XXIII is flatly declared to be "the first pope fully to appreciate the possibilities of the modern economy and its institutions." One comes away from Professor Camp's study convinced that if the Church is to respond adequately to the challenge posed by the move toward secularity, there must be a far more rigorous and exacting discipline and training in the secular studies and the record from Leo XIII through John XXIII gives the impression of a well-intentioned but fumbling amateur.[4]

William McSweeney is also critical of Leo's social teaching. While noting sympathetically that Leo's was a "voice, however faint, that addressed the modern world in a way that none of [his] predecessors had done," he concludes nevertheless that

> the concern for social justice which the Pope advocated was conditional upon the retention of the economic system which exalted private property as a sacred institution....Leo's solution to the social question was, in one respect, an illusion. It created a new sense of freedom for Catholics, of openness towards the modern world and concern for its problems. But the reality was an integrist or totalist movement calculated to subject all areas of thought and action to the judgment and supervision of the Vatican through the local hierarchy.[5]

A third writer, Dr. Christine E. Gudorf, concludes that while each of the popes to have written on socioeconomic matters has linked justice, charity, and peace, "the linkage between these three... has been so influenced by the Pope's static view of human nature and society that the papal treatment of and his understanding of justice, upon which the social teaching is based, has often tended to support the status quo."[6]

If these critics have fallen into the familiar trap of oversimplifying history by hindsight, it is only fair to add that social encyclicals and related Church documents do, in fact, date rather quickly if only because the economies of the world are in such constant flux that official Church documents on socioeconomic problems are, by definition, culturally conditioned to a greater degree than comparable documents on matters such as revelation and therefore in need of constant updating. Furthermore, the Church's view of its own rule has changed somewhat. Whereas some nineteenth-century popes, such as Leo XIII, acted as authorities with exclusive access to ethical and moral truth, more recent leaders have held that the economic order has a certain validity in its own right, that economists and social scientists possess insights and expertise which are indispensable for understanding problems and achieving ends to which a humanistic ethics or Christian morality can only point. In this age of technology and creativity, truth is recognized more as a goal to be pursued than as an object already possessed. Ethical truth is to be sought by way of dialogue, in which both the believer and the scientist have something to share with and learn from the other.

A number of scholars—and notably the distinguished French Dominican theologian Marie-Dominique Chenu—have argued in this connection that, theologically, it is no longer accurate to speak of the Church's "social doctrine." According to Chenu:

not only the imperfection but the ambiguity of the term and the notion have become apparent: Vatican II, in its pastoral constitution on the Church in the modern world, *Gaudium et Spes* deliberately eliminated the expression and replaced it with formulae that are lexically similar but intentionally different in meaning: the term "the social teaching of the gospel" speaks of "teaching" rather than of "doctrine" and refers directly to the gospel and its inspiration. In this way a dissociation is effected between the general sense of a social content consubstantial with the Christian economy and a particular sense, historically tied to and conditioned by the sociotheological analysis contained in the positions and formulations proclaimed in the texts of the popes from Leo XIII to John XXIII, between 1891–1960.... Nothing has changed, and yet everything has changed. The pluralism that is henceforth to be regarded as the norm is not merely a material consequence of the diverse situations in which Christians find themselves in the world, it is also a matter of principle, stemming from the very nature of the Church which defines itself in terms of its presence in the world and not as an institution endowed with absolute reality.[7]

It is significant that Pope Paul VI opted for a dialogical approach in his last major document on socioeconomic matters, the 1971 apostolic letter *Octogesima Adveniens*, written to commemorate the eightieth anniversary of *Rerum Novarum*. The style of this apostolic letter closely parallels that of Pope John's major social encyclicals *Mater et Magistra* and *Pacem in Terris*. It is written in the form of a familiar dialogue not only with Catholics or with Christians in general, but with all those of goodwill, and carefully avoids the more pontifical style of teaching which so often characterized similar documents in the not-too-distant past.

On some matters, of course, the Holy Father states his own convictions very firmly, but never in such a way as to force his opinion on the reader or to short-circuit or foreclose the dialogue. On matters which are purely contingent, those open to varying viewpoints which lend themselves to a variety of solutions, he carefully refrains from trying to say—or even leaving the impression that he is trying to say—the last and final word. Indeed, he goes out of his way to emphasize that it is neither his ambition nor his mission "to utter a unified message and to put forward a solution which has universal validity." His purpose is the more modest one of "confiding" his own thoughts and preoccupations about some, but by no means all, of today's more pressing social problems and of encouraging individual Catholics and groups of Catholics, in dialogue with other Christian brethren and all men of goodwill, "to analyze with objectivity the situation which is proper to their own country," and, in addition, "to discern the options and commitments which are called for in order to bring about the social, political and economic changes seen in many cases to be needed."[8]

Again, one is reminded of Pope John's distinctively pastoral style of teaching by Pope Paul's repeated emphasis, in several different contexts, on the legitimate variety or plurality of possible options which are open to men of goodwill, his related emphasis on the obligation of individual Catholics to form their own conscience on these matters in the light of the Gospel message but without waiting for directives from their ecclesiastical leaders, and last but not least his urgent plea for the kind of basic humility which "will rid action of all inflexibility and sectarianism" and for "an effort at mutual understanding of the other's position and motives."[9]

All the popes have begun with the conviction that the material goods of this world are intended for the benefit of the whole human race. For material goods to fulfill this purpose, two things above all are necessary: development and distribution. The former requires human initiative, intelligence, and creativity in order to promote an ever-higher standard of living; the latter implies that every human person has a right to what he needs to provide for himself and his family, not only on a day-to-day basis but also, in reasonable measure, for the future: "The Creator himself has given man the right of private ownership that individuals may be able to provide for themselves and their families."[10]

Traditional ethics from at least the time of Thomas Aquinas has held that private ownership not only of what is necessary for one's life but also of superfluous goods—even the means of production—most effectively promotes development: "each one is more solicitous for promoting that which is his alone than that which is common to all or to many, since we tend to leave to others the tasks that are for the common good; human affairs tend to be more orderly when the task of providing for something rests on an individual than when it is the task of all to provide for everything."[11] However, "the individual must consider them [material goods] not as his own, but as belonging to all—so that the individual should share them easily with others who are in need."[12]

God intended the earth and all it contains for the use of every
human being and people. As all men follow justice and unite
in charity, created goods should abound for them on a reasonable basis. Whatever the forms of ownership may be, as
adapted to the legitimate institutions of people according to
diverse and changeable circumstances, attention must always
be paid to the universal purpose for which created goods are
meant. In using them, therefore, a man should regard his
lawful possessions not merely as his own but also as common
property in the sense that they should accrue to the benefit
not only of himself but of others.[13]

The first principle of this [economic] order [is] the universal
destination of goods and the right to common use of them.[14]

While private ownership and its attendant "personal-profit
motivation" may remain effective means of promoting development, they can and do at times become obstacles to the equitable distribution of available goods. As Pius XI pointed out, the
common welfare may demand state or collective ownership.
Capitalism (private ownership) and socialism (limited collective
ownership) are, therefore, relative values to be weighed in the
light of how well each serves the twofold aim of development
and distribution.

John Paul II expressed the traditional understanding of the
relationship between these two latter principles:

Christian tradition has never upheld this right [private
ownership] as absolute and untouchable. On the contrary, it
has always understood this right within the broader context
of the right common to all to use the goods of the whole of
creation. The right to private property is subordinated to the
right to common use, to the fact that goods are meant for
everyone....From this point of view the position of "rigid"
capitalism continues to be unacceptable, namely, the position
that defends the exclusive right to private ownership of the
means of production as an untouchable "dogma" of economic
life.... [The means of production] cannot be possessed against
labor, they cannot be possessed for possession's sake, because
the only legitimate title for their possession—whether in the
form of private ownership or in the form of public or collective
ownership—is that they should serve labor and thus make

possible the achievement of the first principle of this order, namely the universal destination of goods and the right to common use of them.[15]

Leo XIII treated of the same principles almost a century earlier when he observed that "the fact that God gave the whole human race the earth to use and enjoy cannot in any manner serve as an objection against private possession."[16] But Leo was addressing a situation entirely different from that of John Paul. The "socialism" which he roundly condemns entailed an out-and-out denial of any right to private property[17] and was, therefore, an entirely different concept from that to which John Paul II accords the same conditional status as capitalism (private ownership of the means of production). Pius XI, who writes at the midpoint, chronologically, between Leo and John Paul has some very harsh things to say about socialism, but he also states: "Certain kinds of property... ought to be reserved to the State since they carry with them a dominating power so great that they cannot without danger to the general welfare be entrusted to individuals."[18]

A third concept, that of subsidiarity, functions to integrate the traditional understanding of society and state and assure balance in the relationship between private ownership and common use. Pius XI formulates it in this way:

> That most weighty principle, which cannot be set aside or changed, remains fixed and unshaken in social philosophy: just as it is gravely wrong to take from individuals what they can accomplish by their own initiative and industry and give it to the community, so also it is an injustice and at the same time a grave evil and disturbance of right order to assign to a greater and higher association what lesser and subordinate organizations can do. For every social activity ought of its very nature to furnish help to the members of the body social, and never destroy or absorb them.[19]

The state should exercise its authority in order to promote activity on the level of individuals and private organizations.

> It is lawful for states and public corporations to expand their domain of ownership only when manifest and genuine

requirements of the common good so require, and then with safeguards, lest the possession of private citizens be diminished beyond measure, or, what is worse, destroyed....Those in authority should favor and help private enterprise in order to allow private citizens themselves to accomplish as much as is feasible.[20]

To illustrate how these principles are applied in practice we will examine three particular subjects, using *Mater et Magistra* as a starting point.

Socialization

The most widely publicized and perhaps the most controversial section of *Mater et Magistra* is the one dealing with the phenomenon of socialization. "Socialization"—a word which, to the best of my knowledge, had never before appeared in a papal document—is understood as the "progressive multiplication of relations in society, with different forms of life and activity, and juridical institutionalization." It finds its expression, for the most part, not in governmental programs but in "a wide range of groups, movements, associations, and institutions ...both within single national communities and on an international level."[21]

Mater et Magistra holds that socialization brings many advantages:

It makes possible, in fact, the satisfaction of many personal rights, especially those called economicosocial, such as, for example, the right to the indispensable means of human maintenance, to health services, to instruction at a higher level, to a more thorough professional formation, to housing, to work, to suitable leisure, to recreation.[22]

Pope John says that while socialization "restricts the range of the individual as regards his liberty of action," it does not necessarily reduce men to automatons. He explained:

Actually, increased complexity of social life by no means results from a blind drive of natural forces. Indeed, as stated above, it is the creation of free men who are so disposed to act by nature as to be responsible for what they do. They must, of course, recognize the laws of human progress and the development of economic life and take these into account. Furthermore, men are not altogether free of their milieu.

Accordingly, advances in social organization can and should be so brought about that maximum advantages accrue to citizens while at the same time disadvantages are averted or at least minimized....

Now if social systems are organized in accordance with the above norms and moral laws, their extension does not necessarily mean that individual citizens will be gravely discriminated against or excessively burdened. Rather, we can hope that this will enable man not only to develop and perfect his natural talents, but also will lead to an appropriate structuring of the human community. Such a structure, as our predecessor of happy memory, Pius XI, warned in his Encyclical Letter *Quadragesimo Anno*, is absolutely necessary for the adequate fulfillment of the rights and duties of social life.[23]

There are three possible ways of misinterpreting what this encyclical has to say about socialization. The first would be to confuse socialization with socialism. The second, which is similar, would be to equate socialization exclusively with governmental action. The third would be to equate socialization exclusively with voluntary action by nongovernment organizations or associations, thus ruling out almost every kind of governmental action.

The first two mistakes are more likely to be made by extreme liberals who do not subscribe to the principle of subsidiarity, according to which "it is gravely wrong to take from individuals what they can accomplish by their own initiative and industry and give it to the community," and it is "also an injustice and at the same time a grave evil and disturbance of right order to assign to a greater and higher association what lesser and subordinate organizations can do."[24] The third mistake is more likely to be made by ultraconservatives, Catholics included, who interpret the principle of subsidiarity so rigidly as almost to exclude the possibility of effective governmental action. To make this mistake would be to ignore the numerous references in the encyclical to legitimate governmental programs in the field of social welfare and social reform.

At the present time we are probably in danger of making the last of these three mistakes, as witness some of the public statements being made about the role of government by administration spokesmen, notably David Stockman, former director of the Office of Management and Budget. People are not "entitled" to any federally funded social service, Stockman said on the television program "Issues and Answers." "I don't believe that there is any entitlement, any basic right to legal services, or any other kind of services.... The idea... that almost every service that someone might need in life ought to be provided, financed by the government as a matter of basic right, is wrong. We challenge that. We reject that notion."[25]

While it is true that Stockman was prepared to put a "safety net" under the "truly" needy, his statement indicates that he does not believe even the truly needy are *entitled* to such protection. Many church-related social agencies expressed their disagreement with Stockman's cold-blooded social philosophy, charging that the administration's approach to budget-cutting lacks compassion. Their criticism should not have surprised Stockman. As a former Harvard Divinity School student, he must have known that the majority of religious authorities in social ethics disagree with his philosophy, holding that citizens are entitled to certain essential services from their government in cases of necessity.

Pope John XXIII summarized Catholic tradition on this issue in the encyclical *Pacem in Terris:*

> Experience has taught us that unless these [government] authorities take suitable action with regard to economic, political and cultural matters, inequalities between the citizens tend to become more and more widespread, especially in the modern world, and as a result human rights are rendered totally ineffective and the fulfillment of duties is compromised.[26]

The encyclical points out that governments must make efforts to see that insurance systems are made available to the citizens, so that in case of misfortune or increased family responsibilities, no person will be without the necessary means to maintain a decent standard of living. The majority of Protestant and Jewish social ethicists agree.

Church social agencies are not about to get involved in a partisan controversy with the administration. Nor do they oppose federal budget cuts in principle; they understand the need to trim the budget and to curb inflation. They argue, however, that many of the proposed cuts will cause the poor and disadvantaged undue hardship. If Stockman's philosophy prevails in the administration, these church agencies will have no choice but to break with the administration and stand up for the rights of the poor and disadvantaged.

The So-Called Industry Council Plan

During the 1930s and 1940s a number of American commentators on the social encyclicals placed great emphasis on the so-called Industry Council Plan as a means of reorganizing the American economy according to the principles outlined in Pius XI's *Quadragesimo Anno*. The program of social order advocated in that encyclical envisaged (1) an organized and orderly economic society, with organizations of each industry and profession and a federation of such organizations; (2) an economic society which is self-governing, subject only to the superior power of the state to intervene when the public good demands it; (3) social institutions organized to seek the common good for their members and for all economic society; (4) the predominance of such organizations and institutions as the primary means of putting justice into economic life; and (5) the rule of the great virtues of justice and charity through the functioning of these organizations.

When *Mater et Magistra* was issued in 1961, some writers observed that the new encyclical seemed to be less interested in the so-called Industry Council Plan than was Pius XI. This was only partially true. Pope John carefully avoided giving his approval to any particular method of organizing or reorganizing economic life. Moreover, even his terminology was somewhat different from that of Pius XI in his encyclical *Quadragesimo Anno* and in his later encyclical on communism, *Divini Redemptoris*. Pius XI used the terminology of "corporativism," which, in English, has been freely translated into "Industry Council Plan." Pope John XXIII, on the other hand, was mostly preoccupied with the practical aspects of the problem and so carefully avoided using this kind of terminology. He was a pastor and not a jurist. He knew all the discussions raised by the formulas of Pius XI and Pius XII and the misunderstandings these discussions had caused. So he kept from any formulizing and even went so far as to avoid using the words "corporation" and "corporative organization."[27]

It would appear to be partially correct, then, to say that Pope John XXIII was less interested than Pius XI in the so-called Industry Council Plan. Pope John's approach to the problem of social reconstruction like his terminology was less theoretical—more flexible, if you will—than that of Pope Pius XI. But it would be a serious mistake to conclude that Pope John was any less interested than Pius XI in the basic principles of social reconstruction underlying the so-called Industry Council Plan. The basic principles of social reconstruction outlined in *Mater et Magistra* are the same as those which are to be found in Pius XI's encyclical *Quadragesimo Anno*. They can be summarized as follows:

Economic order will not come naturally, only by free competition, free enterprise, and free initiative, although a certain degree of freedom must always be safeguarded. Intermediate bodies are natural and necessary if we want to avoid state totalitarianism. Institutional cooperation at all levels must be organized between the agents of the economy. Intermediate bodies must cooperate among themselves and with the government in order to help it play its positive role in the economy for the common good, national and international.

These are the basic principles underlying the Industry Council Plan. Pope John did not tell us, in detail, how they were to be put into practice. His approach, I repeat, was very flexible. He opened the doors to all kinds of institutional cooperation among those interested at the different levels of production, strongly insisting on any organization of the economy which takes into account the national and international common good. The state has a positive role to play, and this role must be accomplished with respect for legitimate autonomies and with the participation of all interested groups. In substance, this is what proponents of the Industry Council Plan have been saying all along. At times, perhaps, their approach and their terminology have been rather inflexible. If so, *Mater et Magistra* can serve as a timely corrective.

One way of moving in the direction of the Industry Council Plan would be to develop a system of comanagement or co-determination. In some European countries, following World War II, labor and management did in fact move in this direction. In the United States, however, organized labor showed little if any interest in comanagement or codetermination. At the present time, however, in the face of the current economic crisis in the United States, one of our major unions has demanded and has been granted a limited form of codetermination by the Chrysler Corporation.

The United Auto Workers (UAW) is reacting pragmatically to the current economic crisis in the auto industry. When the UAW agreed—as it simply had to—to reopen its contract with Chrysler, and voted to make drastic wage concessions in a last-ditch effort to keep that near-bankrupt corporation afloat, it demanded in return a seat on the Chrysler board of directors and a compensatory share in any future Chrysler profits. These demands were negotiated, not imposed by law.

Once it was announced that the UAW had agreed to take a drastic pay cut to keep Chrysler alive, other corporations with which the union has collective-bargaining contracts began to ask for similar concessions. Presumably the UAW will consider each request on its merits. If a company's economic condition warrants, the union will probably agree to adjust its demands. But in return it will demand, as it did in the Chrysler case, a structured form of comanagement, a profit-sharing plan, and a requirement that the corporation "open the books" and give the union a voice in layoff decisions. If these demands are not met, the industry will be asking for a potentially disastrous labor-management struggle of monumental proportions.

Socialism

A recent trip to Poland and Pope John Paul II's new encyclical *On Human Work* demonstrate how much Catholic teaching on the subject of socialism has changed over the course of the years. Pope John Paul's new encyclical, unlike some of the earlier documents referred to above, does not condemn socialism as such; it states that from "the principle of priority of labor

(human work) over capital" and "the primacy of man over
things" the Pope concludes that

> the justice of the socioeconomic system and, in each case, its
> just functioning, deserve in the final analysis to be evaluated
> by the way in which man's work is properly remunerated in
> the system. Here we return once more to the first principle of
> the whole ethical and social order, namely the principle of
> the common use of goods.... Hence, in every case, a just wage
> is the concrete means of verifying the justice of the whole
> socioeconomic system and, in any case, of checking that it is
> functioning justly. It is not the only means of checking, but it
> is a particularly important one and, in a sense, the key
> means.[28]

The principle of the "common use of goods," an ancient one
in Catholic social teaching, leads the Pope to reject "the position
that defends the exclusive right to private ownership of the
means of production as an untouchable 'dogma' of economic
life. The principle of respect for work demands that this right
should undergo a constructive revision both in theory and in
practice."[29] This is not to say that Pope John Paul II rejects all
forms of capitalism. He does not. But neither does he reject all
forms of socialism. While pointing to weaknesses and dangers
in both systems of ownership, he does not choose between them
at the theoretical level. As noted above, his key criterion for
judging either system is the degree to which it recognizes in
practice as well as in theory "the primacy of man over things."

Some of the earlier documents condemn socialism—with
good reason, given the antireligious bias of much of nineteenth-
and early-twentieth-century European socialism. But time
marches on, and systems do change. Pope John XXIII made an
opening in his celebrated encyclical *Pacem in Terris*. Pope Paul
VI went even further in his 1971 apostolic letter *Octogesima
Adveniens*. He called upon Catholics to exercise "careful judgment" in distinguishing between those forms and features of
socialism which are compatible with Christian social teaching
and those which are not. This kind of careful discernment, he
said, "will enable Christians to see the degree of commitment
[to socialism] possible along these lines, while safeguarding the

values, especially those of liberty, responsibility, and openness to the spiritual, which guarantee the integral development of man."[30]

Michael Harrington's book *Socialism* is recommended as useful background reading on this subject.[31] Harrington is a dreamer in the best sense of the word, but he is also a hard-headed realist. While convinced in his own mind that socialism (democratic socialism, be it noted) is desirable and necessary, he knows very well that it is not inevitable and is the first to admit that, if it starts from the wrong premises or takes the wrong turn, it can become—and, indeed, has become in many cases—a curse to humanity rather than a blessing. Harrington is also very realistic concerning the future of socialism in the United States. While arguing that "most of the people in the world today call the name of their dream 'socialism,'" he notes that the United States is the "great exception" in this regard. The United States, he says, is "almost the only country on the face of the globe where 'socialism' is a bad word."[32]

This being the case, Harrington's book is required reading for serious-minded Americans. We owe it to ourselves to try, at the very least, to understand why socialism, for better or for worse, has such great appeal in many countries of the world. In this writer's judgment, Harrington is undoubtedly correct in arguing that it has such an appeal and that "its tremendous resonance obviously tells of a deep yearning for fundamental change among hundreds of people."[33]

Perhaps the clearest sign that its appeal is growing rather than declining is the fact that so many Catholics in other lands are now openly espousing some form of socialism or, short of that, are at least openly contending that democratic socialism is a perfectly legitimate option for committed Christians. The 1972 Christians for Socialism meeting in Santiago, Chile—which went on record as favoring socialism for Latin America—was rather dramatically indicative of this trend. Those Catholics in the United States who were inclined to write off this particular meeting as a ragtag gathering of unorthodox Christian radicals or revolutionaries had something to learn, I think, from a lengthy document on socialism issued by the French hierarchy at the very time that Christians for Socialism were meeting in Santiago. This French document (intentionally dated May 1, the traditional feast-day of the international working class) was entitled "First Reflections of the Episcopal Commission on Working Class Affairs in Dialogue with Militants Who Have Opted for Socialism."[34]

The document was addressed to the bishops of France by an episcopal commission (of fifteen) presided over by Archbishop Maziers of Bordeaux. The preamble stated that the commission wished merely to "hear the views of militant Christian workers and to respond to their questions." The commission reported that all of the workers consulted had rejected capitalism and had adopted a form of socialism. For them, a unified human development was possible only by means of socialism. Most of the working-class leaders believed that the transition from capitalism to socialism would involve a radical break. They were in principle against the use of force, but were afraid that the resistance of the ruling classes would make violence inevitable. The commission then went on to say, in its own name, that "there are major elements of Marxism which have been adopted by Christian workers, and which do not seem to be incompatible with their faith." It concluded that "the economic and political system of socialism is wholly reconcilable with Christianity, so long as human rights are guaranteed.... This first attempt at discussion with militant Catholic workers who have chosen socialism shows us yet again how distant—despite all good will—we are from the working class, its language, culture, spontaneous responses and basic aspirations."[35]

This conclusion undoubtedly came as a surprise to many American Catholics and a severe shock to others. They should bear in mind, however, that the members of the commission were doing precisely what Pope Paul VI, as noted above, advised all Christians to do in his apostolic letter of May 15, 1971. That is to say, they were exercising "careful judgment" in distinguishing between those forms and features of socialism which are compatible with Christian social teaching and those which are not. This kind of careful discernment, the Holy Father noted in his apostolic letter, "will enable Christians to see the degree of commitment [to socialism] possible along these lines, while safeguarding the values, especially those of liberty, responsibility and openness to the spiritual, which guarantee the integral development of man."[36]

This is what the French commission set out to do and what Michael Harrington also attempted to do—and, in large measure, succeeded in doing—in his book *Socialism*. A careful reading of the French document and of Harrington's book will help American readers to play a more intelligent and more constructive role in the continuing worldwide debate about the future of socialism as a viable and legitimate socioeconomic system.

Arthur F. McGovern, S.J., presents a carefully balanced conclusion on the pros and cons of socialism and, more specifically, on the role of Christians in contemporary economic society which can serve as an appropriate epilogue to this brief article on the present state of Catholic social teaching:

> If socialism cannot claim to have "the" solution, capitalism certainly does not. Socialism points to an important alternative possibility, and offers a needed critique of capitalism. For a Christian to work for a democratic socialism would seem a perfectly justifiable option. The very uncertainties about socialism might be all the more reason for Christians to be part of the movement, to help shape its direction and values.... Christians must work not simply for social change, but for a social change that minimizes violence and hostility, that insists on respect for the dignity and freedom of every individual, and that accepts human limitations.... All religious faiths and political ideologies share in common some vision of a truly just and humane society. My own loyalty to the Church and deep love of my faith give expression to this vision in a Christian way, in work and prayer that looks to "a new heaven and a new earth." At present this vision exists largely in hope, but a hope that God has expressed as promise: "The world of the past is gone.... Now I am making the whole of creation new." (Rev. 21:4–5).[37]

Notes

1. P.T. Bauer, "Ecclesiastical Economics Is Envy Exalted," *This World* 1 (Winter–Spring 1982): 69.
2. James V. Schall, "Catholicism and the American Experience," *This World* (Winter–Spring 1982): 8.
3. L. Camp, *The Papal Ideology of Social Reform: A Study in Historical Development, 1878–1967* (Leyden: E.J. Brill, 1969).
4. *American Historical Review* (October, 1970): 1713.

5. William McSweeney, *Roman Catholicism: The Search for Relevance* (New York: St. Martins Press, 1980), pp. 77–79.

6. Christine E. Gudorf, *Catholic Social Teaching on Liberation Themes* (Lanham, Md.: University Press of America, 1980), p. 1.

7. Marie-Dominique Chenu, "The Church's Social Doctrine," *Concilium*, 1980, pp. 72–73.

8. Pope Paul VI, *A Call to Action* (Washington, D.C.: United States Catholic Conference, 1971), p. 3.

9. Pope Paul VI, *Octogesima Adveniens* (The Gospel of Peace and Justice), ed. Joseph Gremillion (Maryknoll, N.Y.: Orbis Books, 1976), p. 510.

10. Pope Paul XI, *Quadragesimo Anno*, n. 45; cf. Leo XII: "Let it be regarded, therefore, that... this principle before all is to be considered as basic, namely, that private ownership must be preserved as inviolate" (*Rerum Novarum*, n. 23).

11. *S.T.* ii–ii, q. 57, q. 2,3; q. 66, q. 2.

12. Ibid., ii–ii, q. 66. a. 2.

13. Vol. 2, *Gaudium et Spes*, n. 69.

14. Pope John Paul II, *Laborem Exercens*, n. 14.

15. Ibid.

16. Ibid.

17. Ibid., nn. 5–14.

18. Ibid., n. 114; see also nn. 111–125.

19. *Quadragesimo Anno*, n. 79.

20. Pope John XXIII, *Mater et Magistra*, nn. 117, 152.

21. Pope John XXIII, *Mater et Magistra*, par. 59, in *The Gospel of Peace and Justice*, ed. Joseph Gremillion (Maryknoll, N.Y.: Orbis Books, 1976), p. 155.

22. Ibid., pars. 63–67.

23. Pope John XXIII, *Mater et Magistra* (Washington, D.C.: U.S. Catholic Conference, 1961), pp. 20–22.

24. Pope Pius XI, *Quadragesimo Anno*, par. 79.

25. Quoted in *New York Times*, March 23, 1981, p. D6.

26. Pope John XXIII, *Pacem in Terris* (Washington, D.C.: U.S. Catholic Conference, 1963), pp. 16–17.

27. Most of the misunderstandings of *Quadragesimo Anno* centered around the subject of fascism. Some people thought Pius XI was in favor of the fascist corporate state, whereas in fact he opposed it.

28. Pope John Paul II, *On Human Work* (Washington, D.C.: U.S. Catholic Conference, 1981), p. 42.

29. Pope John Paul II, *On Human Work*, par. 14.

30. Pope Paul VI, *Octogesima Adveniens* p. 17.

31. New York: Saturday Review Press, 1972.

32. Ibid., p. 109.

33. Ibid.

34. The full text was reprinted, in French, in the May 21, 1972 edition of *La Documentation Catholique*. An adequate English summary was made available in the May 20, 1972 edition of *The Tablet* (London).

35. Ibid.

36. Pope Paul VI, *Octogesima Adveniens*, par. 31, in *The Gospel of Peace and Justice*, ed. Joseph Gremillion (Maryknoll, N.Y.: Orbis Books, 1976), p. 500.

37. Arthur McGovern, *Marxism: An American Perspective* (Maryknoll, N.Y.: Orbis Books, 1980), pp. 323, 328.

The Critical Issue in the Quest for Social Justice: A Jewish View

Eugene B. Borowitz

Though esteeming highly the spiritual worth of the individual, the Bible authors give priority to the corporate human relationship with God. I would speculate that they do so largely because they view humankind as essentially social. Looking at Adam, they have *Adonai* say, "It is not good for man to be alone: I will make a fitting helpmate for him."[1] And the tower of Babel story comes to explain why the history of humankind is essentially a record of the conflict of peoples and nations.[2] Even the account of the Israelite patriarchs serves to introduce the emergence of the Hebrew nation and explain its possession of Canaan.[3] The historical books then tell what happened to the covenanted people, and the prophetic books criticize, threaten, remotivate, and redirect its efforts to create a communal life holy to God. Social ethics is obviously fundamental to the religion of the Bible.

We shall have little difficulty specifying the content of biblical social ethics as long as we see it as a body of abstract ideals. Can there be much doubt that the Bible, in all its diversity of authors, attitudes, voices, and concerns, unambiguously aspires to a time when people live together in plenty and not in poverty, in justice and not in oppression, in love and not in hatred, in peace and not in war?

Our difficulties in accepting and applying biblical social ethics arise as we move from the Bible's idealism to its profound human realism. Its writers accept as axiomatic the premise that human beings are no longer in the Garden of Eden because we

188

are creatures who regularly will to sin. They see our stubborn, perverse rejection of God's will as the motive power of human history and the problem that God's loving, saving power must overcome. The biblical lawgivers, envisioning people this way, created statutes by which they might effectuate their God-inspired social ideal in their immediate, concrete social situation. The prophets, by divine revelation, clarified what God was doing in the particular local and international affairs of Jewish history.

In due course, direct revelation ceased in Israel, and altered social circumstances demanded a more appropriate statement of what God now wanted of the people of the Covenant. The rabbis in their unique way then continued the Bible's practical social concern in the exquisite details of talmudic law and the inspirational lessons of midrashic lore. That tradition of vision and application, of text and interpretation, of precedent and application, of enlargement and augmentation, of creative development and new enactment, goes on to the present day. A substantial body of classic Jewish writings treats of ethical issues, and a not inconsiderable and growing contemporary literature seeks to apply them to our time.[4]

From this point on, the characterization of contemporary Jewish social ethics confronts two difficulties. The first of these it shares indistinguishably with the field of Christian ethics. The move from ethical ideal to specific injunction increases the pluralism of opinion among learned, thoughtful, faithful students of these matters. The classic differences over how idealistic we ought to try to be at this moment or how little we should settle for, human nature being so refractory, are exponentially multiplied today by the irremediable ambiguities created by the technical complexity of many social issues. How does one discover which economic theory provides the most reliable foundation for a program to lessen poverty, or which perception of military realities explains what hardware we require, or worse, how to combine the two of them in a time of stagflation?

More troubling than specifying content, I believe, is the challenge arising from those people who loyally come to the synagogue or church and consider social ethics in its broad sense peripheral if not irrelevant to their central spiritual concerns. This problem takes on special form today in the Jewish

community but one which reflects the present situation of all
biblical religions in America. I think I can best be of help in
clarifying the central issue of biblical social ethics as well as of
making plain the unique contours of contemporary Jewish religious thought by dealing with the metaethical rather than the
material level of our question. I propose to expound and respond
to the arguments of those who question why pious Jews in our
time ought to have a major commitment to transforming society.

Like all our other visible, voluble pietistic movements, the
American Jewish social quietists gain their strength largely in
reaction to the liberal, activist interpretation of the Jewish
social ethic which dominated our community for the first twenty
years following World War II. One must keep in mind that our
secularization had started earlier and proceeded more effectively
than that of American Christians due to our heavy urbanization,
our commitment to higher education, and our identification of
the secular as the realm where we would meet less prejudice.[5]
Liberalism had become the essence of Judaism for much of our
community in a movement far more intense than the parallel
Christian activity. Indeed, by the late 1960s, when this identification of Jewish social ethics with activist, liberal politics
peaked, there had been over a century of unprecedented Jewish
involvement in every cause for human betterment in which
Jews had been permitted to participate. Surely this must be
ranked among the proudest achievements of Jewish history.
Not only did Jews devote themselves to the general welfare in
strikingly large numbers, disproportionately so, and give creative leadership in almost every field they entered, they did so
without long-established models to emulate but in spontaneous,
enthusiastic response to their emancipation from centuries of a
degraded social status.[6]

The rejection of Jewish social ethics as equivalent to liberal
political activity has been gathering power for over a decade. It
substantially derives from the universal American shift to the
right.[7] With the American economy stagnating or in decline, the
rising expectations of many once-quiescent groups in our society
can no longer be met. Fierce competition for limited means has
become common, and self-interest has increasingly replaced
the common welfare as an immediate political concern. In this
atmosphere, ethnics have turned to their roots rather than to the

American future to find a sense of security, and old social coalitions have broken down as the groups seek greater gains for themselves. They have also lost their program of change. Increasingly people feel that liberalism did not and cannot resolve our social problems. Rather it created a host of new ones in the name of social improvement. To some extent this mood draws on the historic prejudices of Americans against various minority groups, for they are vulnerable and subject to attack in ways that were unthinkable a decade or so ago. Less debatably, the concern with the self and its satisfactions has for a growing number of people been understood in more isolated and less social a fashion than previously, the notorious narcissism of our times.

The American Jewish community reflects all these currents but does so in forms refracted by Jewish ethnic experience and values. Consider the issue of social class. Political liberalism had appealed to a community of acculturating immigrants who were poor in means, experience, and even opportunity but rich in hope. The overwhelming portion of the native-born, unretired American Jewish community is now solidly middle-class, and perhaps more of it is upper-class than any other religio-ethnic group. It may have had to make its way through a relatively unfair and discriminatory system, but its present status and privileges depend on the continuing functioning of that system. Today, by sharp contrast to fifty years ago, American Jewry has a stake in not greatly altering this country's socioeconomic structure.[8]

Moreover, a small but significant community role is now played by a relatively recent group of Jewish immigrants, those who arrived as refugees during the Hitler period or, more importantly, since then. A large proportion of this group had not previously come to the United States for religious reasons. The country was synonymous with assimilation and nonobservance. In many cases, too, their form of Orthodoxy required limited participation in general society. Having survived the Holocaust and determined to continue their Jewish lives, they have little desire to learn from or accommodate to gentile ways. Their attacks on English-speaking, beardless, university-attending, American-oriented Orthodox Jews has mitigated much of the social concern visible among what, in the 1960s, came to be called "modern Orthodoxy."[9] Their presence and Jewish militance have posed a special challenge to what remains of the old, outer-directed American Jewish communal leadership. It had already been discredited by the heavy burden of guilt which historical reconsideration had fixed upon it for failing European Jewry during the Hitler years. American Jews had been so concerned to be part of the American war effort that they would not break ranks and press the special claims of the Jews the Nazis were murdering en masse. Worse, research disclosed that the liberal leaders the Jews had adulated had not cared enough for the Jewish victims to give such help as might have been possible, for example, bombing the death camps.

These special Jewish factors intensified the effect of the new general American ethnic assertiveness. As a result, many voices in the Jewish community began to oppose the dogmatic liberal identification of Jewish interests with those of all other American minorities.[10] The liberal political agenda, they charged, takes no account of the special needs of the Jews as a religio-ethnic group and ignores the unparalleled heritage of Western anti-Semitism that still functions against this people. To hope governmental social and economic programs will create a society of such widespread contentment as to vitiate the old Jew-hatred is as naive as was the Jewish Communist dream that the proletarian state would eliminate anti-Semitism. To the contrary, liberal-sponsored programs like busing, affirmative action, and opposition to government aid to Jewish all-day schools directly lessen the chances of American Jews building a strong Jewish community life in the future.

The emerging Jewish right, as it has gained the economic strength and political sophistication to express its will—again paralleling Christian phenomena—has pressed a strong polemic against the Jewish authenticity of the Jewish liberals. By identifying Judaism with general ethics, they legitimated assimilation. Those who wanted to escape their Jewish identity could claim that by helping humankind they were, in fact, being good Jews. Generally they could be counted on to fight for the rights of every people except their own. Thus on the university campus, they impeded or fought the introduction of courses in Jewish studies. Consistent with their devotion to humanity, the liberals' Jewish religious practice tended to be minimal and their knowledge of Judaism superficial. Even the articles written by those who sought to show the harmony of Judaism and universal ethics are little more than a few biblical verses or rabbinic apothegms, often snatched from their context, utilized to Judaize a Western intellectual position. A Judaism which has no discipline and demands no sacrifice is unworthy of being called a religion. How then could such people speak authentically in Judaism's name and hope to apply its values to the problems of society as a whole?

Rather than pretentiously assert a Jewish mission to all humankind, Jewry should devote itself to what its millennial history best suits it for, sanctifying the lives of individuals and families. If Jews were properly observant, they would also be decent citizens. Devoting themselves mainly to the preservation and enhancement of their community, they could not help also being a positive force in society and making a major contribution to its welfare. Besides, in this time of social peril, Jews need to base their lives on the primary lesson of the Holocaust: in a crisis, no one else can be counted on to help Jews but other Jews. We are historically mandated and ethically entitled to make concern with our people's welfare the sovereign content of our social ethic.

This account of the ideology of the new Jewish right has thus far omitted one major factor which, in quite complicated ways, makes its appeal quite compelling, that is, the deep American Jewish concern for the State of Israel. No other Jewish cause remotely comes close to motivating American Jewry as does the survival of the Israeli state. It represents our people's primal, life-affirming response to the Holocaust and, in the face of excruciatingly difficult political pressures, exemplifies in its democratic, social-welfare orientation the age-old social values of Judaism. As the State of Israel perceives its needs, or better, as American Jewish leaders, eager not to repeat the failures of the Holocaust, understand their need to lobby for Israeli causes, the agenda of American political liberalism—domestic welfare—is soft and unrealistic. The major problems of our day are, rather, international. Hence America needs to become staunchly anti-Soviet and thus militarily unimpeachable.[11]

The reeducation of American Jewish leadership in this regard may well be dated to 1967. Lyndon Johnson informed a

group summoned to the White House that if the State of Israel
was to get the jet planes it desired, American Jews would have
to stop backing the protests against the Vietnam War. Similarly,
the lesson of the critical dependence of the Israeli army on the
American arsenal for resupply in the decisive early days of the
1973 war was not lost on many American Jews. If the State of
Israel is to survive, America must be militarily strong—and it
would help if the Pentagon saw the American Jewish community
as its backers.

From those days to the present, the rhetoric and formal
organizational stands of most American Jewish organizations
have shifted rightward, that is, general human concerns have
essentially been displaced by ethnic and Israeli ones. This move
has been justified by the ideology that Jewish concerns are the
proper, authentic focus of a Jewish social ethic. It must be
noted, however, that all this has not yet produced a clear-cut,
major statistical reorientation in Jewish voting patterns, if the
presidential elections of 1980 and 1984 have been rightly
assessed.[12] The old liberal ethics of most American Jews has, in
any case, surely lost its old elan and weakened to the point
where it may well soon become empty. Historically, it is far too
early to say what is likely to happen or when, and events in this
century have been so unpredictable that speculation is most
unwise.

Intellectually, the issue before Jews as individuals and as a
community may be put this way: should the social ethic of
contemporary Judaism as it concerns general society be achieved
indirectly, as a side effect of particular Jewish observance, or
should it be another major, direct, active concern of faithful
Jews, comparable in some measure to their devotion to the
Jewish community in its service of God?

I respond to this question speaking officially for myself
alone, but articulating a position which I suggest many American
Jews roughly share socially, though not perhaps theologically.

We too are deeply concerned about Jewish authenticity and
therefore have no wish to gloss over the failings of doctrinaire
Jewish liberalism. Any Jewish ethic worthy of that name cannot
be purely universalistic, so concerned with humanity it has no
interest in the Jewish people. Jews loyal to the Covenant with

God must necessarily accept the responsibilities that places upon them to build their specific community and through it bring humankind to its messianic goal.

With all that, a word is in order in defense of a previous generation of Jewish universalists. They may have allowed their enthusiasm at the emancipation of the Jews to carry them too far in jettisoning Judaism's protective particularity. They should also have had a more realistic view of human nature and social change. For all that, their radicalism accomplished much for their less adventuresome fellow-Jews. They articulated the ethic by which Jews still participate in general society, developed a style for Jewish involvement in general causes, accomplished much to improve human welfare, and served as living proof that one can be a proud Jew and thoroughly involved in the great social issues of our time. The challenge of their stance still cannot be ignored: will we long remain a vital community if in our democratic situation we try to reinstitute a ghetto orientation to Judaism?

By this brief digression I wish most emphatically to deny that the faults of Jewish liberalism totally invalidate its substance. The choice before us is not the either/or of a tarnished liberalism versus a refurbished, modernized traditionalism. Modern Orthodoxy and right-wing Conservatism, both strongly linked with the move to right-of-center or rightist political stands, would not exist had they not adopted much of the pioneering liberals' ideology. Right-wing Orthodoxy, as indicated by its fanatic, antipluralistic acts in the United States and the State of Israel, is too self-centered for most of us to accept it as an authentic Judaism for modern Jews. An excessive universalism need not be replaced by a particularism so overwhelming it has little direct interest in the pressing concerns of humankind. There are many Jews who counsel that we withdraw from the social arena except where Jewish interests are at stake or our allies in achieving them require our help. The older liberals have convinced many of us that Jews, having been welcomed as equals in society, should now understand that our faith demands of us that we share in seeking to meet the problems all human beings now confront even as we give special attention to the specific needs of our own people.

Our ethical choice hinges largely on our interpretation of our recent history. What does our experience of Emancipation from the ghetto mean to us? Ought it to bring us to introduce a major change in the traditional Jewish social ethic, making it more universally oriented and activist in seeking to attain its newly inclusive goals, or, in limited response to our new freedom, ought it to cause us only to extend when necessary our classic inner-oriented social ethic? On theological as well as practical grounds, I believe the Emancipation should influence our understanding of Judaism as profoundly as it now seems to us the destruction of the Second Temple did when it ushered in the era of rabbinic Judaism. Further, as I shall explain in due course, I do not consider the Holocaust to have invalidated the universal imperative of the Emancipation but, if anything, further to have reinforced it.

Let me begin my response on the practical level. The Jewish people, through its major centers in the State of Israel, the United States, and other free countries, has indissolubly linked its destiny with the other free peoples. Should there be a major energy crisis, an economic collapse, radical atmospheric pollution, a global failure of democracy, an atomic war, the Jews will not escape unscathed. I cannot respond to such threats as easily as Jews of the ghetto era would have done by saying, as some Jews still do today, "What has all that to do with us? The people of Israel is eternal. God will guard us." Most of us live too intimately as part of Western society not to be deeply affected by its failures and successes, and all but the most self-isolated of our Hasidim would suffer significant spiritual dislocation if they could no longer live as free, emancipated Jews.

If so, we have a simple ethical responsibility to help those among whom we live shape our mutual destiny. Jews of other centuries were not allowed to share in the determination of their society's policies. We, having both the situation and the incentive, have become socially involved in ways unknown to other Jewries, and rightly so. Any retreat from this activist stance ought to be fought as inappropriate to our radically altered sociopolitical situation.

That argument can legitimately be extended. Having gained exceptionally from our freedom, as the result of great industry and application, to be sure, Jews have a special responsibility to give of their gains to society. To make a contribution only to the extent others do would seem too little on several counts. Most people do not give very much of themselves for the sake of society, one reason conditions are as bad as they are today. Many others, having benefited modestly from our social order, have neither the means, the energy, nor the know-how to do very much for anyone but themselves. It seems only morally right that those who have had greater success should give a greater proportion of their strength and their means to help those less fortunate. Then the Jews, who have fared spectacularly well in the United States, have a simple ethical responsibility to work for the common good in special devotion. And the long heritage of Jewish social concern should spur Jews on to bolster a society which makes it an important part of its life to promote the welfare of its indigent, handicapped, and otherwise deprived citizens.

On a more spiritual level, I want to argue that two of the great experiences of Diaspora Jewry in our time mandate a strong commitment to a universal ethic. In the first case, the Holocaust, I partially agree with the Jewish right. Jews ought to continue their exemplary response to the death of the 6,000,000 and the threat to all of us by vigorously upbuilding and furthering Jewish life today. I differ with those Jews who argue that the cruelty of the Nazis, the indifference of the "good Germans," and the callousness of the Allies' leaders demonstrates that Jews have no genuine share in Western society.. We have been the classic outsider for millennia, they say, and despite surface changes we remain the great available victim.

I readily concede that Jews ought not to underestimate the continuing virulence of anti-Semitism or overestimate the changes wrought by some decades of democracy, goodwill, and ecumenism. But if we deny that a common standard of goodness applies between all human beings, strongly enough to command them to override their group concerns so as to respect the humanity of those their folk considers aliens, how can we fault the Germans for their bestial ethnocentrism? If there is no universal ethics which one should follow even under extraordinary social pressure, how can we condemn the Nazis and those who quietly went along with them? And if out of the bitterness of our suffering we insist upon the paramount importance of such interhuman responsibility, then how can we not exemplify it in our own lives? Instead of responding to the utter negativity of the Holocaust by confining our social concern largely to ourselves, thereby validating group moralities, we ought to demonstrate its evil by our own active concern for people far removed from our immediate situation.

I cannot leave the argument there. I do not see that we can insist today that the promise of the Emancipation finally be fulfilled by the Western world if we do not ourselves resolutely affirm and live by universal ethical standards. We may claim rights among humankind because all people are part of one human family and ought to live in equal status, though that requires them to overcome millennial prejudices in which, as individuals and as classes, they have many vested interests. And, again, if we demand that others ought to effectuate that ideal, so should we who proclaim it, presumably because it is true and not merely because it now benefits us.

To me the Emancipation, for all its equivocation and unrealized promises, is a religious experience reminiscent in its own lesser way of the great revelatory exodus of our people from Egypt. Recent generations of Jews also passed from a long, painful "slavery" to a new freedom, and that passage should become a new motive for Jewish social behavior even as the ancient redemption motivated our people's social legislation— "you know the heart of the stranger, for you were strangers in the land of Egypt." Particularly as we begin to move personally away from that transition, we need to memorialize the experience of our release from the ghetto, *shtetl,* and *mellah* so that it can shape our social consciousness. Few people in our society know intimately what it means to suffer for centuries as pariahs and then come to positions of power and influence. Our own family histories teach us that a society is judged best by the way it treats its most powerless people, those the Bible once identified as the widow, the stranger, and the orphan. Today, Jews are in a unique position to identify with and help do something for such sufferers. We ought to accept that as our modern Jewish duty in order to be true to what we ourselves have endured and what we know we share with all other human beings.

In responding to the Holocaust and our Emancipation by dedication to action for the redemption of all humanity, I believe we can set a proper model of human behavior before all creatures. That is a far cry from the old liberal notion of the mission of Israel to all humankind, but in our contemporary confused and troubled human situation, it is hardly less an exaltation of the people of Israel's potential historic role. And its high estimation of the Jewish people comes from no assertion of Jewish spiritual superiority or expectations of what we shall actually accomplish, but only of what may result when we respond in Covenant faithfulness to what has happened to us.

Two pragmatic considerations seem to me to prompt the Jewish community to take an activist stance in social-ethical matters. The first is a reiteration of the classic modernist perception of the best long-range strategy for securing Jewish security, that Jews will fare better in a society more adequately meeting the needs of its citizens. If so, for their own sake, Jews ought to be involved in trying to overcome the major problems of the society. In doing so, they should be particularly concerned about the rights of underprivileged groups, for their treatment mirrors what may next happen to the Jews.

None of the recent traumas of Jewish history has changed the truth of these assertions. True, there are no guarantees of Jewish security; and Jews cannot do very much to change society or decisively alter its established patterns of inequity; and these social tasks do not nearly conduce to Jewish survival as much as will direct involvement in traditional Jewish responsibilities. Differently put, an outer-oriented Jewish social ethics ought not to take on the messianic dimensions for us that it did for a previous generation. Our hard-learned realism may temper our immediate expectations. It constitutes no reason to deny what our ideals and our enlightened self-interest motivate us to do with our lives.

I should like to suggest a second practical reason for not confining our energies largely to our own community. When we need political allies to help us fight for our cause should some Jewish interest be at stake, we shall be unlikely to find them or to find them receptive if we have not been available when they were carrying on their own struggle for greater social justice. Being a tiny minority in America—perhaps 5,800,000 in a population of over 220,000,000—we must depend on the goodwill of others in order to sway the democratic process. Our potential allies need to be able to count on us for regular aid. Better yet, we may best expect to gain the support we seek when the people we desire it from already stand in our debt for our having long been at their side in their fights.

We cannot, however, any longer assert unequivocally that the liberal rather than the conservative political program is necessarily the better or the more ethical way of achieving Judaism's vision of the good society. The old, dogmatic equation of Jewish ethics with political liberalism no longer is convincing. The transfer of religious ideals to concrete social plans always involves highly complex and contingent considerations. No point of view may reasonably claim that it invariably has the whole truth on such matters. Liberalism can assert a special affinity to biblical ethics because of its concern with benefiting the masses directly and its insistence on taking immediate social action to do so. Nonetheless, its recent record of ambiguous results has vitiated much of its theoretical promise and made it necessary to ask whether in any given instance the conservative option may not better effectuate our ethical goals. As with so much of our life, a revitalized Jewish social ethic must make room for a vigorous pluralism, in this case of political judgment, and out of a thoughtful dialectic over appropriate means, speak to the inquiring Jew.

In one fundamental respect, however, the liberal position seems to me to have special validity to anyone who takes the modern Jewish experience seriously. The Emancipation of the Jews did not come about by benignly waiting for internal developments, market forces, the private sector, or personal growth to grant Jews rights. It came by government initiative. Only in countries where governments acted and formally granted Jews equality and then demanded, if slowly, that their often unwilling citizenries live up to that grant, did Jews truly enter society. Unless Jews are prepared to deny the experience of their own families and ethnic group, they must emphatically reject the notion that government has no proper role in the moral improvement of the social order. Without resolute government leadership in furthering the goals of democracy—in America so closely linked to those of the Bible—the ethical dimensions of our social life may be counted on to contract. Human nature and social interaction being what they are, exploitation, injustice, and what the rabbis poignantly call "free hatred" will slowly but certainly strengthen their hold on our lives. Conservatives, who claim to be realists about human beings, ought to see that as clearly as they see the corruption of good government by those who must operate it. Whenever we are sensitive to the distance we still remain from our social ideals, we must ask what we can all do together, through government, the one "community" through which we all can act as one, to achieve them. And that is not to say that governmental action is always indicated because we consider it the only, the infallible, or the ultimate source of social transformation.

But for me and some other Jews, the most compelling reason for an activist Jewish social ethic is theological. The Emancipation has simply changed our view of what God wants of Jews in relation to all humankind. Or more precisely put, the changed horizon of effective Jewish social ethics exposed by the new scope given Jews for their lives has helped us realize that until recently Jews were only partially able to envisage and effectuate their duty to God. Having gained a broader vision of humankind, Jews like me can no longer delimit what we intuit God wants of us as overwhelmingly, if not exclusively, consisting of acts oriented to our own community.

The classic biblical and rabbinic chasm between Jews and gentiles does not yawn as deeply between us and our neighbors, and many bridges connect us with one another. We all stand before the same God. To be sure, we still find continuing merit, some would say cosmic significance, in sustaining our side of our people's distinctive Covenant with God. At the same time, we have come in ever more intimate ways to recognize our common humanity with gentiles. In very many ways, particularly in many moral and spiritual aspirations and not merely in our joint human needs, we are very much like one another. Working with one another, studying together, cooperating in various community projects, we cannot easily ignore how precious all humankind is to our God and therefore needs to be to us. And our personal postghetto perspective, so radically extended by our education outside of classic Jewish texts and now regularly stretched by the wonders of electronic communication and jet travel, keeps expanding. We can envisage a day when we consider the entire globe our neighborhood and everyone in it the neighbor we are called upon to love even as we love ourselves.

For us, proclaiming God is one must freshly mean appreciating and living out God's active care and concern for all human beings. Acting on that faith, we must devote ourselves in considerable measure to working with all people and not just with other Jews to make the sovereignty of God real on earth.

To this extent the Emancipation has been revelatory; it has given us a more extensive intuition of what God expects of us by having set us in these radically changed social circumstances. For all our disappointments and suffering in these near two centuries of freedom, Jews such as me still believe in the promise of the new, inclusive social order into which we have come and now comprise so integral a part. Authentically living by our people's Covenant with God in this time and place necessarily yields a conception of Jewish duty expanded from that which evolved in the previous fifteen hundred years of isolation, segregation, and persecution. And that has led some Jews to an activist Jewish social ethic which we believe our community as a whole will ignore or forget only at the cost of its great spiritual peril.

Notes

1. Gen. 2:18.
2. Gen. 11:1–9.
3. Note the command as well as the promise in Gen. 12:1–3, the first mention of the Covenant relation and its entailments.
4. See the most helpful article by Sid Z. Leiman, "Jewish Ethics 1970–75: Retrospect and Prospect," *Religious Studies Review*, 2, no. 2 (April, 1976): 16–22. It not only provides a listing of all the relevant writings for those years, but includes translations and other materials dealing with the history of Jewish ethics. I know of nothing comparable for the years since. Leiman's qualifications notwithstanding, I suggest that Sh'ma: *A Journal of Jewish Responsibility* remains the best way of remaining in touch with the scope and variety of contemporary

Jewish ethical concerns, though I am not a disinterested observer.

5. So already my "The Postsecular Situation of Jewish Theology," *Theological Studies*, 31, no. 3 (September, 1970): 460–475.

6. Dawidowicz and Goldstein, "The American Jewish Liberal Tradition," in *The American Jewish Community*, ed. Marshall Sklare (New York: Behrman, 1974), and see the bibliography there on "The Politics of American Jewry," pp. 372 f. Also Eugene B. Borowitz, *The Mask Jews Wear* (New York: Simon & Schuster, 1973), chaps. 2–4.

7. Much of what follows is speculative, but it is not uninformed or essentially ideological pleading. In general, minorities reflect majority trends; Jews, still quite eager to belong and not be thought too different, reflect majority currents faithfully if in idiosyncratic ways. Indeed, they are so sensitive to certain winds of social change that they often serve as a good indicator of the new directions most Americans will one day take, e.g., the almost universal adoption of contraception among modernized Jews in the 1920s.

8. Milton Himmelfarb, an astute observer of the American Jewish community and an early, trenchant critic of its unreflective liberalism (*The Jews of Modernity* [New York: Basic Books, 1973]), denies that a class shift is responsible for any Jewish voting change. Jews in poor, not well-to-do precincts are more likely to vote Republican. See his "Are Jews Becoming Republican," *Commentary* 72, no. 2 (August, 1981): 27–31 and Lucy Dawidowicz, "Politics, the Jews, and the '84 Election," *Commentary* 79, no. 2 (February, 1985): 25–30.

9. Because this sector of the community is inner-directed, where it publishes, it tends to do so in a Jewish language, Yiddish (*sic*), but not modern Hebrew. Being wary of the gentile world, it confines the full strength of its views to oral communication. Some sense of these subterranean attitudes may be gained from perusing the issues of the weekly English newspaper, the *Jewish Press*. A more accommodationist but still militantly rightist stance is taken by the *Jewish Observer*, the slick monthly publication of Agudath Israel, the somewhat non-Zionist Orthodox international religious organization.

10. For an early statement of a thoughtful revisionism, see Charles S. Liebman, *The Ambivalent American Jew* (Philadelphia: Jewish Publication Society, 1973), chaps. 7 and 8. In reading Jakob Petuchowski's "The Limits of Self-Sacrifice" (in *Modern Jewish Ethics* [Columbus: Ohio State University Press, 1975]), one should bear in mind that "self-sacrifice" means the liberal suggestion that Jews put devotion to the general welfare ahead of certain specific Jewish interests.

11. For a more detailed statement of the argument concerning the State of Israel plus a deeper analysis of those points on which I

argue that the old liberalism needs to be modified, see my "Rethinking the Reform Jewish Attitude to Social Action," *Journal of Reform Judaism* 27, no. 4 (Fall 1980): 1–19.

    12. See the data and attitudes of the articles cited in note 8.

Social Justice in the Other Protestant Tradition: A Hispanic Perspective

Orlando E. Costas

The question of social justice in the Protestant tradition is both complicated and relative. It is complicated because it has involved an impressive variety of approaches, movements, and ethical theologians.[1] Yet this variety is sharply reduced the moment one notes the sociohistorical context of the literature on the subject: it reflects by and large the world of those who have shaped (and deformed) history in the last five hundred years. Indeed one is amazed at the way this literature assumes a universal character when in fact it is situated in the experience of the North Atlantic world.

There is, however, another Protestant tradition, situated in a different sociohistorical reality. On a worldwide level, this tradition is linked with the Third World. In the United States, it is represented by oppressed racial minorities.[2] As a member of one of these minorities, I have chosen to analyze the question from that perspective. This means that we will have to examine the social role of the minority church in the American socioreligious milieu because it is in the relationship of minorities to the dominant society that we can detect how that other Protestant tradition has coped with the issues of social justice.

Religion and society in the United States have been shaped by people of different cultural, racial, linguistic, and national backgrounds. For many years, however, "ethnicity" was seen as a stumbling block in the American historical project. The emphasis was put on the so-called melting pot. The quicker a group lost its language or cultural and national identity, the greater the reward it would receive from society.

But the "melting pot" theory failed; ethnicity remained. It is a stubborn reality that won't go away! A series of novels, films, academic programs plus more than one hundred cultural groups that communicate in their own language and dialects are a living demonstration of the cultural pluralism of the United States.

Why and how did the melting pot fail? It failed for at least two reasons. First, ethnicity provided political-economic power to many non-Anglo-Saxon European migrants. Irish, Jewish, Central European, and Italian migrants and their descendants were able to gain a strong political and economic base thanks to their ethnic solidarity. Second, ethnicity made possible the survival of other, non-European marginated groups. Racial prejudice and socioeconomic hostility condemned these "ethnic" groups to impoverished rural communities, urban ghettos, or reservations. They were able to survive their oppressed condition through ethnic solidarity.

Protestant and Catholic churches as well as Jewish temples and synagogues have always been in the center of the ethnic problem. American religious institutions are a direct offspring of the ethnic experience.[3] Among Protestants, however, many argued, for many years, that ethnic churches were destined to disappear. Such predictions turned out to be totally false. Today one finds ethnic churches along the length and breadth of this country.

How does the ethnic-minority church appear in an oppressive society like the United States? What is its role in view of the fact that it must live and carry its mission in a society that has traditionally expressed its value system, prejudices, and unjust structures through religious communities? In other words, what does it mean for the church of oppressed American ethnic minorities to live and work under a dominant church and society? Before we can give a credible response to this question, we need to trace the roots of the ethnic resurgence of the last decades and locate the sociohistorical context of ethnicity. This will enable us to note a basic difference between the traditional ethnic groups (European) and the racial minorities (non-European), which in turn will help us to identify the social role of the minority church and outline its ethical response.

THE ROOTS OF THE ETHNIC RESURGENCE

Already in the late 1950s and early 1960s the melting pot theory began to show signs of collapse. In 1963, Nathan Glazer and Daniel Moynihan published their book *Beyond the Melting Pot.*[4] In this work, they demonstrate how the largest city in the country, New York, was a mosaic of strong ethnic groups (Blacks, Hispanics, Irish, and Jews). By 1975, the melting pot theory had become so outmoded and, conversely, "ethnicity" had become so widely recognized as a fundamental aspect of American society, that these same authors edited a new book, this time showing how ethnicity was an *international* phenomenon[5] (something which cultural anthropologists have been saying for years!). The United States was not so unique after all! Yet it was not until the sixties that this truth began really to hit home.

During this decade the impracticality of the melting pot model became ever more evident. Mainstream society became aware of the fact that in the United States there were many groups with diverse cultural backgrounds which carried out their lives in accordance with their cultural roots and had begun to openly challenge the assimilationist pattern of mainstream society. American society began to be called a "stew pot" rather than a "melting pot."[6]

But how did these groups gather enough courage to make such a challenge? What was the turning point? While some European ethnics would argue that it was due to the sheer presence and militancy of the various cultural institutions that have existed all along the twentieth century,[7] I would insist that the decisive blow to the melting pot theory was given by the black cultural awareness movement.

This movement was spearheaded by the political struggle for civil rights, which came to a head in the mid-sixties. At first, the focus of this struggle was institutional racism. It got its support from liberals and had an assimilationist bent to it. Within a few years, however, the civil rights movement spilled over into a sociocultural awakening.

A new generation of black leaders, such as Stokely Carmichael, Eldridge Cleaver, and Malcolm X, saw that the road to integration was a dead end. They concluded that whites as a whole would never allow blacks really to assimilate. White racism would continue to impede the black community from becoming an equal part of American society. Whites would not relinquish power; they would not only continue to control the basic institutions of American society, but would see to it that the black community as such was kept from them. These leaders concluded, further, that the only way that the black community could become truly free was by gaining political power. Thus the civil rights movement gave way to the black power movement. The "white way of life" was formally rejected. Blacks began to rediscover the beauty of their own race and culture and launched a fascinating process of reverse acculturation which included a vigorous quest for their historical roots in West Africa.[8] They stopped apologizing for their "blackness"; they stopped imitating "whitey"; they affirmed with pride that "black is beautiful."

Neither a growing cultural awareness nor the acquisition of political power could, in and of itself, liberate blacks, however, from the situation of poverty and marginalization that the majority of Afro-Americans had been condemned to in the ghettos of our northern, midwestern, and southwestern cities, and the rural communities of the South. This abject condition called for a deeper struggle—the struggle for socioeconomic justice. It was the awareness of this reality that led to the celebration of the National Black Economic Development Conference in Detroit, Michigan, in April 1969. This conference adopted a Black Manifesto, presented by James Forman, which declared:

> We have come from all over the country burning with anger and despair...with the miserable economic plight of our people....There can be no separation of the problem of our economic, political, and cultural degradation....We...are fully aware that we have been forced to come together because racist white America has exploited our resources, our minds, our bodies, our labor. For centuries, we have been forced to live as colonized people inside the United States, victimized by the most vicious, racist system in the world. We have helped to build the most industrial country in the world.[9]

Therefore, the manifesto goes on to demand reparations totaling $500 million from "white Christian churches and Jewish synagogues, which are part and parcel of the system of capitalism." Leaving aside our positive or negative judgment of the political wisdom of this document, its strong economic language suffices to underscore the fact that by the end of the sixties Blacks were no longer talking the language of racial integration but rather of socioeconomic justice.

Such a process could not but have a "conscientizing" effect on other oppressed sectors of American society. Native Americans resumed their struggle against the American government and society, after years of seemingly quiet resignation.[10] The descendants of immigrants from Asia and the Pacific, some of whom had a long history of labor protest in Hawaii, began to make their voices felt in the mainland; native Hawaiians began to do what in their gracious, tolerant ways they had failed to do during the nineteenth century: resist! For their part Hispanics, especially in their Chicano (Mexican-American) and Puerto Rican variants, began to experience a cultural awakening of their own and entered a process of politicization.

By the beginning of the seventies, the dominant (white) society was feeling threatened. Traditional European ethnic power groups began to react. Political analysts like Michael Novak[11] and sociologists like Andrew Greeley[12] began to argue that blacks and other non-European minorities were not the only ones who had been oppressed in American society; they too had been victimized by the same sector, namely, white Anglo-Saxon Protestants![13] Novelists like Taylor Caldwell[14] and Howard Fast[15] dramatized the rise of European ethnics from poverty and powerlessness to wealth and power.

To the resurgence of European ethnics there must be added the emergence of the feminist movement. An impressive list of books authored by a long list of women theologians, philosophers, and historians, coupled with the historic strength of women's organizations, gave a new visibility to the oppressed and powerless reality of American women. Rightly, they too raised their voices, demanding equal treatment as a bona fide oppressed American minority. Interestingly, though, the American feminist movement, like European ethnics, not only marked a devastating attack against white Anglo-Saxon male–dominated culture but also marked a protest movement whose members are by and large *white*.[16]

The traditional Anglo-Saxon sectors responded to the white ethnic and feminist offensives with the idea of a "new pluralism." Increasingly admitting that the United States was not a melting pot but rather a stew pot, these sectors began to accentuate the beauty of cultural diversity. Thus, rather than forcing each group to be like the other, every group began to be encouraged to "do its own thing." No longer was assimilation required to be a good red-blooded American; the important thing now was belonging to a cultural group and finding your roots.

American individualism, which had looked suspiciously upon any citizen or resident who searched for a cultural identity outside the "American experience," was now transformed into a new sociopolitical line: the identity-by-group individualism. Hence, any group or sector can have a piece of the pie—and non-European minority groups can continue to have the same piece they always had!

THE NEW PLURALISM AND THE MAJORITY CHURCH

The fact of a new cultural pluralism has extraordinary implications for the church. For one, it implies that people prefer to worship God in a culturally comfortable environment; hence, the confirmation of the "homogeneous unit principle" (HUP), advanced several decades ago by the American missiologist Donald A. McGavran as a result of his pastoral/missiological observations in India. According to McGavran, "people like to become Christians without crossing cultural barriers." In other words, the less culturally threatened they feel, the easier it is to lead them to conversion.

The new pluralism implies, secondly, that the so-called divisions of the church along ethnic lines should not be considered a liability for the church's mission, but rather an asset. The old expression, "Eleven o'clock Sunday morning is the most segregated hour in America," can now be seen as a tremendous potential for the growth and expansion of the church. The church does not have to let itself be bogged down by its ethnic diversity; it can encourage these groups and grow in the process.

The acceptance and celebration of ethnic pluralism in the church implies, thirdly, that white Anglo-Saxon Protestant

(WASP) churches need not feel guilty about their homogeneity. Their conscience has been set free. They can continue to concentrate their evangelistic and pastoral ministry among "their own kind" seriously and enthusiastically.

These implications have been defended by C. Peter Wagner, McGavran's protégé and successor at the Fuller School of World Mission, in his book *Our Kind of People*.[17] This book attempts to be an ethical defense of HUP. Working largely on the sociological theory of Andrew Greeley and the ethnopolitical analyses of Michael Novak, Wagner tries to apply McGavran's principle to ethnic American society. For Wagner, the fact that assimilationist and integrationist models for understanding society have been proven inadequate is reason enough to call for pluralistic models of sociological interpretation. He argues that McGavran's "image of cultural mosaic, separate pieces which together compose a beautiful whole, is a pluralistic model." He claims that "whites such as Wilt Campbell and Joseph Hough and blacks such as [Gayraud] Wilmore and [Reuben] Shearers" have developed "positions similar to McGavran's."[18] Whether these authors would agree with Wagner's contention remains to be seen. Be that as it may, Wagner's real point is not as much to prove the relevance of HUP for American society as to show its strategic importance for the American church.

> The new climate for accepting a diversity of peoples as proper in American society favors the development of Christian churches along homogeneous lines. The great majority of America's 330,000 churches are, of course, already homogeneous. But many of them have been made to feel guilty about their homogeneity by the theological attitude that condemned eleven o'clock on Sunday morning as being the most segregated hour in America.[19]

He further argues that in a society that celebrates pluralism, churches should be allowed to "develop freely within just one piece of the sociological mosaic."[20] Indeed not only does such development guarantee a faster rate of growth, but it overcomes the problem of racial and cultural barriers. Consequently, the homogeneous unit principle is for Wagner both sociologically correct and ethically valid.[21]

I see several loopholes in Wagner's argument. One of them is its pragmatic base. Pragmatism is an indigenous American philosophical thought that locates truth in what works. For Wagner developing homogeneous unit churches is ethical, first and foremost, because it brings about rapid (numerical) church growth. The melting pot theory, assimilationist models, and integration are wrong because they have not worked. The stew pot theory is correct because this is the reality of American society. Success or failure makes a practice right or wrong.

In my opinion, however, the melting pot theory is wrong, not because it has not worked, but rather because it has a wrong (hidden) agenda: the overpowering of minority groups by the dominant society. Integration, as a social, political, and economic goal, is not wrong because it has not worked, but rather because mainstream American society has persistently refused, except under pressure (as with the Japanese in Hawaii), to share its *collective* wealth, privileges, and power with racial ethnic minorities. Eleven o'clock Sunday morning is not the most racist hour in the country because it is bad for people to worship God in their own language and culture. Rather it is a racist event because segregated worship services are the outcome of a consistent policy of rejection and exclusion of people of different race, language, and nationalities on the part of many mainstream Christians. This is evident today in the lack of concern one can witness in many mainstream worship services over the plight of oppressed ("nonwhite") minorities. The hymns that are sung, the sermons that are preached, the announcements that are given, and the distribution of the offerings that are collected show what little priority is given to these minorities. For all practical purposes they do not exist.

To be sure, one could (and should) make a *pastoral* case for homogeneous unit churches. To start, such churches would be legitimate on pastoral grounds because that is where people are at, and the only way one can reach them with the gospel and minister to their needs is by meeting them on their own turf. In so doing, however, one should maintain the integrity of the gospel, refusing to reinforce their prejudice and alienation and enabling them to experience liberation from the immoral and antigospel values of the surrounding milieu.

But to argue for homogeneous unit churches on a pragmatic basis, to promote church growth on church-condoned racial/ cultural segregation and socioeconomic exclusivism, is to assume that evil *as such* can be made an instrument of good. Indeed, it is to say that the end (people becoming Christians, or simply church growth) justifies the means (the reinforcement of segregation and exclusivism).

Secondly, Wagner's argument reflects historical insensitivity. He is quick to point out the disillusionment of many blacks with integration. He quotes generously ethnic-liberation theologians who rightly castigate the cultural/ideological chauvinism of mainstream church and theology. He pulls out numerous statistics, shares illustrations, calls social researchers to the witness stand, to show why it is better to evangelize "our kind of people."

Wagner, however, fails to explain why black and other racial-minority churches came into being in the first place. For him the problem is simply one of "feelings" or culture ("doing things our way"), even of social class (income, education, and vocation). But he does not ask what *really* led to such a radical difference between "white" (ethnic or WASP) middle-class churches and their "nonwhite" (largely poor, but also middle-class) counterpart.

It is true that people like to meet with their own kind. It is also true that white ethnics felt the need to have their own churches and institutions in order to provide cultural, social, and psychological solidarity. Many of these institutions, however, were brought along from the old country. It was their bridge to the past as well as to the present.

But most black and other racial-minority churches owe their existence, first and foremost, to their *rejection* by dominant churches. White churches did not want to receive blacks into full membership, and those who later agreed to do it, did it, by and large, on their own terms: they accepted them as long as they remained a voiceless minority; once they became active and numerous, the white membership started to flee or retrenched into covert, and at times overt, racist policies. It was, therefore, out of the painful experience of *racism* that many non-European minority churches came into being. To bypass this fundamental reality is to be historically insensitive. To forget this historical calvary is to make the celebration of ethnicity in the church empty and shallow. It is like having an Easter celebration without Good Friday.

Thirdly, Wagner's thesis suffers from a shallow hermeneutic. He locates the theological rationale for HUP on creation. Wagner sees in the biblical doctrine of creation, God's endorsement of cultural diversity. Indeed, it is God's will that the human race develop in separate groups. Thus, rather than think of the nations in Genesis 11:1–9 as an outcome of God's judgment, as many of the better-known scholars hold, Wagner argues that what God had intended from the beginning was a pluralistic race, but at Babel humankind tried to frustrate God's plan by creating one city, one nation, and one language. He states that

> God intervened and decided to accelerate his program for the decentralization of humankind, so he "confused the language of the earth." (Gen. 11:9) This, of course, was a punitive act, but it was also preventive. It was designed to prove to men and women that they could not frustrate God's plan for human pluralism.[22]

Having read HUP into God's creation plan, Wagner jumps to the New Testament, where he sees a rich cultural mosaic. He sees Jesus as an HUP strategist. According to Wagner, "Jesus knew that the movement he was initiating needed first to be rooted solidly among Aramaic-speaking Jews, his own homogeneous unit, if it were later to gather the necessary strength to spread among Greek-speaking Jews, then to Samaritans, and then to Gentiles 'to the end of the earth' (Acts 1:8)."[23] He also interprets Luke's recording of the early Christian mission in Acts in homogeneous terms. He argues that Paul did not mix Hebrews and Hellenists, Jews and Greeks, Egyptians and Parthenians in the same local house churches. Wagner sees in Paul a concept of equal-but-separate church development. Therefore, when Paul "speaks of Christian believers being 'all one in Christ,' he is referring not to a normative pattern for local congregations, but rather to the supra-congregational relationship of believers in the total Christian body over which Christ himself is the head (Eph. 1:22–23)."[24]

Wagner is right in arguing that God has endowed all creatures with cultural diversity. But he misses the fundamental issue of the early Genesis account, namely, that the God who created the human family and commanded it to be fruitful and multiply, giving it everything it needed to live harmoniously under his Lordship, had to bring into being one special people in order to bless all the peoples of the earth (Gen. 12:1–3). Wagner does not take account of the fact that it was precisely this universal vocation that Israel failed to fulfill because of the desire to be great "like the other nations," and a concomitant, growing ethnocentrism (revealed in the apparent urban bias of the Babel story). It was this ethnocentric ideology that led many in Israel to see themselves as "the center of the world" (Ezek. 5:5) rather than God's witnesses upon the earth. But a vocal minority (reflected, for example, in the prophecies of Isaiah, especially Isa. 19:18, 23–25) insisted that the goal of God's mission was not to perpetuate nationalistic structures, but rather to do a new thing, namely, create new heavens and a new earth (cf. Isa. 66:18–24). By passing over the tensions in the Old Testament between ethnocentrism and universalism, Wagner is able to use the Book of Genesis to back up his views on ethnicity. That might be ideologically clever, but it is theologically irresponsible.

Something similar occurs with the New Testament. Wagner approaches the Gospels as if they had been written by Jesus and gives them a homogeneous-like quality. He does not give any consideration to the complex mixture of the traditions that shaped them. He says that Jesus was a Galilean, but does not ask about its theological significance in Mark's Gospel. Nor does Wagner consider the probable redactional origin of Matthew's Gospel in a mixed Jewish-Gentile congregation in Syria (ca. 85 A.D.). He quotes at length the Acts of the Apostles, but bypasses the highly significant Gentile/universalistic account of Luke's Gospel. He conjectures about the possibility of several homogeneous unit congregations in Rome, but does not grapple exegetically and theologically with the message of Paul's Roman letter. He elevates the Pauline concept of Christian unity to a "supra-congregational principle" by constructing a "homogeneous unit context" in the churches linked to the Pauline mission, barely noting the significant number of scholars who argue differently, and giving preferential treatment to the few that do, but he does not deal exegetically with the Pauline epistles as such. Thus, rather than seeking to understand the context of the Pauline churches internally (from the text), he determines it from the outside.

From the foregoing, it appears that Wagner has elevated HUP to a biblical hermeneutical key. As an effort to understand the gospel from a particular sociocultural situation, such an attempt is legitimate and commendable. But not every contemporary concept can serve as a key to unlocking the meaning of Scripture. An idea can help unlock the meaning of biblical faith only if it is broad and comprehensive enough to account for the entire biblical message and finds therein a legitimate (natural) correspondence. Unfortunately, Wagner's sloppy treatment of the Scriptures does not help him demonstrate the existence of such a natural correspondence between HUP and biblical concepts like "people" or "nation." Moreover, Wagner's analysis of the biblical roots of HUP appears so smooth and so uncomplicated that it makes the historically, culturally, and theologically complex composition of the biblical tradition appear as a twentieth-century book on church growth! Hence one remains unconvinced that HUP is sufficiently broad even to unlock the meaning of the Pauline mission, let alone the whole of biblical faith.

In my opinion, the homogeneous unit principle is a very useful concept as a pastoral/missiological observation. Used wisely (and thus critically), it can help the church establish an effective missionary link with an unevangelized community. But as an ethical maxim and a biblical hermeneutical key it has yet to prove its relevance. On the contrary, the reality of apartheid in South Africa and the history of racism in the United States and elsewhere shows us too well what can happen when one tries to elevate an empirical observation like HUP to the level of an ethical norm or a theological organizing principle—it can betray the gospel and become the basis for an ethic of neutrality and the reinforcement of the status quo.

There are those who may accuse me of blowing Wagner's book out of proportion. His influence, they would say, is not that broad in numerical mainstream Christianity. Indeed there are significant sectors in the mainstream that would vehemently disagree with his main theses.

My point in analyzing Wagner, however, is neither to magnify his influential role nor to take him as a spokesperson for mainline churches. On the contrary, Wagner is here highlighted because of his effort to defend ethically the homogeneous unit principle in the context of the new American pluralism. Wagner did not invent the latter, nor did he create its relationship with the majority American church. He simply has attempted to justify it ethically and theologically. What I have attempted to highlight in this section, therefore, is what lies behind Wagner's book, namely, the ideology of the new ethnic pluralism and its presence in the majority church.

THE NEW PLURALISM AND THE RACIAL MINORITIES

For those of us who are part of non-European ethnic minorities, the so-called new ethnic pluralism posits a new challenge. We are too well aware of the historical stigma attached to "our kind of ethnicity." Having been rejected for so long on account of the color of our skin, our diets, our speech and our life-style, we find it hard to forget the way the melting pot theory has been used as an ideological tool to force us to be assimilated under the dominant ingredients of the English language, Anglo-Saxon idiosyncrasies, and Caucasian purity. Now that we have rediscovered and reaffirmed our respective racial and cultural identities, and in view of the setback that we are currently experiencing in the small sociopolitical gains we were able to make in the past decades, we find it hard to adjust to the so-called new pluralism. Indeed this sort of pluralism smacks of the politics of *dividir y reinar* ("divide and conquer") that the people of Latin America (as well as Native Americans, Africans, Asians, and Pacific Islanders) are so familiar with.

Several years ago, the Puerto Rican cultural anthropologist Eduardo Seda Bonilla suggested that in order to understand the American ethnic reality, distinction needed to be made between the immigrants of various European nationalities and the racial minorities. He pointed out that historically there have been two possible ways of "adaptation" for American minorities. One was designated for the European immigrants, whom Seda calls "the cultural minorities." The other was reserved for non-Europeans, or "the racial minorities." He states:

For the cultural minorities, the "adaptation" started at a low point of contact with "America"; a point in which the group boundaries, the "differences," were drawn according to ethnic or cultural characteristics in contrast with the surrounding "American way of life." These differences were defined by country of origin, by languages and by religion...,literature (novels, stories, poems) and movies....The life (the culture) the immigrants brought in their emotional and intellectual baggage was condemned to disappear as they sailed past the "Statue of Liberty" into the melting pot where the "greenhorn custom" was washed away to create "full-blooded Americans."

Seda Bonilla goes on to describe the effect of this process on the second type of minorities.

Little Italies, Germantowns, Irish Shantytowns, Frenchtowns flourished throughout America, and when their inhabitants, the "natives" of these slums, had become "American" enough, most of them moved away leaving their golden streets for...the racially discriminated group, who must remain to inherit the filthy, overcrowded, crumbling tenements left behind by the "ethnics"...

For the first type of minority, all they had to do to assimilate was to change the ethnic identification: discard their culture....Once their cultural identity subsided under the American cultural identity, the door to the "silent" or socially invisible world of the majority was open; because they were "white."

For the second type...identified on the basis of "racial" stigma, shedding the cultural items that distinguished it from the American culture and taking over [its] identity, made no difference whatsoever. If anything, it made things black with a foreign accent styled after an alien way of life more attractive than to the "native son." ...Perhaps deep in their hearts majority Americans want to racially stigmatize groups to remain alien, to feel alien; out of sight, out of mind—with a memory of a home somewhere else where "white" Americans hope they will eventually return.[25]

These are strong words, but more accurate than what many would like to believe. They reveal what ethnicity looks like from the other side of the divide. Though Seda Bonilla wrote these words in the latter part of the sixties, his analysis is perhaps more relevant today than it was then, with the New Right and the antiminority socioeconomic policies of the Reagan administration.

The fact of the matter is that historically Asians and Pacific Islanders, Afro-Americans, American aborigines, and Hispanics have been classified by the majority society and mainstream culture as "nonwhites." East Asians have been labeled "yellow"; Africans and Arabs, "black"; American aborigines, "red"; and Pacific Islanders, "bronze." As for Hispanics, while it is true that they have among them Caucasian elements, the over-whelming majority of them (Mexicans, Puerto Ricans, Cubans, and Dominicans) are the hybrid descendants of Europe, Amer-india, and Africa. In the United States, anti-Hispanic feelings have passed through the color ("brown") as well as the linguistic line ("Spanish-speaking"). Hence, their "nonwhiteness" goes along with their "non-English-speaking" status. This explains why Puerto Ricans in New York were first called "Spics" and why Chicanos in the Southwest identified the majority society as "Anglo." ("Anglos are Caucasians/Europeans, not blacks, American Indians, or Asian/Pacific Islanders.)

These "nonwhite" minorities have been structured into a system of social inequality where a "relatively fixed group membership...is utilized for assigning social positions with their attendant differential rewards."[26] The basis of such strati-fication is that of Anglo ethnocentrism, competition, and power. *Ethnocentrism*, in this context, means viewing reality from the limited perspective of one's group; scaling and rating everyone else with reference to it. *Competition* implies a struggle against other social units in the achievement of wealth and prosperity. As for *power*, it is understood, in this case, as the capacity to impose one's will upon another.

Anglo ethnocentrism is the result of a long process of over-powerment and competition on the part of mainstream American society. For decades, and even centuries, mainstream society has both exploited racial minorities and seen them as a social, economic, and political threat to its own future. Thus while individual members of these minorities have been able to make it economically and even politically, Anglos have stratified collectively their respective groups, condemning them, in varying degrees, to a life of poverty, oppression, and marginalization. Black slavery; aboriginal (Indian, Hawaiian, and Alaskan) conquest, subjugation, and broken treaties; territorial occupation; the expropriation of Mexican-American lands; Hispanic, Afro-Caribbean, Asiatic, and Pacific Islander migration to provide cheap labor for American industries and agribusiness—this is the basis of the stratification that American racial minorities have suffered.

It should be no surprise to discover that when these "non-white" minorities are grouped together they represent the regions of the world that have suffered the greatest impact of Western civilization: Africa, Asia, the Pacific, Latin America, and the Caribbean. They are the offspring of those parcels of the world that have suffered the worst social, economic, and cultural rape the world has ever known. They are, therefore, the victims (in varying degrees) of what the Brazilian anthropologist Darcy Ribeiro has called "historical incorporation," i.e., the subjugation of peoples by "societies with a more highly developed technology," causing them to lose their national or group autonomy, traumatizing their culture, and denaturalizing their ethnic profile.[27] While not all American racial minorities have been incorporated historically by the dominant society in the same manner, all of them have experienced a shocking cultural trauma (much deeper than any white ethnic group). Some, like Afro-Americans, not only lost their tribal autonomy, but also experienced a denaturalization of their original ethnic profile. Yet others, like native Hawaiians and Alaskans, American Indians, Chicanos, and Puerto Ricans, became strangers in their own lands and have begun to resist the threat of ethnic denaturalization. We can say, therefore, that American racial minorities are the Third World inside the United States.

THE OTHER AMERICAN PROTESTANT CHURCH

It is out of the shattering experience of military, political, and psychological conquest,[28] economic exploitation, cultural trauma, and ethnic denaturalization that "the other American church" came into being. Such a situation has set the practical boundaries for the minority church. It is in such a context that this other church lives and carries out its mission. How does it appear in such a reality? What role does it play, and how does it understand its social responsibility?

It should be remembered that the church of American racial minorities is diverse, not only culturally but also historically, theologically, and organizationally. In fact, it is as varied and complex as the religious institutions of mainstream society. This warns us against quick generalizations. Indeed, the minority church is a very complicated web of churches.

This ecclesiastical diversity notwithstanding, there remains one common denominator, namely, the fact that minority churches have been affected, directly or indirectly, by similar sociohistorical circumstances and have responded accordingly in varying degrees. Some of them are the direct product of the missionary movement; others are indigenous. Some have been foreign cultural enclaves in their respective ethnic communities; their response to oppression and injustice has been extremely passive. Others have been bastions of cultural integrity and social activism.

Be that as it may, it is my contention that the *most active* and *socially significant* bloc of minority Protestant churches play similar roles in American society. It is the social *role* and ethical *response* of this bloc, as expressed in religious music and poetry, sermons and prayers, theological writings, and socioreligious movements and institutions, that I shall now attempt to outline.

A Place of Cultural Survival

First of all, the minority church is a place of cultural survival. It helps either to preserve or to reconstruct the value system, language, music, art, costumes, symbols, and myths of its respective communities. This has been amply documented in the case of black Americans. The black church gave cohesiveness and meaning to the experience of African slaves and their descendants. It provided them with the space to be themselves, to exercise their musical and oratorical talents, and most importantly, to interpret the meaning of their experience and cultivate hope even against hope. The church enabled Afro-Americans to pick up the pieces of their destroyed ethnic (tribal) life. With the help of white philanthropic and missionary organizations, the black church also promoted education in the Afro-American community and set the stage for the civil rights and cultural awareness movements of the last decades.

Though not as large as the Black Protestant church, Hispanic, Chinese, Japanese, and most recently Korean Protestant churches have helped preserve their respective languages and cultures. In a time when there was no bilingual education, when schools encouraged monolingualism and discouraged parents from speaking to children in their own tongue, when the "old ways of life" were ridiculed and the "American way" was exalted, the church of these minorities kept their languages, values, and customs alive. Even when there was a break with certain values of the indigenous culture, as in the case of the Holiness and Pentecostal churches, their withdrawal into a countercultural enclave has often meant the repossession of cultural values that were lost in the process of acculturation by their mainline sister churches.

Thus, for example, while Hispanic mainline Protestant churches (Methodist, Presbyterian, Baptist, etc.) assimilated, in varying degrees, the worship patterns of their Anglo counterparts, it was the Pentecostals who brought into the church the musical creativity of the Latin American world. Indeed Pentecostals not only legitimized the use of indigenous instruments like the guitar, maracas, and güiros in worship, but also encouraged the spontaneous rhythmic expressions of the Hispanic soul. The Hispanic Pentecostal church had to withdraw from the larger cultural-church milieu in order to recover and preserve fundamental traits that are today recognized in many mainline churches as essential aspects of Hispanic culture.

A Signpost of Protest and Resistance

Secondly, the minority church has been a signpost of protest and resistance, "the heart of a world that has no heart" (Marx). The very fact that it has survived against all sorts of odds—from financial and political to ecclesiastical and theological—speaks for itself.

Historically, the dominant church has viewed its minority counterpart as either an esoteric foreign enclave, a threat to the unity of the universal church, or a "mission station." The fact of the matter is, however, that the minority church has been a disturbing sign on the fringes of an unjust society. By its sheer presence, it has been a prophetic indictment against the racism, political oppression, economic exploitation, and sociocultural marginalization which have been such a constituent part of the American way of life. Unfortunately, the mainstream church has had way too many vested interests in the policies, practices, and institutions that shape national life. Therefore, it has sought, consciously or unconsciously, to protect those interests and thus justify, ethically and theologically, the behavior of its mainstream constituency. Yet it has had to contend with the gospel's commitment to the poor and the oppressed, its passionate denouncement of personal and social sin, and its anticipation of a new order of life where justice, peace, and freedom prevail. In this context, the majority church has been torn between its vested interests and the gospel. On the one hand, it has found itself embarrassed by the prophetic witness of the minority church. On the other, it has felt morally, theologically, and missiologically compelled by the gospel to cooperate with the minority church in its ministry to its poor and oppressed constituency. The minority church is, thus, a sign of protest not only against an unjust society, but also against the legitimizing role of the majority church and its theological and social betrayal of the gospel.

A Liberated and Liberating Community

Thirdly, the minority church appears as a liberated and liberating community. It provides an environment of personal freedom where oppressed women and men can recover their dignity and self-worth; where they can overcome the loneliness and hardship of poverty and powerlessness without becoming prisoners of alcohol, drugs, and other dehumanizing vices; where they can express their fears and hopes without inhibition; where they can be comforted, strengthened, edified, and can celebrate with joy the God who gives abundant life.

Moreover, the minority church carries out its ministry in the world with dignity, dedication, and joy, even though it has never had the material resources of its mainstream counterpart. Way before there were any special seminary study programs for minority ministers, the minority church, especially in its black and Hispanic variants, was running its own leadership-development programs. Even to this day, one finds all across the major cities of the land dozens of black and Hispanic Bible institutes staffed and paid for by minority churches.

By the same token, the minority church has created its own ecclesiastical structures and has organized its own foreign and national missionary endeavors. It has faithfully evangelized its own people and has been growing consistently and overwhelmingly. (The American minority church is one sector that by and large does not need "church growth strategists" to stimulate its numerical growth. Even among mainline Protestants, minorities can start two and three new congregations for what it costs Anglos to start one.) In short, the minority church has established oral and written ecclesiastical, theological, and missiological traditions of its own that are clearly distinguishable from those of the majority church.

The minority church has done all of this while living, as it were, in captivity and exile. Indeed the prophetic genius of the minority church is that it has learned to "sing the Lord's song in a strange land" (Ps. 137:4). It has been able to give its respective communities a vision of a more fraternal, just, and peaceful world, enabling them to hope even when there seems to be no hope. Its ethic has been clearly one of liberation.

An Agent of Reconciliation

Fourthly, the minority church appears as an agent of reconciliation. Because it is a liberated community, it is committed to reconciliation. Because it has an ethic of liberation, it can play a major role in bringing about a new, reconciled national church and society. Such reconciliation can only be built upon the principle of *efficacious love*, which implies just structures, economic as well as political freedom, and social as well as personal peace or well-being.

Reconciliation between races, classes, or cultures is costly. It has a high price-tag. It passes through a painful process of social awareness in which false assumptions, prejudices, and hidden agendas are brought into the open. It involves repentance and restitution. And it can only take place in a liberating setting where people are set free from fear and guilt.

The minority church is a powerful agent of reconciliation because it is free. It is not inhibited from unmasking, in love, the dominant American church and society and calling them to conversion. Moreover, by demanding socially just laws, an equitable distribution of wealth, and equal social opportunities, it has sought to establish the conditions for reconciliation with justice.

The minority church does not make its contribution to a reconciled national existence by selling its dignity and prophetic birthright for the few crumbs that the dominant sectors of society are too pleased to give the so-called disadvantaged or less fortunate. Rather it serves the cause of social reconciliation, and validates thereby its personal reconciliation with God, by working for structures that make it socially and politically difficult for the strong to oppress the weak, for the majority to exploit the minority, for the greedy to get richer and the needy to get poorer. By the same token, the minority church expresses its love toward its majority counterpart by challenging it to repentance and restitution and inviting it to join forces in the struggle for a new moral order, wherein the poor, the powerless, and the oppressed are liberated from their misery, and the rich and powerful are transformed from their greedy values and oppressive behavior into a more meaningful existence and fraternal life-style.

Notes

1. For a summary of the classical Protestant views on social ethics, up to the mid-sixties, see Edward LeRoy Long, Jr., *A Survey of Christian Ethics* (New York: Oxford University Press, 1967).

In the last decade and a half there have been many publications on social justice in the English-speaking, North Atlantic Protestant world. In so-called conciliar Protestantism (related to the World Council of

Churches), see, out of a vast selection, the following publications: *Official Report of the World Conference on Church and Society* (Geneva: World Council of Churches, 1967); Richard D.M. Dickisson, *To Set at Liberty the Oppressed: Towards an Understanding of Christian Responsibilities of Development/Liberation* (Geneva: World Council of Churches, 1975); Julio de Santa Ana, ed., *To Break the Chains of Oppression* (Geneva: World Council of Churches, 1975), and *Separation Without Hope? Essays on the Relations Between the Church and the Poor During the Industrial Revolution and the Western Colonial Expansion* (Geneva: World Council of Churches, 1978); Julio de Santa Ana, *Good News to the Poor: The Challenge of the Poor in the History of the Church* (Maryknoll, N.Y.: Orbis, 1979), and *Towards a Church of the Poor* (Maryknoll, N.Y.: Orbis, 1981); Robert McAfee Brown, *Religion and Violence* (Philadelphia: Westminster Press, 1973); *In Search of a Theology of Development* (Geneva: Sodepax, 1969); and Frederick Herzog, *Justice Church: The New Function of the Church in Northern American Christianity* (Maryknoll, N.Y.: Orbis, 1980).

Among evangelical Protestants, the following can be singled out, from an equally varied selection: J. Andrew Kirk, *Theology Encounters Revolution* (Downers Grove, Ill.: Inter-Varsity Press, 1980); David O. Moberg, *Inasmuch: Christian Social Responsibility in 20th Century America* (Grand Rapids: Eerdmans, 1965); David O. Moberg, *The Great Reversal: Evangelism and Social Concern*, rev. ed. (Philadelphia and New York: Lippincott, 1977); Ronald J. Sider, ed., *Living More Simply: Biblical Principles and Practical Models* (Downers Grove, Ill.: Inter-Varsity Press, 1980); Ronald J. Sider, ed., *Lifestyle in the Eighties: An Evangelical Commitment to Simple Lifestyle* (Exeter: Paternoster, 1981), and Ronald J. Sider, ed., *Evangelicals and Development: Towards a Theology of Social Change* (Exeter: Paternoster, 1981); Ronald Sider, *The Chicago Declaration* (Carol Stream, Ill.: Creation House, 1974); Ronald J. Sider, *Rich Christians in an Age of Hunger: A Biblical Study* (Downers Grove, Ill.: Inter-Varsity Press, 1977), and *Christ and Violence* (Scottdale, Pa.: Herald Press, 1979); John Howard Yoder, *The Politics of Jesus* (Grand Rapids: Eerdmans, 1972); Sherwood Eliot Wirt, *The Social Conscience of the Evangelical* (New York: Harper & Row, 1968); Waldron Scott, *Bring Forth Justice* (Grand Rapids: Eerdmans, 1980).

2. Literature on social justice from minority Protestants is growing. Some of the best-known Protestant black studies are: Allan A. Boesak, *Farewell to Innocence: A Socio-Ethical Study on Black Theology and Power* (Maryknoll, N.Y.: Orbis Books, 1977); James Cone, *Black Theology and Black Power* (New York: Seabury Press, 1969); James Cone, *A Black Theology of Liberation* (Philadelphia: Lippincott,

1970); and James Cone, *God of the Oppressed* (New York: Seabury Press, 1975); Major J. Jones, *Christian Ethics for Black Theology* (Nashville: Abingdon Press, 1974); Deotis J. Roberts, *Liberation and Reconciliation: A Black Theology* (Philadelphia: Westminster Press, 1971); and *A Black Political Theology* (Philadelphia: Westminster Press, 1974).

Among Hispanic Protestants in the United States, books are not as abundant, but the following treat, in varying degrees, the question of social justice: Orlando E. Costas, *The Integrity of Mission: The Inner Life and Outreach of the Church* (San Francisco: Harper & Row, 1979); Justo L. Gonzalez and Catherine G. Gonzalez, *Liberation Preaching* (Nashville: Abingdon, 1980); Piri Thomas, *Savior, Savior, Hold My Hand* (New York: Doubleday, 1973).

Among Asian/Pacific Islanders the following are representative works: Clifford Alika, "Haole: American Racism in Hawaii," mimeographed (Berkeley, Calif.: PACTS, 1977); "The Institutionalization of American Racism in Hawaii," mimeographed (Berkeley, Calif.: PACTS, 1976); Paul M. Nagano, "Is Hate Ever Justified?" mimeographed (Berkeley, Calif.: PACTS, 1974); "Ethnic Pluralism and Democracy," mimeographed (Berkeley: PACTS, n.d.); Roy I. Sano, "Toward a Liberating Ethnicity," mimeographed (Berkeley: PACTS, 1973); "Ethnic Liberation Theology: Neo-Orthodoxy Reshaped—or Replaced?" mimeographed (Berkeley: PACTS, 1975). See also the following works, among others, of the Chinese-American ethicist Robert Lee, *Religion and Social Conflict* (ed. with Martin Marty) (New York: Oxford University Press, 1964), *The Schizophrenic Church: Conflict over Community Organizations* (Philadelphia: Westminster, 1969), and *Faith and the Prospect of Economic Collapse* (Atlanta: John Knox Press, 1981).

3.   See for example H. Richard Niebuhr, *The Social Sources of Denominationalism* (Cleveland: World, 1929), which is the classical Protestant study on the subject. For more recent and comprehensive materials on the subject (especially among Catholic ethnics), see below the studies of Andrew Greeley. For the Jewish side, see Arnold Dashefsky and Howard M. Shapiro, *Ethnic Identification among American Jews: Socialization and Social Structures* (Lexington, Mass.: Heath, Lexington Books, 1974).

4.   Nathan Glazer and Daniel P. Moynihan, *Beyond the Melting Pot* (Cambridge: Harvard University Press, 1963).

5.   Nathan Glazer and Daniel P. Moynihan, eds., *Ethnicity: Theory and Practice* (Cambridge: Harvard University Press, 1975).

6.   Cf. Andrew Greeley, "Catholics Prosper while the Church Crumbles," *Psychology Today* (June, 1976), p. 44.

7. See below (nn. 11 and 12) the works of Novak and Greeley, and Glazer and Moynihan, *Ethnicity.*

8. See for example Alex Haley, *Roots* (New York: Doubleday, 1976).

9. National Black Economic Development Conference, "The Black Manifesto," in *Black Theology: A Documentary History, 1966–70,* Gayraud S. Wilmore and James H. Cone, eds., (Maryknoll, N.Y.: Orbis, 1979), pp. 80, 84.

10. Cf. Vine Deloria, *Behind the Trail of Broken Treaties: An Indian Declaration of Independence* (New York: Dell, 1974) and *The Indian Affair* (New York: Friendship Press, 1974).

11. Cf. Michael Novak, *The Rise of the Unmeltable Ethnics: Politics and Culture in the Seventies* (New York: Macmillan, 1971).

12. Cf. Andrew Greeley, *Why Can't They Be Like Us? America's White Ethnic Groups* (New York: Dutton, 1971); idem, *The Most Distressful Nation: The Taming of the American Irish* (Chicago: Quadrangle Books, 1972); idem, *Ethnicity in the USA* (New York: John Wiley, 1974).

13. Most recently, the conservative American black economic historian Thomas Sowell has added his indirect support to Novak and Greeley in his controversial (and questionable) book, *Ethnic America: A History* (New York: Basic Books, 1981). For an objective critical assessment of this book, see David Herbert Donald's review, "What Americans Bring to America," in the *New York Times Book Review,* August 2, 1981, pp. 1, 20.

14. Cf. Taylor Caldwell, *The Captains and the Kings* (Greenwich, Conn.: Fawcett, 1972).

15. Cf. Howard Fast, *The Immigrants* (New York: Dell, 1977).

16. Cf. Rosemary Radford Ruether, *New Woman, New Earth: Sexist Ideologies and Human Liberation* (New York: Seabury Press, 1975), where she warns of the danger of white middle- and upper-class women doing an abstract analysis of their "oppressed status" that ignores their racial and class privileges. This is precisely what happened with the feminist movement in the nineteenth century, which only sought electoral rights and became a tool in the hands of white male-dominated society to maintain the political supremacy of white society.

17. Cf. Peter Wagner, *Our Kind of People: The Ethical Dimensions of Church Growth in America* (Atlanta: John Knox Press, 1979).

18. Ibid., p. 31. Cf. Will D. Campbell, *Race and the Renewal of the Church* (Philadelphia: Westminster Press, 1962); Joseph C. Hough, Jr., *Black Power and White Protestants: A Christian Response to the New Negro Pluralism* (New York: Oxford University Press, 1968); Gayraud

S. Wilmore, Jr., "The Case for a New Black Church Style," in *The Black Experience in Religion*, ed. C. Eric Lincoln (Garden City, N.Y.: Doubleday Anchor books, 1974); Reuben A. Shearers II, "Beyond White Theology," *Christianity and Crisis*, November 2 and 16, 1970, p. 234.

19. Wagner, *Our Kind of People*, p. 79.

20. Ibid., pp. 79–163.

21. Cf. Ibid., pp. 78–163.

22. Ibid., p. 112. Wagner's claim is questionable because the story of Babel speaks of the phenomenon of urbanization, not decentralization or human pluralism. Cf. Samuel Noah Kramer, "The 'Babel of Tongues': A Sumerian Version," *Journal of the American Oriental Society* 88 (1968): 108–111. To be sure, Bernhard Anderson ("The Babel Story: Paradigm of Human Unity and Diversity," in *Ethnicity*, ed. Andrew Greeley and Gregory Baum [New York: Seabury Press, 1977], pp. 63 ff.) is right in stressing the connection between Gen. 10 and 11. It is no less true that the relationship between 11 and 12 is even stronger. Gen. 10 is part of the Priestly Code, which belongs to the postexilic period. Gen. 12, which is the heart of the Yahwist tradition (J), is preexilic. It was written at the moment in which Israel saw its ethnicity as a blessing for all the nations. It is not possible to read Gen. 11 without taking into account the sinful reality of humanity, whose root lies in Gen. 3. The scattering of the race can only be understood in the context of human sin, just as the promise of universal salvation (Gen. 12) can only have meaning in the light of a broken humanity.

23. Wagner, *Our Kind of People*, p. 119.

24. Ibid., p. 132.

25. Eduardo Seda Bonilla, *Ethnic Studies and Cultural Pluralism*, reprint from *The Rican: A Journal of Puerto Rican Thought*, 1969, pp. 2–3.

26. Donald Noel, "A Theory of the Origin of Ethnic Stratification," in *Majority-Minority: The Dynamics of Racial and Ethnic Relations*, ed. Norman R. Yetman and C. Hoy Steele (Boston: Allyn & Bacon, 1975), p. 32.

27. Darcy Ribeiro, *The Americas and Civilization*, trans. from the Portuguese by Linton Lomas Barrett and Marie McDavid Barrett (New York: Dutton, 1972), p. 35.

28. For an excellent analysis of military, political, and psychological conquest in an American minority (Mexican-American), see Virgilio Elizondo, *Mestizaje: The Dialectics of Cultural Birth and the Gospel* (San Antonio: MACC, 1978).

Index

.